International Political Theory

Sage Politics Texts

Series Editor
IAN HOLLIDAY
City University of Hong Kong

SAGE Politics Texts offer authoritative and accessible analyses of core issues in contemporary political science and international relations. Each text combines a comprehensive overview of key debates and concepts with fresh and original insights. By extending across all main areas of the discipline, SAGE Politics Texts constitute a comprehensive body of contemporary analysis. They are ideal for use on advanced courses and in research.

International Political Theory

Rethinking Ethics in a Global Era

Kimberly Hutchings

SAGE Publications
London • Thousand Oaks • New Delhi

SAGE Publications Ltd
6 Bonhill Street
London EC2A 4PU

SAGE Publications Inc.
2455 Teller Road
Thousand Oaks, California 91320

SAGE Publications India Pvt Ltd
32, M-Block Market
Greater Kailash – I
New Delhi 110 048

British Library Cataloguing in Publication data

A catalogue record for this book is available
from the British Library

ISBN 0 7619 5515 1
ISBN 0 7619 5516 X (pbk)

Library of Congress catalog card number 99–73845

Typeset by Mayhew Typesetting, Rhayader, Powys
Printed in Great Britain by Athenaeum Press, Gateshead

This book is dedicated to the memory of
Vera Hooley
1902–1997

Summary of Contents

Contents

Preface

This book is the product of several years of work. During that time I have had cause to be grateful to a variety of institutions and individuals. I am particularly grateful to the University of Edinburgh for granting me sabbatical leave in the Autumn Term of 1998 to complete the manuscript. I have also benefited greatly from opportunities to present some of the arguments contained here at conferences of the British International Studies Association and the Political Studies Association and at seminars at Edinburgh, Dundee, University College, Cork and the Centre for the Study of Democracy, Westminster. The Gender and IR group of the British International Studies Association and the Society for Women in Philosophy have both provided forums in which I can articulate and test out ideas. I am grateful in addition to colleagues who have read and commented on my work during this time, including Zenon Bankowski, Roland Dannreuther, Tim Hayward, John Holmwood, Russell Keat, Moya Lloyd and Andrew Thacker, and grateful in particular to Chris Brown, Andrew Linklater, Susan Stephenson and Rob Walker for offering to give me feedback on the manuscript as a whole. Ian Holliday and Lucy Robinson have also provided great encouragement in their respective editorial roles. As always, however, one's greatest debts are to those whose friendship and support has sustained one through the difficulties of thinking and writing. In addition to friends already mentioned, I therefore also offer my thanks to Susan Pryse-Davies and Bernadette Joslin in London and to the friends who have enhanced my life in Edinburgh, Richard Freeman, Fiona Mackay and Paddy Rawlinson.

Introduction

This book has two main purposes. Its first purpose is to provide an overview of the competing schools of normative international theory.[1] This will not be accomplished by furnishing the reader with an exhaustive account of all of them, but by mapping them in relation to the constitutive conceptual oppositions which have been embedded in and challenged by normative international theory over the past twenty years. The second purpose of the book is to work through the examination of the debates within and between the different schools towards an account of how to do normative international theory in such a way as to move beyond theoretical deadlock between realists and idealists, cosmopolitans and communitarians towards something which would properly be called international political theory (Brown, 1995; Bellamy and Warleigh, 1998).[2] In this latter ambition I join with an already extensive set of developments in ethical and political theory generally as well as with the normative international theorists discussed in this volume under the headings of critical theory, postmodernism and feminism. My particular answer to the question of how to do normative international theory is grounded in an approach which combines Hegelian and Foucauldian insights into the impossibility of disentangling ethics from politics and into the nature, scope and limitations of normative judgement. The extent to which it is convincing is something which, on good Hegelian and Foucauldian grounds, can only be judged by the reader.

The argument of the book is articulated in three stages. Part One, which comprises the first two chapters, involves an exposition and analysis of standard, mainstream approaches to normative international theory. Chapter 1 considers the construction of normative international theory as a debate between realism and idealism. In recent work on international theory, both explanatory and normative, this is excessively well trodden ground. For some readers it might seem odd to bother to look at the 'tired and fruitless dialectic between idealism and realism' again (Dillon, 1998), particularly since in explanatory international theory the rapprochement between neoliberal and neorealist theoretical positions is now well advanced. Both realism and idealism can now be presented as outdated and transcended theoretical paradigms in standard accounts of the recent history of international theory (Bayliss and Smith, 1997; Brown, 1997a; Neumann and Waever, 1997). However, in the case of normative theory I argue that the conceptual oppositions in which the idealist/realist debate is grounded continue to exert massive influence on theoretical work. This is not, as is sometimes suggested, because realism outlaws consideration of normative values in the international sphere. It is because the presumptions of realism and idealism combine to confirm that the consideration of normative questions in international politics must take on the form of an applied ethics. That is to say, a form in which it is assumed that morality must be brought to politics through the application of standards arrived at in abstraction from politics. In Chapter 2, I explore precisely this phenomenon in the revival of normative international theory which has occurred over the past twenty years in the Anglo-American academy.

The examination of idealism, realism and the ethics of international politics in the first two chapters demonstrates two things. First, it demonstrates that the conceptual oppositions between reason and nature, universal and particular, state and inter-state, morality and international politics continue to dominate normative international theory. This means that normative international theory is condemned to the eternal repetition of theoretical positions which depend on that which they purport to exclude. Idealists depend on realists, cosmopolitans on communitarians and vice versa. This does not mean that theoretical work carried out within this framework is either meaningless or useless, but it is confined within conceptual limits that subvert the theoretical ambition of this work, which is always to cross the lines between reason and nature, universal and particular, state and inter-state, morality and international politics which have been drawn so clearly. This is the second of the points which the first two chapters aim to make – that there is an in-built tension between the conceptual framework within which idealism and realism, cosmopolitanism and communitarianism operate and the purposes of their normative theorizing. This is manifested in the many recent attempts in ethical theory to break out of the choice between cosmopolitanism and communitarianism and it is with a brief account of some of these attempts that Chapter 2 concludes.

The second stage of the argument of this book, presented in Part Two, takes its cue from the ambitions of mainstream normative international theory to synthesize the oppositions which ground its ontology of international politics and its epistemology of normative judgement. Here I am following a well established path of recent critical thinking in

normative international theory which builds on older theoretical traditions. In Chapter 3, therefore, I examine the work of critical theory,
postmodernism and feminism in relation to the rationalist and Marxist
traditions, all of which are informed by the desire to transcend the conceptual oppositions entrenched in idealism and realism. The argument of
this chapter yields insights into the double deconstruction which is
required for the realist/idealist dichotomies to be properly undone. In the
first place, on the ontological level, the interdependence and interconnection between individual, collective, intra-state, inter-state and trans-
state politics, between economics and politics and between international
politics and the ways in which it is understood and judged are
demonstrated. In the second place, the deconstruction of the ontology of
international politics is accompanied by the recognition that at the
epistemological level, the theorist does not operate in abstraction from the
object of analysis. This does not only imply that the theorist is necessarily
implicated in international politics but also that theory is inherently
political. It is this latter claim which, I argue, poses particular difficulties
for critical international theories. It is all too tempting for the theorist to
identify the politics of their theorizing with an ideal that operates in
abstraction from the complex of ontological interdependencies which
characterize the actual world. The claim that theory is political can very
easily degenerate into repetition of the tiresome academic hubris which
wants to substitute writing for revolution by identifying the theorist's
judgement with transcendental ideals or progress in history. In which
case the critical theorist, postmodernist or feminist theorist does not
advance much beyond the position of the Kantian cosmopolitan who
presents the truth about international distributive justice without considering the conditions of possibility for the recognition of that truth.
However, although this remains a danger in the kinds of critical theories
which I examine in Chapter 3, it is not a necessary implication of the
recognition of the politics of theory. All that the latter need involve is an
appreciation of the conditions of possibility and exclusive effects of any
normative judgement.

Chapter 4 follows through the lessons learned in Chapter 3 and
articulates an account of how to do international normative theory which
draws on readings of Hegel's and Foucault's work. The upshot of the
argument of the chapter is that normative theory should aim to
substitute phenomenological adequacy and genealogical honesty for the
fixed ontologies and authoritative epistemologies on which it traditionally relies. Phenomenological adequacy means that the categories
through which theorists understand and judge the world should be
expounded as fully as possible in terms of their conditions of possibility

in principle and practice. To take an example, a theory which relies on the category of the nation-state to, for instance, underpin a prescriptive commitment to democratic self-determination will be phenomenologically inadequate if it ignores the sub- and trans-state conditions of possibility of nation-states which problematize as well as enable the realization of democracy within them. Genealogical honesty involves the theorist in being clear both about the conditions of possibility and implications of any given judgement. What histories underly the commitment to a version of the ideal of self-determination and how would the world have to change to fulfil the ideal, who would be included and who would be excluded? The requirements of both phenomenological adequacy and genealogical honesty force normative theorists to abandon the ideal for the real world and to recognize the irrelevance of normative judgement which uses the ideal as a short cut to a clear conscience. At the same time, however, in recognizing the ideal as part and parcel of the second-best real world which normative theorists inhabit and construct in the same way as everyone else, normative theory of a Hegelian and Foucauldian kind offers no comfort to those who use the gap between real and ideal worlds to confirm the impossibility of normative judgement as such. Normative judgement and prescription is not unrealistic when it envisages a world radically different from the way it is now, it is unrealistic when it fails to think through the foundations on which it must build in order to change the world, and what negative as well as positive implications that building may have. Most of all, normative theory is unrealistic when it substitutes rigorous analysis of how political agency can be generated within international politics with the illusory fast track power of privileged, non-exclusive insights into truth or history.

In Part Three, the conclusions about how to do normative international theory drawn from the first two sections are illustrated by exploring and assessing normative debate in two specific areas. In Chapters 5 and 6 debates surrounding the concepts of self-determination and democratic political cosmopolitanism are examined. In both cases it is argued that contributions to debate generated by the critical theories of international politics examined in Chapter 3 display greater phenomenological adequacy and genealogical honesty than those coming from the ethics of international politics (examined in Chapter 2). Although it is also argued that none of the theoretical perspectives lives up entirely to the requirements set by Hegelian/Foucauldian theory. In particular, it seems that genealogical honesty is a difficult goal for normative theory. The temptation is always to underplay the problems in the realization of a particular normative goal by identifying it with a transcendental ideal which is guaranteed by reason or history to be recognized by others. In fact, however, it is precisely to forward the goal of having one's ideals recognized and realized that genealogical honesty is so important. It is an uncomfortable truth that ideals and their realization are inextricable from a variety of conditions. These conditions are likely to be neither unambiguous in their ethical potential nor to have the capacity to ground their universal recognition. There are always dangers and there are always exclusions implicit in any normative position. Unless this is clearly understood, the theorist is unable to grasp fully his or her own ethical commitments. This is of crucial importance at the purely theoretical level since it exposes theorists again and again to charges of hypocrisy and inconsistency when the phenomenological inadequacies of their analysis are made evident (something which ensures the repetitive nature of most normative debate). It is equally crucial in its practical implications, because the conditions of possibility of normative judgement effectively draw the line between argument and coercion (violent or non-violent) as means of resolving normative issues.

This book is about theory and, for that reason, it might be a somewhat frustrating read for those anxious to arrive at answers to questions of how to tackle world poverty, human rights abuse, ecological crisis, political violence and disempowerment in the contemporary international order. If it furthers such projects at all it does so indirectly by arguing that certain ways of approaching the theoretical consideration of such questions are better than others. Perhaps the most obvious contribution it makes to such debates is a reminder that the blocks and incentives to change in international politics are comprised of the relative identity of real and ideal worlds. The primary responsibility of the normative theorist is towards the articulation of this truth and its ethical potential – an articulation which is always partial and will be effective only to the extent that others identify with it in their turn. Normative theory in itself changes nothing; if it appears to change things then the chances are that the world is changing already.

Notes

1   I use the expression 'normative international theory' as a generic term to cover a range of work which is most commonly labelled as 'normative international relations theory' or 'international', 'world' or 'global' ethics. As the title of this book makes clear, the kind of normative international theory for which I am

arguing is referred to as 'international political theory' (see note 2 below). However, this term is not appropriate for much of the work discussed in Chapters 1 and 2, which either relies on the notion of 'international relations' (assuming a fundamental distinction between intra- and inter-state politics) or effectively treats normative international theory as a branch of philosophical applied ethics. Nevertheless, the expressions 'normative international theory' and 'international political theory' both pose problems in continuing to rely on the concept 'international'. The term 'international' is normally used to signify inter-state, but in the context of this book I use it more generally to refer to a much broader range of political actors and contexts than simply states and the inter-state system.

2   The use of the term 'international political theory' to refer to normative international theory remains relatively rare (see Donelan, 1990 for one exception), largely because (as mentioned in note 1) most work in this area relies on drawing distinctions between international (inter-state) and political (intra-state) and between politics and morality. As will be demonstrated in Chapter 3, there is now a great deal of work that challenges the validity of both of these distinctions, but in doing so that work has problematized the term 'international' and therefore looks for alternative expressions such as 'world' or 'global' political theory. I have chosen to hold onto the term 'international' because it seems to me that to abandon it assumes too much about the extent to which the inside/outside distinctions on which it relies have ceased to be relevant. However, as the full title of this book suggests, *International Political Theory: Re-thinking Ethics in a Global Era*, I am sympathetic to the idea that contemporary international politics combines aspects of 'international relations' as traditionally conceived with globalizing processes which sometimes reinforce but also undermine the significance of states and the state system.

PART ONE

MAINSTREAM DEBATES: NORMATIVE INTERNATIONAL THEORY

1

Idealism and Realism

CONTENTS

Introduction

An investigation into contemporary normative international theory cannot take place without some explanation of what the term 'normative international theory' means. However, this is not a straightforward question of definition, since the term, as will be evident in much of the argument of this book, is essentially contested in the theoretical literature. For the moment, a preliminary and abstract statement of the range of meanings it holds must suffice. *Normative theory* is a very broad term which refers to any theorization of reality which is in some sense evaluative; this applies to the premises on which it is based and the questions it sets out to answer. Normative theories are usually explicitly or implicitly prescriptive, that is they are concerned with how to criticize, change and

improve the world as it is. Within the study of politics in the Western
tradition normative theories archetypally have been those concerned
with the question of the best ways to organize and structure political,
economic and social life (whether it be in the context of city-state, state or
empire). This means that normative political theories are concerned with
ontological questions about the elements which make up political, economic and social life, with epistemological questions about the justification
of normative judgements and with the prescriptive implications which
follow from those judgements. It follows therefore that normative international theory will be concerned with the question of the best ways to
organize and conduct international political, economic and social life.
This broad question is understood in terms that vary widely depending
on the version of normative international theory under consideration. For
the bulk of the post-1945 period, normative international theory has
occupied a largely discredited place within the Anglo-American international relations academy and a marginal place within the disciplines of
philosophical ethics and political theory. For much of this time consideration of normative questions in international politics has been
largely confined to debates over the ethics of war and deterrence.[1] Over
the past twenty years, however, this situation has changed and there has
been an enormous growth of normative theory about issues in international politics other than war. Examples include work on international
human rights, global distributive justice, nationality and nationalism,
cosmopolitan citizenship and democracy.[2] In a recent work on normative
international theory, Brown defines it as follows:

> By normative international relations theory is meant that body of work which
> addresses the moral dimension of international relations and the wider
> questions of meaning and interpretation generated by the discipline. At its most
> basic it addresses the ethical nature of the relations between communities/
> states, whether in the context of the old agenda, which focussed on violence and
> war, or the new(er) agenda, which mixes these traditional concerns with the
> modern demand for international distributive justice. (Brown, 1992a: 3)

Normative theory in politics is closely intertwined with two other kinds
of theorizing. On the one hand, explanatory theory (including theories of
history), which describes and seeks to understand and explain the nature
of politics as such, is, as will become evident below, inextricably bound up
with normative assumptions. The question of what international politics
is cannot be answered without reference to conceptual frameworks that
are normatively inflected. On the other hand, moral theory, as suggested
above by Brown, provides frameworks for judgement and prescription
which have been adapted for use in the international political context.

One of the crucial, perennial questions for normative theories of politics, and particularly of international politics, is the question of the extent to which normative political theory is an at least partially distinctive endeavour, i.e., something that is not reducible to either social scientific explanations of politics on the one hand or moral theory on the other. This is a question which dominates the debates with which this chapter is concerned. Different kinds of normative theory posit both different ideals and different understandings of the possibility of mediating in practice between the world as it is and the world as it might be; some are a good deal more pessimistic than others. Nevertheless all such theory is concerned with the possibility of explaining, arguing for, and defending political values, and with critically engaging with the world as it is.

In the discussion which follows I will be analysing international normative theory in terms of three elements: *ontological, epistemological* and *prescriptive*. These elements are heavily interdependent within any given normative theory but they are logically distinctive and any given example of normative work may be explicitly concerned with one (or two) of these elements rather than others. In this context, when I refer to the ontological component of normative theory, I am referring to the range of claims made in the theory about the *stuff* of which international politics is made. Traditionally, a distinction is made between two kinds or levels of stuff. On the one hand, there is *metaphysical* stuff, on the other hand there is *empirical* stuff. Metaphysical stuff refers to truths about existence which are not subject to direct empirical verification and are established through philosophical argument. These may include truths about nature, human nature, morality, politics and history. The claim that human nature is essentially bad or the claim that there is a teleological pattern to human history are examples of such metaphysical assertions which are made about the nature of international politics by different schools of normative international theory. In contrast to metaphysical assertions, according to the traditional account, are empirical truths about the real, concrete institutions and practices of international politics. Just as in domestic political theory arguments about the notion of punishment rest on empirical claims about the nature and operation of state and law in practice (as well as deeper assumptions about human nature, guilt and responsibility), so in normative international theory arguments about international justice rely on a large range of claims about the nature of states, inter-state relations, international law, the global economy and so on (as well as deeper assumptions about human nature and history).

However, on reflection, the traditional distinction between metaphysical and empirical types of stuff within international politics is a good deal more problematic than initially it seems. The problem is that the apparently straightforward matter of identifying the empirical substance of international politics turns out to be a metaphysical minefield. This is very well exemplified in the difficulties currently surrounding the concept of 'international' as it is used and criticized in normative arguments about international politics. The meaning of the term *international* is traditionally understood as referring to the modern state system in which states are conceived as independent authorities over whom no transcendent authority holds sway. It is commonly used as the contrary of *domestic* and refers primarily to the space/realm within which states are located and relate to one another. However, this whole picture is part of a conceptual scheme which does not and never has simply reflected the way the world is. Rather it is one of the (more influential) ways in which explanations and judgements of international politics have been constructed. Different normative theories disagree profoundly over the claim inherent in the traditional conception of the international realm that states are the only source of legitimate authority within that realm. These disagreements have as much to do with metaphysical disagreements about the sources of political authority (such as natural law, moral law, contract, individual right and so on), and with conceptual disagreements about the nature and scope of politics (how it relates to economics or morality for instance), as they do with the empirical facts of the case. In summary, the question of what international politics is is always a theoretical question. This is not because the concrete institutions and practices of international politics are irrelevant to international theory, it is because the issue of what is or is not relevant is a conceptual question. It is a question that is equally important to explanatory as to normative theory, and this is the principal reason why, as noted above, normative international relations theory is inextricably bound up with the social science of international relations and vice versa.[3]

Epistemology refers to the theory of knowledge, a branch of philosophy which is concerned with establishing how (and in relation to what) knowledge claims can be assumed to be reliable. The preoccupation of epistemology is with establishing what knowledge is and with identifying the distinction between valid and invalid claims to knowledge. In normative international theory the epistemological element concerns the question of how to validate normative judgements about how the international realm is or ought to be. Are the grounds for the legitimacy of such judgements to be found in rationally accessible universal principles or ideals? If so, what are these principles/ideals? If not, what weight do judgements of right and wrong in international politics carry? These kinds of questions are inextricably entwined with the question of normative truth, whether it exists and how it can be known and demonstrated. This epistemological element of normative international theory is where its interrelation with moral theory is most evident. Many of the answers to the question of normative truth in the international context are borrowed from or depend on claims derived from moral theory. This is particularly evident in the debates between cosmopolitans and communitarians in international ethics, which will be discussed in Chapter 2. However, epistemological concerns are also inseparable from questions concerning the referents of the substantive claims being made, which takes us back to the ontological element of normative theory considered above.

The prescriptive element of normative international theory follows from its ontological and epistemological claims. In the light of substantive, valid claims about how the world is or is not, normative theory purports to provide the resources from which both to judge whether the world is or is not as it ought to be and, insofar as is and ought are estranged, to prescribe how the world should be changed. Thus one of the key focuses of normative theory is on practical policy, what aspects of contemporary international politics are benign and should be supported or, alternatively, what aspects of contemporary international politics are dangerous and should therefore be discouraged. Sometimes the prescriptions of normative international theory are highly specific, such as proposals for the introduction of global redistributive taxation. Sometimes they are much more general, such as open-ended demands that the world should be made more peaceful or more just.

In this chapter and in Chapter 2 I will be tracing the predominant ways in which debates within normative international theory have been structured. The purpose of the first two chapters is to demonstrate the patterns of thinking which dominate most work in normative international theory and the problems raised by those patterns of thinking. I will begin the characterization of the dominant patterns of thinking in normative international theory by identifying two versions of it which have traditionally occupied the outer limits of what it is understood to mean within the international relations academy. These are the supposed extremes of *idealism* on the one hand and *realism* on the other. Idealism and realism are terms deriving from the vocabulary of international relations theory since the 1930s. However, as we shall see, they reflect broader traditions of thinking in political theory and philosophy. These theoretical alternatives continue to set the agenda for current debates both in their positive influencing of different theoretical approaches and as positions to be challenged and transcended. I will explain the ways in which the contrast between realism and idealism emerges, in relation to certain readings of canonic thinkers in international political theory, as part of establishing a distinctive framework for the study of international politics, particularly in the post-1945 period. It will emerge that the predominant characteristic of both idealism and realism is that these frameworks of thinking are distinctively structured in terms of a series of tensions which, I will argue, are governed by the ruling conceptual oppositions between reason and nature, ideal and real, universal and particular. These tensions create peculiar conceptual difficulties in formulating normative international theory. The result of this is that such theorizing tends to become bogged down in a perpetual and never-ending argument between apparently opposed, but actually complementary, positions.

The study of international relations as a distinctive academic discipline is very much a twentieth century phenomenon. It is not, of course, the case that international politics was not a matter of study prior to 1919 (when the first Chair of International Relations was established at Aberystwyth). Generations of philosophers, theologians, historians and legal scholars have had plenty to say about international relations (or its pre-nation-state correlates) in pre-modern and modern periods. However, the historical canon of international political science and political theory was and continues to be constructed in retrospect in the academic study of the international, a process which, as far as normative theory is concerned, has been distinguished by the invention of the past in terms of seemingly infinite variations on a standard theme. The standard theme is the distinction between idealist and realist understandings of the actuality and potentiality of international politics (to be explained below). This theme is read back into the history of political thought in order to identify forerunners of these schools (e.g., Kant is claimed for the idealists, Hobbes for the realists) or representatives of a 'middle way' between them (e.g., Grotius).[4] What follows is a schematic account of idealism and realism, which uses particular thinkers (modern and canonic) to pick out key elements of the two poles of normative international theory. It is intended to identify paradigmatic features of opposed schools of thought in international relations rather than as an account which does full justice to the complexity of the work of any particular theorist.

Idealism

One of the most difficult things about grasping the different approaches to understanding and judging international politics is the variety of labels with which one has to deal. For purposes of clarity I use the term 'idealism' to refer to normative international theory with predominant features which are also present in approaches referred to in the literature under the headings of moralism, utopianism, revolutionism and liberalism.[5] To speak of idealism as a tradition of thinking in international theory is in a sense misleading. Idealism is not a coherent ongoing chain of thinking. It would be more accurate to see idealism as referring to a set of overlapping themes which achieved significant influence in late eighteenth and nineteenth century liberal and socialist ideology and exercised a profound effect on the theory (and, possibly but contestably, the practice) of international politics in the period immediately following the end of the First World War until the early 1930s.[6] Idealism has become identified as a substantive tradition very much in hindsight with the discrediting of its tenets in the work of the political realists (see below). For some time after the Second World War, idealism existed as little more than a suspect and shadowy other of realism in the common-sense thinking of international relations. For this reason it is easiest to identify idealism by looking back at its acknowledged canonic exponents.

In terms of canonic accounts, idealism as a perspective on international politics has its most obvious origins in late eighteenth century Enlightenment thought about human perfectibility, international law and the possibilities of peace between states. Because he is the theorist most commonly cited as a reference point for idealism in contemporary work, I will draw out the themes of idealism through an examination of the work of Immanuel Kant. In a very famous essay, 'Perpetual Peace: A Philosophical Sketch', Kant envisaged a combination of moral and self-interested factors leading to the setting up of a peaceful international federation of states, in which relations between states would be governed by cooperation and mutually agreed rules and norms (Kant, 1991a: 93–130). There are three elements to Kant's argument in 'Perpetual Peace' which are of particular importance to the ways in which the idealist option has come to be understood in international theory.[7]

The first element is the clear distinction made by Kant between morality and politics (Kant, 1991b: 40–7). This distinction is one aspect of Kant's complex critical philosophy and it is impossible to explain it fully in a few sentences. However, it depends on a prior distinction between two different but related spheres of human action and motivation: reason and nature. The sphere of reason refers to human action which is governed by purely rational self-determination. According to Kant, to act rationally in this sense means to be motivated by principles which are legislated by a purely good will (Kant, 1969: 11). That is, a will which is oriented solely in terms of doing what is right. This is a capacity that human beings have, but which they cannot exercise automatically and Kant provides various aids in his practical philosophy to help individuals to know and do what is right.[8] The sphere of nature is the sphere of natural necessity or of causal relations. According to Kant, to act naturally is to act on the influence of natural passions and sentiments (Kant, 1969: 13–15). This is not something which human individuals are obliged to do, otherwise they would be equivalent to animals. Human beings possess a capacity of free will which means they can resist determination by their desires and fears (Kant, 1991b: 42). However, in so far as humans allow themselves to be determined by such natural influences then they participate in a realm of nature rather than of reason. Morality, for Kant, is defined in terms of the sphere of reason, so that even a good action which is done from impure motives cannot count as fully moral. In contrast, politics, for Kant, is the realm of practice in which people obey principles of right (embodied in the state and positive law) for pragmatic, self-interested reasons, most obviously through fear of punishment. Such behaviour is, in Kant's terms, naturally determined or heteronomous as opposed to the rational self-determination which is characteristic of morality. To refrain from theft because you know it is wrong is to act morally, to refrain from theft because you know you will be punished is to act legally or politically.

Kant's mapping of morality and politics onto a deep metaphysical distinction between reason and nature leaves politics in an oddly ambivalent position. On the one hand, in so far as politics relies on the mechanisms of natural determination it is completely opposed to morality. On the other hand, however, the story does not end there, since in Kant's political theory the purpose of politics (i.e., the establishment of state and law) remains governed by the demands not of pragmatism but of a purely rational principle of right which is inextricably bound up with the demands of the moral law (Kant, 1991b: 56–7). Kant argues that ultimately politics is in the service of morality, in the sense that the goal of politics should be to approximate as closely as possible to the moral ideal of a 'kingdom of ends', that is, of the state as the embodiment of principles of self-legislation. It seems, therefore, as if politics is caught somewhere between reason and nature rather than being clearly identifiable with either.

The second significant element of Kant's argument for idealist approaches in normative international theory, is the role played by individual, state, inter-state and cosmopolitan levels of right. For Kant, the state is the political order in which the principle of right can be realized – essentially the principle of respect for individual freedom (Kant, 1991b: 57–8). It is therefore crucial that states be the right kind of states. Kant argues that the right kind of states are ones which have a republican (liberal) constitution and protect the right to property, i.e., ones which maximize individual rights (Kant, 1991a: 74–9, 99–102; 1991b: 123–49). Moreover, Kant argues that this kind of state is likely to be pacific in its relation with other states and that republican states will therefore work to establish inter-state laws to regulate inter-state behaviour (Kant, 1991a: 87–92, 102–14, 1991b: 150–7). These laws are designed to protect states from the possibility of war and promote conditions for peace and prosperity; they are, however, based on the agreement of equals (agentic states) and there is no transcendent authority to enforce obedience. Right remains located in states. However, when it comes to cosmopolitan law, the story is rather different. Kant claims that in addition to state-right and international mutual obligation there should be a level of obligation in international politics which is cosmopolitan in character (Kant, 1991a: 105–8). That is to say one that covers all individuals as such, regardless of citizenship status. Kant's notion of what falls under the cosmopolitan level of obligation is very narrow; nevertheless, he insists that this obligation is not based on the right of states but on the invocation of explicitly moral duties to individuals which are prior to the rights of states and upon which the rights of states are ultimately founded. According to Kant, if the three levels of state, international and cosmopolitan obligation are properly constituted in the light of the principle of right, then perpetual peace becomes a possibility.

The third element of Kant's argument which forms a reference point for idealist international relations theory is his reliance on philosophy of history to strengthen his normative argument for the possibility of perpetual peace. A large section of Kant's 'On Perpetual Peace' is concerned to demonstrate that even if humans (or even devils) and states are not capable of recognizing the normative force of his recipe for perpetual peace and acting on that recognition, there are forces of nature which are capable of doing the job (Kant, 1991a: 108–14). Fear of others in a state of nature and fear of the increasing destructiveness of war will push humanity first into states, then into federations based on international agreements and the recognition of cosmopolitan obligations (Kant, 1991a: 112). Moreover the economic interests of both individuals and states in the increase of international/global trade will further reinforce the requirements of the principle of right (Kant, 1991a: 114). Kant supplements his account of the necessary direction of human development with an account of the normative significance of reading history as progress, whether or not there is clear cut empirical evidence that this is the case. He argues that the role of the political philosopher is to enhance the possibilities of progress in history by always interpreting history in such a way as to sustain hope for the future of mankind in the light of universal moral principles (Kant, 1991a: 51–3).

What emerges from Kant's international political theory is a curious interplay between conceptions of morality and politics. This interplay is conducted at different levels of individual, state, international and cosmopolitan right, through both reason (autonomy) and nature (heteronomy) in history. It is not the case that all idealist perspectives on international relations share all of these features equally, however the elements highlighted above in Kant's argument are characteristic of idealist approaches to international politics in general. First, such approaches assume the potential of rationally derivable principles to be universally applicable to the regulation of the realm of politics. Secondly, such approaches attach an ultimate moral significance to the individual. Thirdly, such approaches assume that the state instantiates rational principles which implicitly transcend it (the state) and that the establishment of international or cosmopolitan institutions is both possible and desirable in accordance with tho^e rational principles. Fourthly, such approaches are either attached to a full-blooded progressive philosophy of history or, more cautiously, at least presume the possibility of progress in history as well as the ready accessibility of the standards by which progress in history should be judged.

These general idealist notions gained much broader currency in nineteenth century liberalism. Utilitarianism, the great rival to Kant's moral and political philosophy and an equally important influence on the liberal tradition, also shared an idealist attachment to the ultimate moral significance of the individual, the universality of moral principles and the possibility of historical progress in terms of peace, international trade, law and institutions.[9] For utilitarians, the fundamental moral principle is that one should act always to maximize the greatest happiness of the greatest number of people, with each person counting as equally important in the calculation. The main difference between the idealism of Kant and that of the utilitarians is that the distinction between morality and politics is less fundamental in utilitarianism. This reflects the fact that utilitarianism is not premised on a basic distinction between rational and natural determination. For utilitarians, acting rightly as opposed to acting in terms of self-interest is to be understood as a distinction of degree rather than of kind. The applicability of rational principle (the principle of utility) to political action is therefore more straightforward than it is for Kant and the ethical significance and necessity of the state (as the body which mediates between reason and nature) as such is less powerfully present. Both Bentham and James Mill were clear that the thrust of utilitarianism is both ethically and politically cosmopolitan – states and nations have importance only in so far as they are instrumental in enabling the regulation of politics by the principle of utility (Bentham, 1843: 537–8; 1992).

The optimism of both Kant and utilitarianism about progress in history was reinforced by two other ideological developments in nineteenth century liberalism which were either cosmopolitan or internationalist in their political implications. First, faith in free trade as a means to undermine the significance of state sovereignty and pave the way for a more cosmopolitan world became a central part of liberal ideology (Smith, 1992; Burchill, 1996a: 43–54). Secondly, the belief in the principle of democratic self-determination as the basis for the legitimacy of the state began to spread (Burchill, 1996a: 35–9). J.S. Mill was one of the thinkers to take up this theme and famously argued that when a people reached a certain level of maturity it had a right to self-government (Mill, 1992; Walzer, 1992: 87–95). The link made between maturity and democracy fits in with the idealist emphasis on the priority of individual over state right. Any possible tension between the principle of nationality and the idea of perpetual peace is resolved as commitment to the right to self-determination becomes combined with the Kantian claim that states organized according to the principle of right would be peacefully oriented in relation to other states and able and willing to cooperate to establish international law and protect individual rights.

In the aftermath of 1918, the resources of idealism became identified by some of the victorious powers as a buffer against the repeat of what was then seen as the outcome of national self-aggrandizement and great power politics (Burchill, 1996a: 39–42). It is at this point that there is the first systematic attempt to bring something like the international federation of states envisaged in Kant's essay to fruition. The end of the First World War saw the setting up of the League of Nations as an international institution created to protect rights to self-determination of sovereign peoples, state rights, and to prevent war and punish aggression. The institutionalization of Woodrow Wilson's ideals in the Versailles Settlement of 1919 expressed a faith in the possibility of eliminating war from the international system through the promotion of democratic self-determination. Underlying this faith are assumptions which are clearly identifiable with Kant's much earlier consideration of the prospects for international politics. First, it was assumed that certain principles of right must take precedence over national self-interest (i.e., that the higher, rational principles of morality must be capable of regulating the lower, natural motivations of politics); secondly, it was assumed that the principles instantiated by the liberal state transcended state right and were of universal relevance, having fundamental reference to the rights of individuals; thirdly, it was assumed that international institutions could replicate the work done by states in the domestic context to ensure the realization of rational principles of right in the international sphere; fourthly, it was assumed that self-interest, in the form of the natural determinations of fear and greed, could be yoked in tandem to the moral law when it came to the project of preserving perpetual peace and that progress in history was therefore possible (Brown, 1997a: 25).

In order to sum up the key features of idealism it is helpful to analyse it in terms of the ontological, epistemological and prescriptive elements identified above as constitutive of normative theory in general. Ontologically, for Kant, the world has a fundamentally double aspect. The human being is split between autonomy (a realm of rational self-determination) and heteronomy (a realm of natural necessity). The former *ought* to subsume the latter in the sphere of human action, including politics, but in practice it only predominates in so far as it wins the battle against the power of natural desires or, alternatively, through the fortunate (providential) correlation of heteronomous with autonomous ends. From this point of view the human world can always be read ambivalently. In contrast, utilitarian thinking suggests a much weaker duality between the worlds of 'is' (nature) and 'ought' (reason), since to act according to the principle of utility is to act according to the way in which human beings are naturally motivated. Whereas Kant keeps reason and nature perpetually apart, utilitarianism identifies reason with nature. There is therefore a greater degree of struggle and of difficulty inherent in the Kantian account of how to establish and institutionalize domestic, international and cosmopolitan principles of right. However, the ontological claims made by the two kinds of idealism overlap in many respects. This applies in particular to the priority given by both to the individual, with state, international and cosmopolitan right all gaining their legitimacy essentially by reference back to individual right. Idealism does not identify states or political collectivities as having intrinsically a special normative status – such status as they have is always reducible to individuals on the one hand and universal principles on the other. The conceptual framework through which idealism explains international politics accepts the reality but dismisses the necessity of the state system as well as inserting both individuals and economic processes as important elements in explaining the past and future of that system. Over against the actually existing world, idealists pose the shadowy picture of the world as it ought to be. However, this has the odd consequence that not only the ideal but also the real world of international politics becomes shadowy and insubstantial. A void waiting to be filled by the principles of right and the march of world history.

Idealist perspectives assume the possibility of authoritative normative judgement in the international sphere and explain that possibility in terms of a moral law which is grounded in certain metaphysical assumptions and is universally applicable to human and/or rational beings. Nevertheless, it is clear that idealist theories do not agree with each other about the basis on which they make their claims about what ought to be. This raises the epistemological question of how either Kantian or utilitarian variants of idealism establish the validity of their normative claims. In both cases the key to gaining access to the principles which ought to govern international politics is reason, and it is presumed that rational argument will be able to solve the problem of which account of normative truth is to be preferred. Partly because there is a large amount of overlap in the ontological and prescriptive elements of idealist theories the epistemological question of how normative judgements are authorized takes on major importance for different versions of idealism. This leads to the phenomenon in much contemporary normative international theory of a great deal of work being devoted, not to the fact that a particular practice is right or wrong, but to the demonstration that the opposing theoretical school thinks it is right or wrong for the wrong reasons. This tendency is particularly evident in work on the ethics of international politics which will be considered in the following chapter.

Idealism premises judgement and prescription on a complex of arguments about actual and possible worlds. It claims that there are ideals about how international politics should operate and that these are possible to achieve through a combination of principle-driven policy and the natural forces of human aversion to death and desire for goods. The world both can and should be changed. Explicit idealist prescriptions are typically either internationalist or cosmopolitan in nature. Some idealisms see progress in terms of the establishment of international law and international institutions, but presume that the legitimacy of such arrangements will be the product of agreements between states as the only sovereign actors in the international sphere.[10] Others argue, more radically, for a sovereign political authority existing over and above the level of the state to guarantee peace and individual rights.[11]

Realism

Proponents of the realist tradition in international relations have been known to trace back its origins to Thucydides' account of the

Peloponnesian Wars in Ancient Greece (Forde, 1992). However, it is perhaps more plausible to trace its modern antecedents to thinking about history and world politics which emerged in parallel with the idealist themes described above. The modern state system has its most clear point of origin in the Treaty of Westphalia (1648), which replaced the notion of the overarching identity of Christendom in Europe with the primacy of state sovereignty. In legal terms international relations became a matter of the interaction of different independent sources of right over whom no overarching authority existed. Over time, two kinds of theoretical development were encouraged by the Westphalian settlement: first, philosophical work on nationality, culture and history in the late eighteenth century (for example the work of thinkers such as Herder, Fichte and Hegel), which emphasized the intrinsic value (and/or destiny) of the nation-state (this work has been picked up in contemporary communitarian thinking which will be examined in Chapter 2). Secondly, conceptions of international politics as being a matter of *raison d'état* and *realpolitik* in which states pursued their interests by the best means available, which might be the achievement of a balance of power through diplomacy or through military intervention (Bayliss and Smith, 1997: 110–24; Waever, 1997: 7–10). These ways of thinking were identified by the victorious powers after the First World War as being complicit in the bringing about of that war. It was these presumptions about the proper means of conducting international politics which the idealist Wilsonian policies sought to combat after 1918. However, the dominance of an idealist 'common sense' in international affairs in theory as well as practice began to be threatened from the early 1930s onwards with the League's manifest inability to contain aggression and expansionism from Japan and Germany (Burchill, 1996a: 42). The outbreak of the Second World War confirmed the end of theoretical optimism about international politics, even though its outcome was a settlement in which international law and institutions became more rather than less entrenched. There were two main reasons for this: first, at a theoretical level, it was accepted by most commentators that idealist perspectives had failed to provide a basis for understanding or preventing the outbreak of more war; secondly, the end of the Second World War marked the beginning of another conflict, the Cold War. In the context of the Cold War the American dominated international relations academy was heavily influenced by the ideological and policy-driven concerns of a bi-polar world (Halliday, 1991; Rothstein, 1991; Gaddis, 1992–3). These two factors combined to produce a post-1945 academic study of international relations which self-consciously formulated its disciplinary identity as much in terms of what it was not as in terms of what it was. It was not moral but political, not internationalist or cosmopolitan but state-centric, not ideal but real (S. Hoffman, 1977). These are claims which are central to the perspective on international politics known as political realism which has been overwhelmingly influential in the study of international relations in the post-war period.

According to many critics (and some defenders) of realism, the notion of 'normative international theory' is a realist oxymoron. This reflects the view that political realism is characterized by the assumption that the international sphere (perhaps the sphere of politics in general) is distinguished by the absence of categorical normativity in the sense of overriding principles of right. On reflection, however, this understanding of political realism is a drastic oversimplification. To begin with, as was seen to be the case with idealism, realism does not constitute a single theoretical tradition as such but more an interconnected series of themes which emerged in response to both theoretical idealism and to the major events in international politics from the 1930s to the 1960s. The normative theoretical resources offered by realist theories of international politics are contingently rather than necessarily connected. In what follows, I suggest that one can categorize these resources as having three distinguishable aspects: tragic, sceptical and systemic.[12] Elements of all of these can be found in the work of the earlier generation of realists such as Niebuhr, Morgenthau and Carr; the more recent variant of realism represented by the work of Waltz is largely sceptical and systemic.[13] Of the canonic forefathers frequently invoked by political realists, the tragic aspect can be traced most obviously to Augustine and Machiavelli, whereas the sceptical and systemic aspects of realism can be seen to derive from Hobbes. Although these aspects are distinguishable, I will argue that they have all worked to reinforce a particular set of claims about the right way to organize and conduct international politics and about the nature and scope proper to normative international theory.

Murray convincingly traces one of the philosophical roots of political realism in Augustine's moral imperfectionism, in which politics is not amoral but is only ever imperfectly moral (Murray, 1997: 31–69). The tragic aspect of political realism is found in its characterization of politics in terms of an ongoing agonistic conflict between what Carr sums up as *utopianism* and *realism* (Carr, 1946: 10). Utopianism refers to idealism and the notion of motivation by moral principle; realism refers to motivation by pragmatic self-interest. In Niebuhr's early work *Moral Man and Immoral Society* (1946), he argues for the persistence of a tragic and unresolvable conflict between the capacity of individuals to act according to ideals (in true Kantian fashion) and the incapacity of collectives to do the same (Niebuhr, 1946: 9). In his later work he refers to the necessary duality of justice and order, community and dominion in political life and the precarious balance which needs to be achieved between them (Niebuhr, 1959: 149; 265). Morgenthau states explicitly that 'Man cannot help sinning when he acts in relation to his fellow men', because a fundamental of politics, the pursuit of power, conflicts with the fundamentals of morality expressed in the Judeo-Christian tradition (Morgenthau, 1958: 247). Carr puts it very bluntly:

> Here, then, is the complexity, the fascination and the tragedy of all political life. Politics are made up of two elements – utopia and reality – belonging to two different planes which can never meet. There is no greater barrier to clear political thinking than failure to distinguish between ideals which are utopia, and institutions which are reality. (Carr, 1946: 93)

This theme of realist thinking, however, can be interpreted in different ways when it comes to international politics. On one interpretation it seems as if international politics as well as domestic politics is simply always the struggle of opposed and incompatible influences, with the balance sometimes working in favour of utopia (the realm of pure reason) and sometimes in favour of reality (the realm of nature). According to this kind of reading the forces of *ought* and *is* push and pull against each other in a perpetual tug of war, but they do not combine, either in terms of a synthesis or in terms of one subsuming the other. On this view, politics is again seen in ambivalent terms, a blank space which may be occupied, temporarily, by either of the two battling forces of reason or nature. Another interpretation, perhaps best exemplified in some passages in Morgenthau's work, is one in which the reality side of Carr's utopia/reality distinction is dominant in politics with morality reduced to a minimal role in which it constitutes the outer limits of permissible behaviour but little else (Morgenthau, 1958: 253). On this account, what becomes crucial to understanding and judging politics are the forces of natural determination which control reality and utopia becomes marginalized as a point of refence both for what is and what can be (if not what ought to be) in politics.

Whichever interpretation is predominant, however, tragic realism has certain substantive implications. First, it is dubious about the notion that moral principle (autonomous reason) has the power to control politics over time and, consequently, it is sceptical of the idealist claim that there can be progress in history judged in terms of rational moral ideals. At best it implies that there may be some kind of accommodation between the forces of reality and the principles of utopia – the stablity of which will be always in doubt. Secondly, it draws attention to the importance of establishing an understanding of the principles that govern reality as opposed to utopia. Political realism focuses attention on the principles or forces which underly non-moral motivation. In the work of Morgenthau this leads to a focus on the notion of interest as the key determining force in human behaviour. From this emerges a preoccupation with human nature and the identification of primary human interests in security and power, which is succeeded by the articulation of purely political norms derived from these fundamental interests. In Morgenthau's analyses of international politics, the idea of 'national interest' emerges as the crucial explanatory factor in inter-state behaviour (Morgenthau, 1985: 3–12). Tragic political realism is not concerned with identifying the governing principles of politics purely for their own sake, however, but as part of grasping how these principles of action may or may not be constrained within or made compatible with higher utopian ends. One consequence of this is that there is a thread of thinking in tragic political realism which is concerned with elucidating a middle way between utopia and reality. However, because utopia and reality are conceived as mutually exclusive in principle in tragic realism, attempts to articulate a synthetic political morality tend always to collapse back into one or other of the elements of the tragedy (see 'International Society or the Middle Way' in Chapter 3 below).

Tragic political realism in the work of Niebuhr, Morgenthau and Carr is a normative perspective on politics in general. It can be associated with the split between city of man and city of God in Augustine's work and his pessimistic assessment of the potential of action in this world to close the gap between them. It can also be associated with Machiavelli's distinction between individual and political virtue and the incapacity of political life to live up to the demands of Christian morality. Most interestingly in relation to its anti-idealism, it can be seen as the pessimistic converse of the Kantian account of the relation between politics and the moral law. However, in the post-1945 period, realism was developed very much as a perspective not necessarily on politics in general but on international politics in particular. The reason for this is that this interpretation of politics as inherently tragic is accompanied by sceptical and systemic aspects of political realism bound up with the distinction between the domestic and the international political sphere. Rather than finding their concerns prefigured in Augustine and Machiavelli, sceptical and systemic aspects of realism have their more obvious founding father in the work of Hobbes.

According to standard accounts, at some point in the early modern era in the history of what is now termed *international* politics a crucial change takes place. The customary and legal recognition of the status of overlapping authorities within a common community of faith which characterized medieval European order is transformed into a system of legitimate, sovereign states. The point at which this transition was made definitively is a subject of much debate but the Westphalian settlement of 1648 provides its most frequently cited marker. Hobbes's place in the canon of international political theory is as one of the earliest thinkers to recognize and draw implications from this historical shift in European politics from the medieval to the Westphalian order. The way in which he does this is through setting up a clear distinction between two dimensions of political authority, internal (in relation to subjects/ citizens) and external (in relation to other political authorities).[14]

As is well known, in *Leviathan* Hobbes argued for setting up a political authority over individual subjects which was virtually absolute. The nature of Hobbes's ideal political order is one in which sovereign power is envisaged in the form of a transcendent being, a collective person with supreme power over the actual persons by whom the state is constituted (Hobbes, 1991: 117–21). Hobbes saw this as the only way in which political order could be achieved, given his argument that there are no natural ordering principles built into human relations which will guarantee the honouring of contractual agreements. In contrast to the internal authority of Leviathan, however, its external authority in relation to other political collectives is analogous to the situation of individuals in a state of nature in which there is an absence of any overarching guarantee of contractual relations (Hobbes, 1991: 90).

The formal character given to relations between particular political authorities in Hobbes's account is of particular significance. First of all, political orders are conceived as plural and absolutely separate, secondly political orders are conceived as states – that is, as unitary political authorities. A contrast between plurality and unity is mapped onto the contrast between the international and the state. What emerges therefore is the sense of the international as a space *between states*. It is this sense of what the international means which is crucial to debates in contemporary international normative theory. However, in addition to the formal characterization of the international which can be derived from Hobbes (although he never himself uses the term 'international'), there are also substantive aspects of Hobbes's account which have implications for the 'normative' component of international normative theory. In the course of his argument for the setting up of Leviathan, Hobbes makes clear that there is no right prior to the commonwealth (Hobbes, 1991: 90–111). Right follows the institution of sovereign authority and exists only where sovereign authority, whose power is the guarantee of right, exists. Hobbes therefore establishes a key distinction through which to make sense of both the nature of international politics and the nature of normative theory. For Hobbes, international politics is distinguished from state politics in a way which maps international politics onto the absence of right, and state politics onto its presence. Normative considerations therefore apply in a different way in the international as opposed to the state context.

Modern political realism takes on board two of Hobbes's most important arguments. First, the notion of order as a central political value which is the effective presupposition of right. Secondly, the idea of a strict distinction between state and inter-state politics. According to the tragic aspect of realism, the norms governing politics in general (domestic and international) tend to be derived from the fundamental human interest in security. What the sceptical and systemic aspects of realism emphasize in addition is that the domestic state and the realm of inter-state relations represent radically different contexts in relation to that fundamental interest. The crucial distinction here is between internal and external sovereignty. Considered domestically as internally sovereign, states are always already defined by the givenness of order. The existence of overarching state authority within a given territory makes it possible for states to institutionalize morally right values and principles, though this is not a necessary consequence. In contrast, in the post-Westphalian European state system which was generalized globally in the twentieth century, there is no guarantee of order because there is no overarching authority. In the international context the political imperative to pursue order and avoid war involves commitment to maximizing state interest (defined as power). States operate analogously to Hobbesian individuals in a state of nature but without the possibility of a social contract. The key means of international politics therefore become the achievement of a balance of power which will guarantee peace or, failing that, deterrence and war.

This Hobbesian 'turn' in political realism is sceptical in two principal ways. First, it identifies international relations as inherently prior to principles of right and therefore justifies the claim that principles of right are inapplicable to international relations. As we have seen, in its 'tragic' dimension political realists both imply the existence of universal principles of right and do not see the norms of politics in the international sphere as entirely divorced from those principles. Nevertheless, it is clear that the distinction between morality and politics and the way it is mapped onto the distinction between the state and international by the legacy of Hobbesian thinking has the effect of severely limiting the scope of realist normative international theory. Secondly, however, the influence of Hobbesian scepticism goes beyond the notion that international relations is an amoral or largely amoral sphere since, in addition, it suggests that principles of right are not universal and necessary but contingent and particular – the product of particular political and historical conditions. The realist thinker who goes furthest along this path is Carr, who argues for the historical relativity of what are presented as universal truths about the international realm (Carr, 1946: 67–8). In the work of Morgenthau, it is more the case that the universal truths about what ought to be the case are inscrutable, whereas the norms governing politics are demonstrable, and that therefore it makes sense to concentrate attention on the latter and be sceptical about any claims to have access to the former (Morgenthau, 1958: 81). This view was very much compounded by what was perceived by realists as the damage likely to follow from misplaced attempts to force the world as it is into the mould of what ought to be. The former kind of scepticism is inseparable from the systemic claims which have come to dominate the work of successors to the earlier generation of political realists in the study of international relations, the *neorealists*. According to this approach, the realm of international politics is distinguished by a completely rigid separation of the *international* from the *normative* if the latter is understood as going beyond systemically generated norms of instrumentally rational action on the part of states.

Neorealism is most commonly exemplified by the work of Kenneth Waltz. In *Man, the State and War* (1959), Waltz argues for a conception of international politics as distinct from politics within the state. The conception of the international is, in line with political realism, one which stresses the international as being fundamentally anarchic, lacking a principle of order. However, Waltz claims to develop this idea much more rigorously than political realists like Morgenthau. Where Morgenthau sees a general distinction between the governing norms of politics as opposed to morality which has particular salience in the international context, Waltz argues for a radical separation of levels of analysis of politics, with individuals and states as the first two levels and the international as a third and distinctive, systemic level (Waltz, 1959: 224–37). Whilst politics within the state and at sub-state levels may be radically different in different states, international politics is always fundamentally the same for Waltz. Internationally states operate in a context of anarchy which dictates certain kinds of priorities and behaviours and a single conception of the good for all states, that is, to ensure international order and relative advantage within it (Waltz, 1979: 88–97). In effect, neorealism reworks the distinction between politics and morality which is common to idealists and political realists alike and which is based on the ambivalent placement of politics between natural and rational motivation. Now we have a distinction between *politics* and *morality* on the one hand, i.e., the normative realm of individual and collective agency, which is confined to the spheres of individual action or domestic state structures, and *rationality* or *relations* on the other. The international sphere, which is the realm of rationality or relations, becomes naturalized in that its operation is structurally predetermined. It is a sphere in which structural constraints dictate the pattern of inter-state behaviour over against the specific nature and ideology of particular political orders. In effect, neorealists reject the notion of normative international theory in principle since within the international there is no room for changing the system and no possibility of bringing together the realm of what is with what ought to be.

We are now in a position to summarize the nature of realist theory in relation to idealism, using the three elements of normative theory earlier identified. Ontologically, realism shares with Kantian idealism the identification of the human condition as split between natural and ideal determination. In the case of tragic realism this tends to result in a mirror image of idealism in terms of presumptions about international politics. Rather than morality determining politics and history, the opposite is assumed. But what differs is the perception of the balance of forces rather than the nature of those forces. However, systemic realism introduces a more substantive difference to idealism by claiming a profound disjuncture between politics within the state and politics outside it. This leads to the state taking on a special status both in terms of its identification as the sole significant actor in the international context and normatively in terms of its capacity to mediate between reason and nature. This excludes consideration of non-state actors as significant participants in international politics. It is also profoundly contrary to the idealist focus on individuals as the fundamental source and location of normative value. Realist conceptions of the international realm itself do differ somewhat between tragic and systemic aspects. Tragic realism emphasizes the contingent and transient nature of all social and political life and the cyclical view of history as a constant reiteration of the same ambivalent political dynamics. Systemic realism emphasizes the structural necessity of the inter-state system and tends to lose track of history, focusing instead on the synchronic, logical relations which dictate the pattern of international politics. Both agree, however, that there is no definitive progress in history whether through natural or rational necessity.

Epistemologically, tragic realism does not necessarily differ from idealism in terms of assuming the possibility of rationally grounding claims about what ought to be the case. Some realist thinkers clearly suggest that there are certain universal principles by which the normative goodness or badness of a situation may be assessed – even if they are dubious about their power to change that situation. However, another theme of tragic realist thinking is that idealism in international politics is often employed to disguise the pursuit of particular interest. On this view, there are always grounds to be suspicious of the deployment of moral principles in the context of international policy-making. Carr goes further than this in arguing that all claims to truth about international politics are relative to the interests of the claimant. In general, realism, in all of its aspects, differs from idealism in arguing for the importance of norms of judgement derived not from moral principles of right but from the determinations of political practice. As stated above, this is not because it isn't possible to judge international politics in terms of moral principles, rather it is because such judgements distort international political reality. To see international politics through rose-tinted spectacles, it is argued, is to be blind to, and thereby collude with, the most dangerous possibilities of international politics. Where idealism gives normative priority to the principles of right deriving ultimately from the moral law, realism gives equal or greater priority to specifically political norms. What is right in international politics in so far as it is the realm of the purely real side of politics can be judged in terms of political norms of conduct to do with the pursuit of security and national self-interest. As with idealism, however, this leaves realism with the question of how it justifies its basic normative principles and the metaphysical assumptions about human nature, states and history from which they are derived.

The judgements and prescriptions of political realism follow from its ontological and epistemological presumptions. Realism condemns actuality in so far as actors bring inappropriate principles of right to the practice of politics and supports the idea of prudence as the key virtue of the political actor. Realism is sceptical about the possibility of radical change and it differs from idealism in terms of the means thought appropriate for bringing about what change (progress) may be possible. Crucial to realist prescriptions for the good of international politics is the preservation of the principle of state sovereignty. For this reason, realists stress the importance of the institutions and practices which support the principle of state sovereignty and enable states to co-exist, such as treaty-making and diplomacy. Above all, the achievement of a balance of power between states is seen as the key to international peace and security. Realism is highly sceptical of the virtues and efficacy of inter-national institutions and even more so of political cosmopolitanism. Not only is there no basis for political authority above and beyond the agreement of states in the international sphere, but also international institutions based on internationalist or cosmopolitan legitimations are regarded suspiciously as an idealistic coating of the real pursuit of underlying state interests.

Conclusion

At the crux of the debate between idealism and realism is a double distinction: the distinction between morality and politics on the one hand and the distinction between state and international politics on the other. The former distinction is common to both paradigms, the latter is an implicit assumption of Western political theory since the seventeenth century, but it is made explicit and rigid in the sceptical and systemic elements of realism which have set the agenda for thinking about international relations in the post-war period. This double distinction is grounded on a yet more fundamental distinction between realms of rational and natural determination. Although Kant provides the most obvious example of a metaphysic in which human action is perpetually caught between autonomy and heteronomy, the presumption of this radical contrast between reason and nature is reflected in the accounts given by all the other variants of idealism and realism of the substance of international politics. Even in the cases of utilitarianism and systemic realism, which give an essentially monological account of the mainsprings of international politics, those theories are only intelligible in terms of the reduction of one side of the reason/nature dichotomy into the other. The different ways in which idealism and realism deal with the double distinction between morality and politics, state and inter-state give rise to a variety of specific disagreements about whether politics (nature) regulates or should regulate morality (reason) and vice versa; about what the status and scope of application of moral or political principles is or should be; about whether it is more dangerous to bring moral principles into politics or to exclude them. But what remains constant is the grounding distinction which the normative theory sets out to bridge. In summary, both idealism and realism accuse each other of illegitimately identifying what is with what ought to be. Realists accuse idealists of seeing reality through a cloud of wishful thinking and therefore making fundamental mistakes about what is possible in the international sphere. Idealists accuse realists of taking the status quo of the state system as eternally given and the basis for international right, thereby endorsing rather than challenging violence and inequality within the international sphere. The interesting question raised by both idealism and realism is whether it is possible to think the ideal and the real together without this becoming transformed into either moralism or *realpolitik*.

The tit-for-tat exchange between idealism and realism has provided the conceptual framework of normative international theory in the post-1945 period. However, it should be borne in mind that this has been a debate conducted until relatively recently from the standpoint of the prevalence of sceptical/systemic aspects of realist theory in both the explanation and normative judgement of international politics. Although it is clear from the above that both idealism and realism are founded on the same conceptual oppositions, the dominance of realism, with its exclusion of the ideal from the real has sustained the notion that the realm of international relations excluded the normative as such. Thus normative theory seemed only to be identified with idealism and its appropriate realm of application with the domestic political sphere. Even the explicit normative content of the tragic elements of political realism was very much marginalized. In mainstream accounts, idealism (and therefore moral judgement and action) has been seen as the shadowy other of international politics, to do with that which international politics both is not and cannot be – and perhaps ought not to be. Just as the domestic state has been the shadowy other of the international. This situation, however, has begun to shift with the development of work that explicitly opposes the exclusion of the normative from the international as a matter of both theory and practice.

Within the study of international relations, the notion of the inapplicability and irrelevance of normative considerations within the international sphere has given way for a variety of reasons and in a variety of contexts. It was noted earlier that the domination of realism in international theory was consolidated by the circumstances of the Cold War. The end of the Cold War, the growing importance of the international/global economy, the increasingly obvious part played by non-state actors in international politics, the upsurge of intra-state ethnic conflict, perceptions of global ecological crisis – all of these have provided external prompts for the re-thinking of realist orthodoxies. This re-thinking is apparent not only within the re-emergence of idealist themes in liberal and a variety of new critical theories of international politics (see Chapter 3) but also in a return to the tradition of realism as a normative theory, particularly in its tragic dimension (Frankel, 1996b; Spegele, 1996; Murray, 1997). Of all of these developments, the most obvious counter to realist orthodoxy is the upsurge of work in international ethics, which will be the focus of discussion in the next chapter. However, what the discussion of realism and idealism in this chapter has demonstrated is that if the revival of normative international theory is simply a swinging back of the pendulum from realism to idealism then very little has been gained. Normative international theory, as was noted at the outset, aims to produce and account for normative judgements and prescriptions in the international sphere. For both idealism and realism this involves the bringing together of morality with politics. However, it is not clear how any approach that continues to rest on a conceptual framework in which morality and politics have radically different relations to the mutually exclusive realms of reason and nature can succeed in bridging the gap between them (morality and politics). The argument of this chapter has made clear that in essence both idealism and realism set themselves an impossible task when they try to think morality and politics together. In the light of this it is not surprising that the two theories have a tendency to reduce to moralism on the one hand and *realpolitik* on the other. It remains to be seen whether approaches in the ethics of international politics are more successful in formulating normative international theory. If not, it seems likely that the problem lies not with either idealism or realism but with the underlying conceptual framework which leads them to identify normative theory with something that must but cannot actually be thought.

Notes

1   There has been a variety of philosophical and theological work on the ethics of war and deterrence in the post-1945 period. Much of this work followed on from consideration of the new forms of warfare, such as mass bombing, experienced in the Second World War and from the war crimes trials at Nuremburg and Tokyo. However, other events were also influential on the flowering of this work at different times. At times of superpower tension during the Cold War, attention was focused specifically on the ethics of nuclear war and deterrence. The experience of the Vietnam War also provoked a wide range of responses in philosophical ethics. See, for example: Clancy (1961); Wasserstrom (1970); Walzer (1992 – first published 1977); Kenny (1985); Paul et al. (1986); Holmes (1989); Norman (1995).

2   Three useful overviews of themes and approaches in contemporary norma-
    tive international theory are to be found in Nardin and Mapel (1992a), Brown
    (1992a) and Dower (1998); see also Held (1995).
3   Brown (1997a) provides an excellent overview of the competing schools in the
    explanatory theory of international relations in the post-1945 period. See also
    Burchill and Linklater (1996); Smith et al. (1996); Neumann and Waever
    (1997).
4   The middle way is most clearly exemplified by the theoretical school variously
    referred to as 'rationalist', 'Grotian', 'international society' or 'English School'.
    This approach will be examined in Chapter 3. A recent and helpful collection of
    essays on this approach is Roberson (1998).
5   *Moralism* and *utopianism* are both terms used by classical realist thinkers such
    as Carr and Morgenthau (discussed in the section on 'Realism' in this chapter)
    to refer to ways of thinking which presume both the possibility of moral
    progress in and the applicability of moral principles to the judgement of
    international politics. Wight adopted the term *revolutionism* to refer to a range
    of similar perspectives, with the emphasis on the possibility of moral progress
    in history (Wight, 1991: 8–12) (see discussion of Wight's classification in
    Chapter 3). *Liberalism* is a much broader term than the others. In international
    explanatory theory it is used to refer to modes of explanation which stress
    factors other than state power and interest and draw attention to cooperation
    as well as competition in the international sphere (Smith, 1992; Burchill, 1996a).
    In normative international theory, however, liberalism is associated primarily
    with both the assumption of the possibility of moral progress in the inter-
    national sphere and the necessity of the application to international politics of
    moral principles grounded on respect for individual right (see discussion in
    Chapters 5 and 6).
6   In the discussion which follows the focus will be on features of liberal rather
    than socialist ideology. The relation between idealism and Marxism will be
    examined properly in Chapter 3.
7   In the account of Kant which follows I will be drawing in particular on the
    following texts: 'Idea for a Universal History with a Cosmopolitan Purpose',
    'On the Common Saying: "This may be true in theory but it does not apply in
    practice"', 'Perpetual Peace: a Philosophical Sketch' (all the above texts are
    collected in Kant's *Political Writings* (1991a); *The Metaphysics of Morals Part I*
    (1991b); *Foundations of the Metaphysics of Morals* (1969). Useful secondary
    source material on Kant's political thought includes: Williams (1983, 1992b);
    O'Neill (1989a); Beiner and Booth (1993); Hutchings (1996b); Bohman and
    Lutz-Bachmann (1997).
8   The most famous such aid is the 'universalization test' by which human beings
    are able to test out the moral validity of a maxim for action. According to Kant,
    if a maxim yields contradictory or absurd consequences when it is univer-
    salized, then this means that the action could not be morally right. This is
    summed up in Kant's first formulation of the categorical imperative for moral

judgement and action: 'Act only according to that maxim by which you can at the same time will that it should become a universal law' (Kant, 1969: 44).

9 A good overview of classical and contemporary utilitarian approaches to international politics is provided by Ellis (1992). Key primary utilitarian texts are Bentham (1970) and J.S. Mill (1962).

10 This version of idealism is often referred to as 'liberal internationalism' and is discussed in more detail in 'Modelling Cosmopolitan Democracy' in Chapter 6 below.

11 This version of idealism is most obviously exemplified in contemporary arguments for cosmopolitan democracy, discussed in 'Modelling Cosmopolitan Democracy' in Chapter 6 below.

12 I am using the term 'tragic' in a different sense to Spirtas (1996), who identifies what I term the systemic element of realism (most pronounced in neo-realism) with tragedy (Spirtas, 1996: 387–9).

13 I cannot pretend to provide an exhaustive account of the different realist thinkers here. The analysis which follows draws on the following texts: Niebuhr (1946, 1959); Carr (1946); Morgenthau (1958, 1985); Waltz (1959, 1979). Useful introductory reading on realism includes: Donnelly (1992); Burchill (1996b); Brown (1997a: 67–122). More specialist work on realism includes: Griffiths (1992); Frankel (1996a, 1996b); Murray (1997).

14 Note that Hobbes was never primarily concerned with international politics in his political theory. Hobbes's preoccupation was with providing secure grounds for political authority within a bounded political order. Nevertheless, Hobbes's account of internal political authority is necessarily entwined with its external other and has been very influential in conceptualizing the limits of normative international theory.

2

The Ethics of International Politics

Introduction

In normative international relations theory, over the past twenty years, the mainstream challenge to realist dominance has been mounted by work on 'international ethics'. This work has its theoretical roots not in the paradigms of international relations theory itself but in Anglo-American philosophical ethics or moral theory. In the past thirty years, in the Anglo-American academy, there has a been a great revival of work in the area of moral theory known as applied ethics. This kind of work is involved in assessing arguments concerning the rights and wrongs of a variety of legal, political and social issues from abortion and punishment to genetic engineering. Applied ethics is premised on the notion that moral justifications for concrete practices are both theoretically possible and practically valuable. Debate within this area of work has been dominated by the theoretical paradigms of consequentialism (largely inspired by utilitarianism) and deontology (largely inspired by Kantianism) (see, for example, Almond and Hill, 1991). This has the consequence that although the purpose of applied ethics is to cast light on the rights and wrongs of particular concrete issues, in practice applied ethics also uses the concrete issues as a way of testing the validity of the particular theoretical paradigms. Thus the focus of discussion has an in-built tendency to shift to the metatheoretical domain of the rights and wrongs of particular moral philosophical paradigms. Over the same period and in parallel with the upsurge of work in applied ethics there has been a revival of work in political theory, marked most obviously by Rawls's defence of liberal and social democratic principles in *A Theory of Justice* (1972). A similar logic is discernible in debates in political theory as is apparent in applied ethics. Although the purpose of the exercise is to establish the right kind of way of organizing the modern, liberal state, a large part of debate is preoccupied with the assessment of theoretical principles rather than practices and institutions. If the debate in applied ethics is dominated by that between Kantianism and utilitarianism then that between liberalism (a term which includes Kantian, utilitarian and contractarian paradigms) and communitarianism dominates contemporary political theory. One of the most striking things about contemporary liberal/communitarian debates is the extent of agreement over practice (most participants support some form of liberal social democracy) and the intensity of disagreement over theory. The notion that contemporary political theory is to a large extent a variation on applied ethics is confirmed by recent developments in applied ethics in which communitarian arguments have begun to be articulated. Thus arguments between different universalist approaches have now been supplemented by arguments from ethical particularism in both moral and political theory.

In general, the pattern of argument in international ethics reproduces debates between theoretical approaches which have been honed in applied ethics and political theory. This was a pattern already set by one focus of debate in international ethics which predates much of the work in applied ethics and political theory in the past twenty years. Since 1945 there have been successive attempts made by ethical and political philosophers to establish ways of distinguishing between just and unjust, legitimate and illegitimate uses (or threats of uses) of violence in the international realm. From the beginning this project was defined in terms of applied ethics. Thus, the conceptual armoury drawn upon in considering the ethics of war and international intervention has been predominantly the familiar one in which consequentialism is pitted against deontology or ethical universalism against ethical particularism.[1] The much more recently formulated arguments in international ethics concerning issues such as human rights, distributive justice, the ethics of nationality and cosmopolitan democracy have taken their cue from just war theories and share the vocabulary of applied ethics and political theory.

When commenting on the dominance of realism in international relations theory in the post-war period, Brown notes that it was accompanied in the Anglo-American academy by the relative eclipse of work in moral theory and (what Brown terms moral theory's sub-discipline) political theory, other than of the most abstract meta-theoretical kind (Brown, 1992a: 84–5). He observes that the marginalization of normative work in international relations was part and parcel of a more general rejection of substantive moral thinking in the immediate post-war period. Brown's point is to suggest a closer link between international relations theory and its sister disciplines of moral and political theory than is often assumed and to indicate the link between a revival in normative international theory (international ethics) and these other theoretical developments. There is no doubt that Brown is correct in his claim, but his point is interesting for another reason. Brown suggests a genealogical link between moral theory, political theory and normative international theory with moral theory as the source and origin for normative thinking about both domestic and international politics. This claim is interesting because rather than international ethics being seen as operating counter to the conceptual assumptions of realism (or indeed idealism), it actually works to confirm them. International ethics is based on the notions that morality and politics are fundamentally distinct, and that normative theorizing is concerned with demonstrating how the latter (politics) can be made to conform to the requirements of the former (morality). In this chapter I will argue that the examination of international ethics confirms that if re-engagement with the normative in international relations is in the form of moral theory, or of political theory dominated by moral theory, then the conceptual tensions through which both realist and idealist alternative readings of world politics have been articulated will continue to structure debate. The ethics of international politics do not challenge the logic which presents a choice between realism and idealism, instead it re-presents that choice at the more rarified level of principles of ethical judgement.

In the discussion that follows, I will examine key approaches in international ethics and how they relate to the conceptual presuppositions of realism and idealism. First, the ethical paradigm summed up by the term 'morality of states' will be considered. It will be argued that consideration of the theoretical justification for a morality of states (which follows from the standpoint of international ethics) leads to the exploration of more fundamental grounds for moral judgement in the international sphere. This exploration of the grounds of moral judgement takes us to the predominant approaches to international ethics. These are summed up under the general heading of cosmopolitanism and will be examined in the second section of the chapter. Thirdly, the discussion will move on to communitarianism, an approach to moral theory which can be seen as complementing certain aspects of the 'morality of states' tradition but which introduces a rather different basis for the notion of 'state right' and is radically anti-cosmopolitan in its implications. I will argue that in the case of all of these approaches we are constantly returned to the conceptual oppositions and choices explored in Chapter 1. Nevertheless, as with the theoretical approaches in the previous chapter, it will also be argued that there is a demand implicit in the aims of these different theoretical approaches for a synthesis of what have been defined as oppositional elements. In the final section of the chapter I will consider certain recent attempts to respond to this implicit appeal, still within the terms of international ethics. In conclusion, it will be claimed, in spite of the best efforts of all of these theorists, the attempt to move normative international relations theory beyond the realism/idealism dichotomies is stymied by its confinement within the cage of international ethics. In order to re-think normative international theory properly the notions of morality and politics have to be re-thought in terms which are antithetical to the idea of an ethics of international politics itself.

The morality of states

The 'morality of states' paradigm in international ethics is the one most closely tied in its intellectual origins to the emergence and development of the post-Westphalian state system in Europe and, in particular, to the development of modern international law. It is profoundly intertwined with the thinking which is to be found in the ideological justifications for the legitimacy of state power in the work of Western political theorists from the seventeenth century onwards. The essential characteristic of a morality of states theory is that it acknowledges that states are the crucial ethical actors in the international context and bases the principles of international ethics on the principle of state sovereignty (Nardin, 1983). Dower identifies the key elements in a morality of states as follows:

1 States have a duty to support the system of states.
2 States have a duty to respect the sovereignty, autonomy or independence of other states.

3   States have a duty not to interfere or intervene in the internal affairs
    of other states.
4   States alone have the right to engage in organized violence.
5   States have a general duty to promote peace but have a right to wage
    war if they have a just cause.
6   States have a duty to observe restrictions in the conduct of war, if
    they are at war.
7   States have a duty to honour agreements.
8   States have a duty not to harm other states, but have no duty in
    general to promote the global common good, the good of other states
    or the good of individuals living in other states.
9   Individual human beings do not have rights against any states other
    than those they live in. (Dower, 1998: 55)

All of the above principles reflect implicit and explicit requirements of
contemporary international law. However, in order to count as a standpoint in international ethics, the morality of states cannot simply rest on
its being a reflection of principles institutionalized in the current international order. This would be to reduce international ethics to realism,
dependent on and relative to the vagaries of history. Unless there is a
higher level moral justification for the above prescriptive principles then
there is no reason why these principles should be seen as having universal scope and binding moral force. There are two prime candidates to
provide morality of states with a derivation from moral ideality rather
than political reality: natural law and contract.[2] Of these the former has a
much longer history as a way of distinguishing right from wrong in
relations between different political powers. I will therefore look briefly
at natural law as a distinctive tradition in moral theory before going on
to show how it has become entangled in contractarian thinking in
modern conceptions of the morality of states.

   The origins of natural law thinking can be traced back to stoic conceptions of a universal law of nature which extended to the government of
human conduct as well as the material natural order (Heater, 1996: 1–26).
In terms of the relevance of natural law thinking to international ethics,
however, it is the Christian development and adaptation of more ancient
ideas which is most significant. In medieval scholastic philosophy the
legitimacy of political power was accounted for in terms of a divinely
sanctioned natural law which reflected a divinely ordained natural hierarchy of rights and obligations. The necessity of coercive political order
was grounded in the need to protect humanity, to the greatest possible
extent, from its own sinfulness by providing a stable context to prepare
for entry into the eternal, divine order after death (Williams, 1992a: 29–

33). However, the legitimation of political rule was linked to the obligations of political rulers as well as political subjects to this higher,
universal order. One of the best-known outcomes of Christian natural
law thinking was what has become known as 'just war theory', a body of
principles designed to govern both entry into war and the conduct of
war. What is interesting about just war thinking is that it combines an
acceptance of the ethical status, indeed necessity, of political authority
with the notion that that authority is sanctioned and limited by a higher
power. Thus although political rulers (and only political rulers) have a
right to declare war, this right is constrained by a range of conditions to
do with the justice of the cause, likelihood of success and so on (*jus ad
bellum*). Similarly, although political authority is entitled to kill or injure
in circumstances of *jus ad bellum*, this right is again circumscribed by a
range of conditions to do with the consequences of the action and the
nature of the target population (*jus in bello*).[3]

In the transition from medieval to modern forms of political order in
Europe, the concept of natural law continued to act as a reference point
in justifying the legitimacy of the emergent political order of the state.
Both the rights of states over their populations and the rights of states in
relation to each other were derived from a higher order set of principles
sanctioned by God and immanent in nature. However, it is at this point
that the idea of natural law becomes intertwined with contractarian
arguments in formulating an ethics of international politics. In the work
of thinkers such as Hobbes the notion of natural law is secularized into
laws of nature that reflect the absolute natural rights of individuals and
the need for those rights to be collectively (through a mutual contract)
surrendered to political authority (Hobbes, 1991: 117–21). In the work of
thinkers such as Locke, the notion of a pre-existing natural law is
married to the necessity for an explicit contractual undertaking to found
a state, a contract in which all individuals abandon their prior natural
right to enforce that law on their own behalf (Locke, 1988: 271–8). The
notion that the rights of states are to be understood in terms of universal, divine principles of right becomes mingled with and subsumed
by the notion that the right of states derives from the natural rights of
individuals which have been transferred to the collective political
authority.

Making contract and individual right the key to the legitimacy of
sovereign political authority has the effect of reducing the distance
between the viewpoint of a morality of states and the viewpoint of
sceptical and systemic realism, although these remain distinguishable
theoretical positions. The positions converge, as we saw in the previous
chapter in relation to Hobbes, in that they both identify legitimate

authority entirely with the state and provide no grounds, other than self-interest, for intervention in the affairs of another state. They diverge in that whereas the sceptical and systemic realist treats all states as being alike, contractarian theories provide criteria for distinguishing between legitimate and illegitimate states and for justifying revolution within states. Moreover, whereas sceptical and systemic realists presume the eternal verity of the competitive state system, contractarian thinking permits, and perhaps even encourages, the extension of contractarian principles between states. Thus the model of the morality of states emerging from the contractarian turn in political theory is one which is grounded in a notion of reciprocity, mutual respect linked to mutual advantage (Mapel, 1992: 194–8). The resulting morality is minimalist but it is some way removed from a state of nature.

In contemporary ethics of international relations, the viewpoint of the morality of states has been most evident in the revival of just war theory. Both Christian natural law and contractarianism have served as bases for condemning or supporting the rights of states to intervene in the affairs of others or resist intervention in their own (Ramsey, 1968; Anscombe, 1970; Elshtain, 1992a; Walzer, 1992). However, in general the notion of the morality of states has been marginal in the discussion of other issues such as international human rights, global distributive justice and cosmopolitan democracy. If anything, with regard to the latter, morality of states has tended to be set up as the moral position in need of transcendence (Dower, 1998: 61–9). The reasons for this are to do both with dissatisfaction with the substantive scope of a morality of states, and dissatisfaction with the basis on which states are assigned ethical status in the morality of states theory. In the case of the former, morality of states theory is accused of being too close to a straightforward reflection and endorsement of the international status quo. By premising principles of international ethics primarily on state sovereignty, the morality of states is argued to depend on the institution which sustains violations of human rights, problems of world poverty and the lack of accountability of elite international actors. In the case of the latter, it is argued that, ultimately, the morality of states viewpoint assigns an ethical value to the state for instrumental reasons. In the case of natural law arguments states acquire moral status in deference to a higher moral order which is given categorically and universally. In the case of contractarianism states acquire moral status on the basis of individual right. According to critics, the morality of states perspective is unable to justify giving an absolute moral status to the state and is only able to do so by introducing extra pragmatic assumptions which echo realist claims about the necessity of the state system. For this reason in much contemporary ethics of international relations, the notion of a morality of states is accused, at best, of ethical confusion in that it is unable to justify the central place it gives to state sovereignty; at worst, it is treated as indistinguishable from realism (MacCarthy, 1993).

The most interesting theoretical outcome of the analysis of the morality of states perspective is that it seems to be unable to carry through the synthesis of ideality and reality, universality and particularity which it promises. The state occupies the uneasy position of being both ideal and real, universal and particular. Yet because these concepts are understood in terms which are radically opposed, the state is always in danger of being reduced to one or the other – real and particular in its actual existence, ideal and universal in its identification with transcendent grounds of right. Moreover, both natural law and contractarian based accounts are caught between the grounding of international right in terms of universal principles (God's law/individual natural right) and instantiating that right in the ethical particularity of the state. It is no accident that arguments from both natural law and contract can be used both to endorse state right and to undermine it. According to critics in international ethics, in order to avoid lapse into realism, the morality of states perspective needs either to acknowledge the instrumental nature of the value attached to the state or provide a more substantive ground for that value. In the case of the former, morality of states merges with moral cosmopolitanism; in the case of the latter, it merges with moral communitarianism.

Moral cosmopolitanism

Cosmopolitanism is an ancient term which shares its origin with the concept of natural law in stoicism and the stoic's famous claim to be a citizen of the universe (cosmopolis) and not simply a citizen of any particular polity (Heater, 1996: 21–3). The meaning of the stoic's claim was not politically revolutionary, but referred to the idea that the standards governing human conduct were inscribed in nature and available to reason. Traditionally, cosmopolitanism as a normative ethos is associated with three different sorts of claims: first, the claim that all human beings share a common moral identity; secondly, the claim that there are universal (cosmopolitan) standards of normative judgement; thirdly, the claim that there should be a cosmopolitan political order. In recent work which has revived the concept of cosmopolitanism to capture the nature of an approach to normative international theory, a standard distinction is made between moral and political cosmopolitanism (Pogge, 1994: 90). Moral cosmopolitanism refers to the first two strands mentioned above, political cosmopolitanism to the latter. It is obvious that these strands may be interlinked in the sense that arguments for political cosmopolitanism may rely on arguments from moral cosmopolitanism (see discussion of political cosmopolitanism in Chapter 6). Nevertheless, it is not the case that moral cosmopolitan approaches are necessarily politically cosmopolitan in the sense that they are bound to argue for a supra-state political order over and above the state system as enshrined in the morality of states. Indeed, in many cases, the state system is taken for granted as a given context into which cosmopolitan moral standards need to be imported.

> . . . cosmopolitan theories which identify human beings as such as the bearers of values . . . and then, given that starting point, claim that in principle any such beings might, in one's relationship with them, generate duties which one has towards them. These theories may be called 'unbounded' or 'open' because the domain of obligation is in principle all humans (or beings more generally) with the relevant value-bearing characteristics. . . . The natural tendency of these theories is to advocate some kind of world ethic for individuals, as belonging to one global moral community – where community is defined in terms of the claimed moral relations, not in terms of established traditions, felt relations and shared values in practice. (Dower, 1998: 23)

As mentioned above, the recent developments in the ethics of international politics in relation to issues such as human rights, distributive justice, nationality and cosmopolitan democracy, are foreshadowed in an older set of arguments concerning the justice of war. Broadly speaking, there are three kinds of moral philosophical reasoning which have dominated consideration of the ethics of war and deterrence: just war theory, deontology (Kantianism) and consequentialism (utilitarianism). The distinguishing feature shared by just war theory, deontology and consequentialism is that they are all premised on the claim that the state does not provide the ultimate source of right in international politics. They all also share the view that the basis on which the actions of states and individuals in war should be judged is applicable universally. In the light of the discussion in the previous section it could be argued that just war theory is a weaker version of moral cosmopolitanism because of the 'relative autonomy' it grants to the notion of state right. Kantianism and utilitarianism, however, are strong versions of moral cosmopolitanism in that their central reference points are the universal standard of right on the one hand (categorical imperative, principle of utility) and the individual human being on the other. It is characteristic of moral cosmopolitanism that it identifies morality as such with a set of standards which are rationally formulated in an abstract, ideal world for application to concrete reality. Thus Kantian and utilitarian theorists ignore the principle of state sovereignty or treat it purely instrumentally, and instead deploy the categorical imperative on the one hand or the principle of utility on the other to analyse and assess, for instance, the rightness or wrongness of mass bombing, nuclear deterrence or the US involvement in the Vietnam War (Hardin et al., 1985; Holmes, 1989; Norman, 1995).

This application of a cosmopolitan principle or set of principles of judgement to an international or global context is also characteristic of the range of work which goes beyond the subject of inter-state violence to other normative issues in the ethics of international politics. As stated above, this cosmopolitanism is not necessarily prescriptively political or institutional (although it may be); it is fundamentally a moral cosmopolitanism, which grounds its universal standards of judgement and ethical prescriptions on claims about universal human commonality. It is important to note that all cosmopolitan perspectives are not the same. They vary both in their substantive prescriptions and in the sense that they differ in their theoretical presumptions about the principles from which conclusions about rights and wrongs in international politics can be derived. Cosmopolitanism can come in maximalist and minimalist versions, from a contractarian version which uses the principle of individual freedom to justify state right and minimize the level of mutual obligation at the international level to strong human rights arguments for international institutions with coercive powers over states in defence of individuals. For this reason, just as debates over just war have been largely debates between different cosmopolitan paradigms (predominantly between consequentialist and deontological frameworks), so the major focus of ethical theory in relation to international human rights or global distributive justice is debate between different versions of moral cosmopolitanism both in terms of theoretical presumptions and substantive implications for judgement and prescription. This can be illustrated by looking briefly at some examples of such work.

Normative work on global distributive justice is essentially concerned with the question of whether there are grounds for the redistribution of wealth from rich to poor across the globe. It is secondarily concerned with how this redistribution, justly, might be achieved. As a theoretical

debate the discussion of international distributive justice takes its cue
from the theories of domestic distributive justice which have flourished
in the wake of Rawls's *A Theory of Justice* (1972). Beitz's work, which
pioneered debate on international distributive justice, was directly
inspired by Rawls's theory and the idea of an 'original position' in which
rational beings worked out fundamental principles of distribution in
isolation from any concrete context (Rawls, 1972: 11–22; Beitz, 1979).
Beitz argued that in confining his principles of distribution to self-
contained political communities, Rawls was accepting a morality of states
view of international obligation without any justification other than the
unreflective incorporation of the international status quo into his thinking
(Beitz, 1979: 35–50). A characteristic feature of the debates on international distributive justice which have followed Beitz's intervention is that
they are premised on a rejection of the morality of states claim that only
minimal moral obligations hold between states and that states and their
populations have no direct obligation to individuals who are citizens of
other states. They also tend to identify morality of states with realism and
see it not simply as an anti-cosmopolitan position but as an anti-moral
position *per se*.[4] Very frequently work on international distributive justice
will begin with a reference to arguments as to the inapplicability of norms
of distributive justice to the international realm only to move on to
dismiss those arguments. This dismissal is sometimes premised on a
weak empirical claim, that the circumstances of material interdependence
in the contemporary world at least justify the consideration of the
possibility of more extensive inter-state moral obligation (as in Beitz's
claim that Rawls's notion of 'circumstances of justice'[5] does apply
internationally). In itself, however, this premise is compatible with
almost any conclusion about international distributive justice, from a
principle of non-intervention (Hardin, 1977) to an argument for a system
of global redistributive taxation (Barry, 1989a, 1989b). In addition,
therefore, the dismissal of the morality of states and of realism relies on
stronger assertions as to the presence of universal moral facts and
principles which provide higher and possibly overriding claims to those
of state right, as in the work of Singer (1972) or Shue (1996). Unsurprisingly, in the light of the above, much work on international distributive justice is focused on the strong normative assertions which different
theorists invoke. Two influential arguments by O'Neill and Barry provide
examples of the kind of work characteristic of moral cosmopolitanism in
international ethics. It is not my purpose to assess these arguments on
their merits, but to establish the type of argument involved. What
follows, therefore, are summaries not full-blown accounts of the arguments in question.

In her article 'Transnational Justice' (1991), O'Neill begins by dismissing the minimalism of a morality of states on the grounds that the 'circumstances of justice' do apply internationally and therefore a search for a principle/principles of international justice is not only justified but unavoidable (O'Neill, 1991: 277). She also dismisses the communitarian position which would suggest a degree of closure of political community which is incompatible with the realities of the modern world (O'Neill, 1991: 282; see 'Moral Communitarianism' below). However, the bulk of her argument is directed at alternative claims as to what is (are) the principle (principles) of international distributive justice. She criticizes utilitarianism on grounds of both problems internal to its promise of calculating outcomes and on the external grounds that it is compatible with the instrumental use of lives and has no criterion for distinguishing between needs other than degrees of preference (O'Neill, 1991: 282–4). O'Neill then goes on to examine a range of liberal and neo-Kantian positions, in particular ones that rely on a notion of basic human rights. In relation to the latter, she develops her own particular neo-Kantian position. A major preoccupation in this article is with the problem raised by reliance on notions of 'rights' in an international sphere in which the position of individual rights holders may be clear but it is far from clear from whom/what those rights can be claimed. In Kantian terms obligations to those in need in the international context appear as imperfect rather than perfect obligations, for which reason some commentators regard aid as a matter of charity rather than justice (O'Neill, 1991: 298–300). In contrast, O'Neill, using an interpretation of Kant's categorical imperative, establishes the categoricality of certain transnational obligations (e.g., to feed the hungry) (O'Neill, 1991: 300–4). The implication of her argument is that international agencies must be established whose duty it is to carry out these obligations.[6]

In Barry's case, his arguments about international justice are oriented entirely in relation to different cosmopolitan theories of justice in response to which he provides his own cosmopolitan solution in terms of a principle of impartiality (Barry, 1989a, 1989b). Barry distinguishes between obligations of humanity and of justice (Barry, 1989a: 456–8). The former are goal-based obligations, which are essentially justified by reference to human well-being and the duty to promote well-being and relieve suffering. The latter are rights-based obligations, which relate essentially to rights of control over material and non-material resources. For example, aid to a famine stricken country is an obligation of humanity, but it would not be wrong for a state to refrain from providing such aid if the donor state was not satisfied that the aid would go to relieve the needy. According to Barry, however, the systematic redistribution of goods to compensate for natural inequality (in terms of differential natural resources in different states) is a requirement of justice, which means that the question of what the recipient state would do with the resources is irrelevant to the question of whether they ought to receive them. Barry makes his case through a demonstration of the problems involved in alternative accounts of justice, setting his own notion of justice as impartiality against various versions of justice as reciprocity (Barry, 1989a: 439–55; 1989b). One concluding recommendation is that there should be a system of international redistributive taxation (Barry, 1989a: 459–62). This redistributive system, as a matter of justice and not of humanity would be without reference to the kind of states which benefited from it (Barry, 1989a: 459). Barry also argues, however, that any state, rich or poor, should be liable to intervention if it transgresses fundamental principles of justice (Barry, 1989b: 492).[7]

There are two things which are particularly striking about the arguments of both Barry and O'Neill. First, the arguments are framed as a response to a variety of other cosmopolitan theoretical positions. In other words, they are geared to the assessment of the strengths and weaknesses of alternative normative assumptions and principles, largely in abstraction from a consideration of the international political context, although it is presumed in both cases that there is something wrong with the actual current distribution of goods at a global level. Secondly, the implications of their arguments are substantial and imply a set of prescriptions for changing the face of international politics. These arguments are clearly fuelled by a strong desire that the world should be changed to close the gap between principle and practice – in the light of the right kind of principle having been discerned. There are two questions raised by the above account of moral cosmopolitanism as a theoretical practice. First, the question of how moral cosmopolitanism establishes its claim to theoretical truth. There has as yet been no resolution of the competing claims of different forms of deontology and consequentialism. If this is so then it seems that moral cosmopolitanism must remain preoccupied with metatheoretical debates. Secondly, and more importantly, even supposing one version of moral cosmopolitanism is convincing in principle, what is the relation between this theoretical truth and the world to which it is to be applied? Obviously cosmopolitans would like their theoretical prescriptions to influence the empirically unequal and divided world, but it is unclear why the truth should be persuasive, particularly when it has been derived from principles abstracted from actuality. There is a disproportion (exemplified in the arguments of O'Neill and Barry but typical of cosmopolitan ethical theory in general) between time spent on abstract theoretical debate between set-piece positions and time spent on reflection on what might sustain the kinds of institutions, practice and policies which these theories envisage. For instance, the question of whether the state system is even in principle compatible with international distributive justice is rarely directly addressed. This makes such theorizing vulnerable to the standard realist critique of idealism, that it operates in a parallel universe and is therefore inapplicable to political actuality.

The preoccupation with establishing ideal principles of judgement is seen as justified because in establishing true grounds for the validity of certain kinds of policy it enables critique of the international status quo. This is evident in work such as that emerging from the 'Quality of Life' conference, organized by Nussbaum and Sen (1993a):[8]

> The search for a universally applicable account of the quality of human life has, on its side, the promise of a greater power to stand up for the lives of those whom tradition has oppressed and marginalized. (Nussbaum and Sen, 1993b: 4)

A key concern of the moral philosophers participating in this conference was the question of whether there were any objective, universal grounds on which to base transnational judgements about what constitutes a good human life. This meant that a great deal of debate centred on epistemological questions about objectivity and relativism in knowledge, including moral knowledge (Nussbaum and Sen, 1993a: 143–276). The purpose of the exercise, for cosmopolitanism, is to establish truths about humanity which transcend and provide a standard for the critique of different political and social conditions, including those of international politics. In the process of attempting to do this, it not only risks being seen as inherently utopian but also returns to debates about the nature and status of judgements that replay familiar idealist and realist positions.

At first sight the cosmopolitan work on the ethics of international relations seems to provide a robust challenge to realism, the morality of states and the making of a fundamental distinction between the norms governing international politics and moral or domestic political norms as such. However, the robustness of this challenge is more apparent than real. Its purpose is to apply ethics, in the sense of moral standards (principles or values) to the judgement of specific practices in order to prescribe what is right and what is wrong. In the case of work on the rightness and wrongness of war, of aid, of international human rights and so on, moral cosmopolitan approaches do not challenge political realism's account of the distinctions between morality and politics, state and inter-state relations which constitute the scope and limits of international politics. Instead, they construct a standard of measurement according to which international politics can be judged. The result of this is that work on international ethics is preoccupied with debates not about international politics but with the standard of judgement.[9] The effect of this is not to undermine but to return us to the realist/idealist distinction, with international ethics remaining confined to the 'idealist' pole and easily sidelined as utopian or impractical by mainstream accounts of international politics.

Moral cosmopolitanism, therefore, can be defined as the universalistic other of empirical and pragmatic realism. However, cosmopolitan theories are not the whole of the story of ethical theories of international politics, although they are a great part of it. A different challenge to the realist settlement in the study of international politics is to be found in a normative approach which takes issue with the realist/idealist distinction from both sides, problematizing the reduction of international politics to pure *realpolitik* on the one hand and the universalism/cosmopolitanism of ideal normativity on the other. This is the challenge provided by what has come to be called the communitarian approach to international ethics, an approach which provides a different way of grounding the morality of states.

Moral communitarianism

The communitarian perspective in international ethics has its most recent origin in a central debate in moral and political theory between 'liberals' or moral universalists and 'communitarians' or moral particularists.[10] The former include schools of thought (Kantian, utilitarian, contractarian) that attempt to derive the legitimacy and universal applicability of substantive social, economic and political arrangements from abstract, rational (liberal) principles. The latter argue that the principles by which social, economic and political arrangements are legitimized are always grounded in concrete practices, traditions and communities. The implication of the communitarian argument is that morality has to be redefined in much more concrete and particular terms. One consequence of this is that the community or collective which grounds the validity of institutions and provides the condition for normative action and judgement acquires an intrinsic value.

As with cosmopolitan approaches in the ethics of international relations, recent attention to communitarian work follows on from work focused on issues of just war and international intervention. In his trailblazing book on the ethics of war, *Just and Unjust Wars* (1992), Walzer set out to argue the case for defence and prosecution in relation to a series of examples of inter-state violence *ad bellum* and *in bello*. During the course of his arguments he deploys elements of traditional just war theory and uses Kantian and utilitarian approaches selectively, according to context. In addition to this, however, Walzer introduces another normative dimension which departs from the usual repertory of sources for thinking about just war and which prefigures his thinking about justice within the domestic state (Walzer, 1983). He argues for the inherent ethical value of the nation-state as the mode of self-determination of a specific people. This claim is one we have already encountered in Mill's idea of a people's right to self-determination which received a liberal, idealist gloss in Wilson's vision of international politics. However, in Walzer's text, the moral significance of the people or nation as such is emphasized in addition to the liberal, contractarian focus on individual right as the source of state right. Walzer is not consistently communitarian in his arguments in *Just and Unjust Wars*, but for the purpose of this chapter I will be focusing on the communitarian emphasis in this work.[11] This emphasis underlies both Walzer's endorsement of the non-interventionist principle of the morality of states (what he terms the 'legalist paradigm') and certain of his arguments for where he thinks the legalist paradigm needs to be supplemented (Walzer, 1992: 58–73).

The ways in which communitarian approaches to ethical issues of inter-state violence challenge cosmopolitanism are fairly obvious. Communitarianism takes issue with the claim that ethical standards, principles and values apply universally given the right of a 'people' to determine itself. The communitarian gives an ethical status to collective right which is not reducible either to the protection of individual right or to its (the state's) institutionalization of universal ethical standards. Instead the source of right is in the particular self of the collective, which thereby acquires a special value (Walzer, 1981). This is evident in some of the arguments Walzer makes in *Just and Unjust Wars*. For instance, Walzer argues in favour of the possibility of legitimate pre-emptive strikes on the part of Israel in the context of the Arab–Israeli conflict. This is justified in terms of the ongoing threat to the state of Israel constitutionally inscribed in its neighbours (Walzer, 1992: 80–5). In other words, the value given to the existence of a particular collective overrides traditional just war criteria which would suggest that states are justified in responding only to direct aggression. Similarly, Walzer invokes a notion of 'supreme emergency' to justify the use of unjust means when the existence of a state as such is threatened (Walzer, 1992: 251–5).

The ways in which communitarianism challenges realism are not as immediately apparent as in relation to cosmopolitanism. This is because although communitarianism is an anti-realist position it can readily be used to support the notion of a morality of states, two positions which moral cosmopolitanism tends to conflate. In many ways, the idea of the ethical privileging of a right of self-determination seems simply to confirm realism's acknowledgement of state sovereignty as the key determinant of international politics. Moreover, it appears to be in accord with the Hobbesian argument that the political order precedes and institutionalizes right rather than vice versa and with the sceptical element of realism which puts the notion of the universality of values and principles into question. Nevertheless communitarianism cannot be identified entirely with realism. In the first place, communitarianism disrupts realism's implicit commitment to the inapplicability of moral norms to international politics. It does this by giving normative significance to collective right in a way which is analogous to Kantian notions of individual right. Moreover, it suggests that collective right may not be coincident with state right to the extent that there are nascent 'peoples' within and between existing states. Thus Walzer gives a particular normative cast to state right which is distinct both from the sceptical/systemic realist version, in which state right follows purely from its institutionalization of sovereign power and therefore of political order, and from that of the cosmopolitan normative paradigms, whose recognition of state right is parasitic on more fundamental sources of right as such.

There is a prevailing assumption in normative international theory that communitarianism provides the obvious ethical counter to moral cosmopolitanism.[12] Nevertheless, with the exception of Walzer's work, there are, as yet, very few examples of communitarian normative international theory.[13] However, I will now go on to argue that what is striking about the communitarian contribution to debates about the ethics of international politics, in so far as it has yet been articulated, is a peculiar kind of indeterminacy. As soon as communitarian views are applied within the international context they acquire a tendency to dissolve back into the perspectives which they seemed initially to challenge – realism on the one hand and cosmopolitanism or idealism on the other.

The tendency for communitarianism to tip the balance from a morality of states back into realism is evident in Walzer's work. In *Just and Unjust Wars*, the notion of the ethical status of a 'people' becomes the justification for the pure *realpolitik* of the use of the preemptive strike to ensure security from possible threats. Likewise, the notion of 'supreme emergency', which justifies the killing of innocents to preserve the state, recalls the Hobbesian logic of sceptical and systemic realism. There is an odd shift from a communitarian vocabulary of immanently articulated rights and obligation to a vocabulary of an absolute right to survival and autonomy. This is because communitarianism relies on the idea of moral judgement as embedded in particular communities, but in the international context, communities are viewed externally rather than internally and therefore take on a strong resemblance to self-contained Hobbesian actors in a state of nature (MacCarthy, 1993; Hutchings, 1994a). If communities are understood as having absolute intrinsic value then it is not surprising that Walzer reconstitutes the legalist paradigm to extend the rights of self-protection and survival of nation-states. Nor is it surprising that the notion of national right to self-determination dominates Walzer's analysis of *ius ad bellum* and in conditions of supreme emergency trumps Kantian and utilitarian considerations *in bello*.

The charge that communitarian international ethics reproduces realism is commonly made by moral cosmopolitans. Such critics object that communitarianism is not a properly moral position, since it simply reflects and endorses the current principles of the international system. In other words, communitarianism provides no ground for the critique of existing arrangements. As noted above, however, communitarianism does provide at least one principle of critique in the form of the idea of the right to self-determination of a people. Communitarianism does not put the moral validity of the state into question as such but it ties that validity to the link between state and culture, community or nation. It is interesting to examine how the critical principle of a right to self-determination operates in Walzer's argument. There appear to be two kinds of argument: the first argument draws on a language of nature; the second argument on a language of reason. The first argument, reminiscent of Mill's vocabulary, stresses the notion of growth, maturity and strength, with the nation-state being pictured in parallel with the human individual moving from childhood to adulthood. According to this argument, the nation wins the right of self-determination for itself and cannot be granted it by any other agency. The second argument draws on an analogy between the nation and the abstract individual of contract theory which is based on the idea of the state as the embodiment of the individual rights of its members. Thus here communitarianism in the international context slips between realism, in which the forces of nature dictate the outcomes of politics, and moral cosmopolitanism in which the ground for collective right is the prior right of individuals (see Frost, 1996: 128–36).

Walzer is by no means oblivious to the charge that his moral position puts him hand in glove with realism and prevents the adoption of a critical or interventionist stance in relation to current international politics. In 'The Distribution of Membership', Walzer argues that although the rights of states over conditions for state membership are crucial, nevertheless the exercise of those rights should be limited by more general principles (Walzer, 1981). In a recent development of his general ethical and political theory, Walzer addresses the issue of whether a communitarian moral theory is condemned to an unquestioning acceptance of the status quo and the impossibility of intervening in the affairs of other communities. In the essay *Thick and Thin: Moral Argument at Home and Abroad* Walzer argues that 'I want to endorse the politics of difference and at the same time, to describe and defend a certain sort of universalism' (Walzer, 1994a: x). By 'politics of difference', Walzer means a communitarian acceptance (and celebration) of a plurality of cultural values and ways of life which are neither reducible to nor transcended by universal values or principles or common human identity. Walzer accomplishes his task by arguing that there is a kind of minimal, 'thin' version of morality which becomes articulated only in relation to very specific purposes. All actual 'thick' moralities have this capacity, although it in no sense constitutes their true and common core (Walzer, 1994a: 2–6). He suggests that we can perhaps recognize the significance of an experience of injustice within another form of life, but if we try to act on that recognition we will almost certainly make bad mistakes (Walzer, 1994a: 18–19). Instead Walzer argues for the importance of immanent criticism and the ways in which alternative values within a way of life harbour the capacity to transform and improve it (Walzer, 1994a, 1994b). For Walzer, the formulation of international moral norms is one example of a 'thin' morality which is necessary for the survival of the 'thick' moralities of particular communities. It is clear that this 'thin' morality of international ethics is governed by a norm of non-intervention. However, this returns us to the question of how such a 'thin' morality is sustained. The value attached to the survival of particular communities in the context of international politics can, it seems, only be grounded in the natural right of communities to exist as sovereign powers. When this right is put into question then communitarianism seems to have only the vocabularies of realism and moral cosmopolitanism at its disposal.

Between moral cosmopolis and moral community

So far in this chapter I have argued that the ethics of international relations, rather than posing a fundamental challenge to the terms of the debate between realism and idealism, actually depends on and reproduces those terms. The idea of international ethics is premised on the acceptance of a gulf between politics (nature, reality, particularity) and morality (reason, ideality, universality). The focus of international ethics is on identifying the principles that morally legitimize or justify the institutions and practices of international politics. Once these principles are identified they provide the basis for either the critique or endorsement of the world as it is. It was evident in the discussion of the morality of states and moral cosmopolitanism that international ethics did little else than repeat a choice between realism and idealism. At the level of judgement particular interest was posed against universal principle, political against moral truth. At the level of prescription state right (community) was countered by individual right (cosmopolis). Even in communitarianism, which breaks the conceptual ordering of realism/ idealism by identifying morality with particularity rather than universality, the same choices reappear in the arguments between communitarianism and realism on the one hand and moral cosmopolitanism on the other. Ironically, the purpose of international ethics, to bring the realms of politics and morality together, is defeated by a framework of thinking common to realism as well as moral cosmopolitanism and communitarianism which keeps the two apart whether in the gulf between ideal and real, reason and actuality or state and inter-state.

Unsurprisingly, the three-cornered conversation between realism, moral cosmopolitanism and communitarianism has been joined by other voices in international ethics looking for ways between these apparently opposed positions (Brown, 1995; Bellamy and Warleigh, 1998). In particular, international moral theorists have been anxious to find a way of accommodating the importance of both state and individual right and of resisting the transhistorical universalism of judgement in moral cosmopolitanism without falling into the located relativism of judgement in communitarianism. I will now go on to consider three suggestions for alternative paths in international ethics: constitutive theory, neo-Aristotelianism and the theory of moral sentiments.

Constitutive theory is best exemplified by the international theory of Frost. In *Ethics in International Relations: A Constitutive Theory* (1996), Frost takes the starting point of his argument from what he calls the 'settled norms' of international politics. These include the morality of states discussed above but are supplemented by a range of modernization and domestic norms which are claimed to reflect the normative reality of the current international order (such as recognition of economic modernization, democracy and respect for human rights as goods) (Frost, 1996: 106–12). Frost argues that most of the norms on his list are dependent on the normative weight attached to the preservation of a society of states and the principle of state sovereignty. However, there are also certain norms on the list that depend on priority being given to the rights of individuals. Frost recognizes that there is a tension here and argues that not arguments from international order, utilitarian arguments nor rights-based, contractarian arguments are able to resolve this tension without subsuming one kind of right under the other and effectively deleting certain norms from the list (Frost, 1996: 137). Frost's solution to the difficulty is to argue for a constitutive relation between state and individual right, based on a reading of Hegel. According to Frost the achievement of individual rights depends on mutual recognition between individuals within the state as autonomous citizens. This possibility in turn depends on the mutual recognition between states within the international system of each other as sovereign. State right and individual right are therefore mutually constitutive and one cannot exist without the other – at least ideally (Frost, 1996: 141–59). In practice, Frost argues that in the contemporary state system, the latter may well precede and condition the former. Thus he suggests that the recognition of new states, even if their internal regimes do not institutionalize mutual recognition, can be part of an educative process in which established autonomous states teach less worthy states how to play the game according to the settled norms of international politics (Frost, 1996: 154–5).

Frost's argument is put forward essentially as a way of synthesizing moral cosmopolitanism's attachment to individual right with communitarianism's insistence on the normative value of the nation-state and the realist's view of the necessity of sovereign power. However, it displays a tendency to disintegrate back into its component parts. Its critical power derives from an essentially cosmopolitan reading of Hegel's philosophy of right as providing a universally valid paradigm for how both state and inter-state politics ought to be organized. Frost uses Hegel to identify the notion of an ethical state and it is only an ethical state which enables the co-existence of state and individual right. However, Frost shifts from moral cosmopolitanism to a communitarian or even realist position when, in practice, all states are identified with ethical or potentially ethical states. If this move is not justified in communitarian or realist terms then it seems to rely on a reversion to Kantian idealism, in which progress is built into history (Brown, 1997b: 285).

In contrast to constitutive theories of international ethics, which are largely concerned with reconciling the norms of state and individual right, the two other alternative approaches which have begun to be developed in international ethics are focused on reconciling (or avoiding a choice between) universal and particular in moral judgement. The target of both neo-Aristotelian and moral sentiment approaches is primarily the assertion of moral cosmopolitanism that there are rationally grounded and universal standards of judgement and that judgement which is not both rationally grounded and universal is therefore not moral. According to neo-Aristotelians such as Spegele (1996), who labels his theory 'evaluative political realism', morality is embedded in a plurality of forms of life within the current world order, including the morality of states. There can therefore be no abstract standard by which the rights and wrongs of particular institutions and practices are assessed in perpetuity. The only way to adjudicate, morally, between different institutions or practices is to exercise reflective as opposed to determinative judgement, that is, to think creatively and dialogically in relation to contexts in which moral conflicts emerge (Spegele, 1996: 191–229). Moral judgement is a matter not of theoretical but of practical reason in the sense of *phronesis*, which mediates between the claims of politics and morality as well as between different moralities (Spegele, 1996: 92–101). Moral judgement is not purely relative or subjective, it is always objectively grounded but in a plurality of communities rather than a singular cosmopolis. What differentiates neo-Aristotelianism from communitarianism is the significance assigned to practical reason as the guard against realism and a pure amorality and contingency of judgement on the one hand, and the imperialism of moral cosmopolitanism on the other.

Unlike Spegele, Rorty objects to moral cosmopolitanism on pragmatic rather than epistemological grounds. Nevertheless, a similar pattern to the neo-Aristotelian approach is discernible in Rorty's contribution to international ethics on the subject of international human rights (Rorty, 1993). He argues that whether or not there is a rational foundation for claims of universal moral principle, the debates within moral cosmopolitanism are doomed to be prescriptively unproductive because they assume a connection between true knowledge and causal efficacy, that is to say, they assume that the truth is inherently persuasive (Rorty, 1993: 119). Rorty accepts, like Spegele, that moral values are embedded in different cultural discourses outside of which they have little meaning. Rather than turning to *phronesis*, however, to provide an alternative to moral cosmopolitanism, Rorty draws on Baier's recent re-working of a Humean theory of moral sentiment (Rorty, 1993: 128–9). According to Rorty, the way between the acceptance of communitarian moral closure

and the consequent amorality of the international sphere is the development of feelings of identification with others. Thus the key to international ethics is not rational argumentation or even practical reason but
the rhetorical devices which will help individuals in one part of the
world feel an echo of the pain of strangers as if it were their own (Rorty,
1993: 133).

To what extent do *phronesis* and moral sentiment move moral judgement away from the choice between universal and particular, cosmopolis
and community which characterizes most discussion in international
ethics? On the face of it, neither moves the terms of the argument very far.
Both in essence embrace a neo-communitarian argument for the
embeddedness of moral practice and judgement and understand their
position in opposition to moral cosmopolitanism. In addition, neither
theory challenges the notion that morality is to be contrasted to politics in
the international sphere. In spite of the emphasis on practice in both
Spegele and Rorty, the synthesis achieved by these positions remains
largely within the domain of moral theory or, more specifically, within the
exercise of moral judgement or moral feeling set against the actualities of
politics. Nevertheless, it is a synthesis which is suggestive of the possibility of moving debate beyond the terms of international ethics, which is
premised on the notion that morality is not but ought to be inherent in
politics. Both Spegele and Rorty suggest that there is something wrong
with the whole conception of international ethics itself, but neither of
them goes so far as to break out of the paradigm entirely. Instead they
become additional voices in recurring debates over the epistemological
status of moral claims.

Conclusion

The main outcome of the development of international ethics as the
normative corrective to mainstream international theory has been the
reiteration of familiar themes, debates and problems. One problem in
particular has become prominent with the introduction of communitarianism as an international ethical perspective. This is the problem of how
to negotiate between notions of the intrinsic rights of peoples, state
sovereignty and individual rights. This preoccupation has been particularly evident in debates about international human rights and about the
ethical significance of nationality which will be examined in detail in
Chapter 5. A good example can be seen in the recent collection of essays

in response to Nussbaum's call for the return of a focus on cosmopolitan citizenship in US education, *For Love of Country: Debating the Limits of Patriotism* (Nussbaum et al., 1996):

> If one begins life as a child who loves and trusts his or her parents, it is tempting to want to reconstruct citizenship along the same lines, finding in an idealized image of a nation a surrogate parent who will do one's thinking for one. Cosmopolitanism offers no such refuge; it offers only reason and the love of humanity, which may seem at times less colourful than other sources of belonging. (Nussbaum et al., 1996: 15)

Many of the respondents to Nussbaum's paper object to the notion of a stark contrast between cosmopolis and community. The problem is that having formulated ethical thinking in terms of this contrast it becomes extremely difficult to break down or to bridge. There have been a variety of efforts to introduce new conceptual schemes into international ethics so as to get beyond the impasse of a restatement of cosmopolitan and communitarian options. Some thinkers invoke Aristotelian ethics (Spegele), others Humean notions of moral sentiment (Rorty), but the same kinds of charges and counter-charges continue to recur. Ethical approaches are condemned as being either relativist or universalist, realist or utopian, concrete or abstract. The arguments get caught in a repetitive rhythm, in which the contrast is drawn, challenged and re-drawn in such a way that distinctions between morality and politics, state and international, universal and particular remain in place.

Does/should morality regulate politics or vice versa? Does/should moral value inhere in the individual or the collective? Is the international sphere morally distinct from the sphere of the domestic state? Are moral judgements universal or particular, necessary or contingent? The approaches to international ethics considered in this chapter all presume certain answers to the above questions – in each case, answers which in opting for one or other of two apparently opposed alternatives in fact perpetuate dependence on certain axiomatic positions. What emerged from the argument between idealism and realism in the previous chapter is reinforced in the argument between cosmopolitan and communitarian moral theories. As long as normative international theory remains conceived as an ethics of international politics, international right remains conceived in terms of an 'ought to be'. In the chapter which follows, I will be considering certain recent developments in international relations theory which are premised on a rejection of the standard assumptions of both idealist/realist and cosmopolitan/communitarian debates. To what extent do the theoretical frameworks of the English School, Marxism, critical theory, feminism and postmodernism break out of the theoretical choices offered by mainstream normative theory?

Notes

1   A striking example of this is Hardin et al. (1985). See also Holmes (1989); Nardin and Mapel (1992b); Walzer (1992); Norman (1995).
2   See Boyle (1992) and Mapel (1992) for an overview of natural law and contractarian traditions respectively.
3   There is a very large literature on just war theory. Origins are traced back to Augustine and Aquinas (see, Holmes, 1989: 114–45; Williams, 1992a: 14–44). More recent work on and debates about just war theory can be found in the following: Ramsey (1961, 1968); Wasserstrom (1970); Walzer (1992); Clark (1990); Elshtain (1992a).
4   Brown provides a useful overview of theoretical work on international distributive justice (Brown, 1992a; 1997b; see also Dower, 1998: 137–57). Work on this topic includes: Hardin (1977); Beitz (1979); Singer (1972); Barry (1989a, 1989b); O'Neill (1991); Attfield and Wilkins (1992); Pogge (1994); Nielsen (1998).
5   'Circumstances of justice' apply when a combination of interdependence and moderate scarcity entail the need for some principle of material distribution – this would be unnecessary in contexts of absolute abundance or complete separation of individuals or communities.
6   O'Neill's argument raises a series of fascinating questions about modes of theorizing in international ethics, but also about issues such as how to understand the nature of individual and collective agency in the international sphere (O'Neill, 1991: 278). Of all the thinkers working on international ethics, O'Neill shows the greatest sensitivity to the problem of ethical theory which operates in terms of an idealized world (O'Neill, 1991: 281; 1992). Nevertheless, O'Neill's argument here remains essentially an engagement with other ethical positions rather than with international politics, which functions rather as the background testing ground for the validity or invalidity of the theoretical position.
7   In Barry (1989b) the argument concludes with a list of maxims which follow from the application of the principle of impartiality to questions of international justice. These are listed as follows:

1 Where aid is given as charity to relieve suffering, it is legitimate for the donor country to insist that the aid be disbursed to the needy within the recipient country.

2 In as far as redistribution is required by the demands of justice, the criterion of justice is that countries, as collectivities, should have their fair share of the world's resources.

3 Failure of a country to have just internal distribution does not relieve donor countries of the obligations of international justice.

4 International pressure, economic sanctions, or even military intervention may sometimes be legitimate as a way of improving the internal justice of a society.

5 The right of other countries to apply such pressure is not increased if the country in question is a beneficiary of international transfers based on justice. Nor is the right decreased if the country in question is a net contributor. (Barry, 1989b: 492)

The distinction Barry draws between justice and humanity rests on the significance of individual autonomy (1989a: 457–8). The extension of this distinction to international affairs is premised on the analogy between individuals and states as autonomous entities, even though Barry is clearly aware that this analogy is problematic in various respects.

8 The papers in *The Quality of Life* (Nussbaum and Sen, 1993a) were the product of an interdisciplinary conference which brought philosophers together with social policy and welfare economics experts to discuss the question of how to assess the quality of life. The key theme of the volume is the tension between objectivism and relativism in measuring human well-being. However, it also illustrates the nature of applied ethics as the application of standards/principles worked out in philosophical abstraction to the world of policy-making and the difficulties which are inevitably involved in this kind of exercise.

9 It is important to note that these debates are highly sophisticated and often sensitive to the charges of idealism and abstraction. In general, however, the response to such charges is to make the 'standard of judgement' ever more complex and nuanced rather than to look more carefully at the object to which this standard is to be applied.

10 For overviews of this debate see Bell (1993), Mulhall and Swift (1996), Paul et al. (1996). Notable protagonists on the liberal side include Rawls (1972), Dworkin (1985), Raz (1986); on the communitarian side MacIntyre (1981), Sandel (1982), Walzer (1983), Taylor (1990).

11 There are tensions within Walzer's argument between a liberal grounding of state right (in individual right or universal principle) and a more substantively communitarian view of the value inherent in the collective self of a people. This reflects a tension within communitarian political theory as such between an 'organic' communitarianism which treats the collective as an individual self writ large and a 'republican' communitarianism, which views

the collective as a construct which in some sense reflects or embodies individual human autonomy (see Chapter 5, 'Which Selves, What Determination?'). The tensions within Walzer's argument in *Just and Unjust Wars* are usefully discussed in MacCarthy (1993) and Frost (1996: 131–5).

12   Brown (1992a) pioneered the introduction of this terminology. The rapidity with which it has been adopted is noticeable, in spite of the underrepresentation of communitarian work in the field. Thus in Nardin and Mapel (1992b) international ethics was classified essentially in term of consequentialist versus rule based approaches, whereas in Dower (1998) cosmopolitanism and communitarianism have become the key modes of classification (see also, Bellamy and Warleigh, 1998).

13   There are elements of communitarianism in the arguments of Frost (1996), Spegele (1996) and Rorty (1993) – see discussion in the following section below – also in the neo-Hegelian argument of Brown (1994b) and the contextualist approach of Rengger (1993). However, at this moment, no one has yet produced a fully fledged communitarian international ethics and the field remains dominated by different cosmopolitan approaches.

PART TWO

CRITICAL CHALLENGES: RETHINKING INTERNATIONAL THEORY

3

Theorizing International Politics

Introduction

The repetitive and unresolvable nature of contemporary debates in normative international theory has not gone unnoticed. There are now a plethora of critical theoretical approaches to international relations which challenge the conceptual parameters of realist versus idealist, communitarian versus cosmopolitan arguments. These include representatives of Frankfurt School critical theory, postmodernism and feminism, but also two important precursors of these three contemporary schools, the theoretical paradigms of the international society approach (sometimes referred to as 'rationalist' or 'English School') and of Marxism.[1] In this chapter I will be surveying and assessing the range of theories which challenge international relations orthodoxy and the relegation of normative theory to the realm of moral philosophy. It will be my contention, however, that the realism/idealism dichotomy continues to exert a certain influence even on those perspectives which aim to open up an alternative normative theoretical vocabulary. This has meant that normative work on substantive issues in international theory tends to retain its marginal position within the international relations academy – it is treated as a critical voice but one which has made only limited progress in the positive reconceptualization of international politics (Brown, 1994c). Nevertheless, the approaches considered here (international society, Marxism and critical theory, postmodernism and feminism) all provide substantial insights which help to furnish the development of an alternative approach to international normative theory. In particular, I will be emphasizing the crucial insight common to all these approaches that understanding normative international theory in terms of a distinction and/or relation between morality and politics is fundamentally unhelpful.

In considering each of these approaches I will frame the analysis in terms of the ontological, epistemological and prescriptive elements distinguished within realism and idealism. I will assess the extent to which each approach mounts a successful challenge to the realist/idealist alternatives and address the question of the relation between these new approaches and the relegation of normative international theory to the ethics of the international. In each case the main aim will be to assess the contributions these approaches make to re-thinking the dominant terms of normative international theory.

International society, or the middle way

In Chapter 1 attention was drawn to the way in which the canon of international theory has been constructed in retrospect in the twentieth century. The identification of Kant as archetypal idealist or Hobbes as archetypal realist was part of the articulation of the idealist/realist debate since the 1930s rather than evidence of its long-standing nature. One of the most influential categorizations of canonic traditions in international theory (particularly within British and Commonwealth scholarship) has been that coined by Wight, who distinguished three key traditions:

realism, rationalism and revolutionism (Wight, 1991: 7–24). By realism Wight refers to the familiar realist paradigm considered in Chapter 1; by revolutionism, he refers to what was discussed in that chapter under the heading of 'idealism' and also, specifically, to Marxism (see discussion of Marxism and critical theory below). Rationalism, is presented as a *via media* between realism and idealism, it is linked by Wight with the canonic figure of Grotius. Grotius was writing at the time of the demise of Christendom and the formation of the modern state system in Europe (Kingsbury and Roberts, 1990: 1–64). What is distinctive about Grotius's analysis is that it both recognizes the pluralism of state right in the emerging European order (contra-idealism) but at the same time argues that this order is not a mere state of nature but a social order in which states are constrained by common rules effectively derived from natural law (contra-realism). The extent to which Grotian rationalism genuinely mediates between realism and revolutionism is clearly open to question. As Cutler points out, the very fact that Grotius relies on natural law as the basis for international social order seems to link him more closely to idealism or cosmopolitanism (Cutler, 1991: 48), whereas the insistence on the idea that states are the only members of international society has obvious parallels with the axioms of realism and the presumptions of communitarianism. It is not my concern to analyse Grotius here, but the fact that his work can be read not so much as synthesizing or overcoming but rather as retaining and re-presenting the tensions between realism and idealism prefigures the critical question for those who identify themselves as contemporary inheritors of the Grotian middle way. Is this a middle way in the sense of a genuine alternative, or is it a mixture of both ways and therefore always prone to be reducible to the terms of the idealist/realist distinction which it is claimed to overcome?

In contemporary work rationalism is commonly understood to be exemplified in aspects of Wight's own work and that of a variety of other scholars, loosely referred to as 'international society', 'English School' or 'neo-Grotian'.[2] As a theoretical paradigm it is intended to provide a better basis for the description and explanation of international politics than realism and idealism, but like both realism and idealism it is also an explicitly normative theory, designed to offer diagnosis and prescription in relation to the rights and wrongs of international politics. What distinguishes this tradition of thinking about international politics most strongly is a focus on the notion of 'international society'. The concept is contrasted with the realist idea of a state system on the one hand and the idealist notion of a community of humankind on the other. The most significant proponent of this middle way is Bull in his book *The Anarchical Society* (1995). I will offer a brief account of Bull's version of the international society approach before going on to analyse it in terms of its ontological, epistemological and prescriptive implications.

The Anarchical Society is focused around two central concepts which within traditional realist and idealist paradigms are normally presented as distinct and potentially opposed: order and justice (Bull, 1995: 74–94). The title of the book sums up Bull's understanding of international order. According to Bull, international order is anarchical in the sense that, unlike order within states, it is not hierarchical. In other words, there is no overarching authority which underpins and enforces political order. However, Bull does not derive from this the systemic realist conclusion that international order is comprehensible solely in terms of a Hobbesian state of nature. In contrast to the hierarchical order characteristic of states, Bull argues that a horizontal order is characteristic of inter-state relations. This order is based on and maintained by common interests, norms and rules which are evident in a variety of international institutions, practices and conventions such as for instance international law and diplomacy (Bull, 1995: 62–73). Like Wight before him, Bull argues that there have been relatively few examples of international society in world history, the current version is distinguished by its scale which goes far beyond that of earlier examples such as the Ancient Hellenic, renaissance Italian city state or the early European state system. Largely because of this scale, modern international society has more difficulty in establishing and maintaining order than has previously been the case – the degree of cultural solidarity between its components is necessarily less. For this reason, Bull recognizes the importance of the realist analysis of the current international system and its essential pluralism, but nevertheless he is insistent that the concept of society is needed in addition to that of system if the nature of international relations is to be properly understood. At the very least, states have common minimal interests in institutionalizing respect for principles such as obligation to honour agreements or protect property. In practice he argues international society is governed by rules which reflect common interests but often also common values.

Bull defines the concept of justice in a strongly Kantian way as moral and categorical and to be clearly distinguished from the realms of legality, prudence and necessity. He distinguishes three kinds of demands of justice: inter-state/international (in which the concern is with the rights and duties of states or with rights to national self-determination); human (in which the concern is with the rights and duties of individuals); and cosmopolitan (in which the focus is on the good of the world as a whole) (Bull, 1995: 78–82). In principle, according to Bull, there is no necessary contradiction between social order in general and observing the demands of justice.

There is, however, incompatibility as between the rules and institutions that now sustain order within the society of states, and demands for world justice, which imply the destruction of this society, demands for human justice, which it can accommodate only in a selective and partial way, and demands for interstate and international justice, to which it is not basically hostile, but to which also it can provide only limited satisfaction. (Bull, 1995: 89)

Bull goes on to argue that in the international context, order must be taken as the value prior to justice. To the extent that the achievement of the goals of justice is possible at all, it can only come about given the prior existence of order (Bull, 1995: 93).

Various commentators have pointed out that the argument in *The Anarchical Society* can be read in a more or less realist or idealist way in relation to the values of order and justice (Cutler, 1991; Neumann and Welsh, 1991; Jackson, 1996; Linklater, 1996a). At one level, Bull emphasizes the inevitable and perpetual tension between order and justice, stressing the plurality of states and the largely procedural and basic norms which underly international society. At another level, Bull suggests the possibility of developing a richer more solidaristic conception of international society in which shared norms and values provide a much stronger link between separate states and the demands of human and world justice might be more likely to be accommodated. Such an international society would be closer to earlier, limited examples of international society, such as those of the Hellenic world, the world of Italian city states and the early European state system. This latter suggestion is, however, counteracted by Bull's perception of the Western dominated nature of the norms underlying the current society of states and the rising importance of alternative cultural norms in a globalized society of states following decolonization. *The Anarchical Society* concludes on the cautious note that the future of international society largely depends on its capacity to evolve cosmopolitan norms that encompass Western and non-Western values (Bull, 1995: 303–5). In the wake of Bull's work international society scholars have remained caught between the more pessimistic pluralist and procedural conception of international society on the one hand, and the more optimistic terms of the solidarist vision of international society on the other (Linklater, 1996a; Roberson, 1998).

Let us now go on to analyse and assess the implications of the international society perspective in relation to idealism and realism, cosmopolitanism and communitarianism. It should already be obvious that this perspective is a mixture of key elements of the two paradigms which it claims to mediate. The ontological assumptions made by the international society perspective seem to incorporate or potentially incorporate the range of both metaphysical and empirical assumptions made by idealism and realism. The Christian distinction between real and ideal modes of existence and motivation which we find in Kantian idealism and tragic realism is reproduced in the distinction between the realms of order and justice. The acknowledgement of both inter-state justice on the one hand and human and world justice on the other reflects both a realist assumption of the special status of the state and the idealist view that individuals and principles have an intrinsic normative status even in the international context. At the level of empirical actuality, the international society perspective both acknowledges the realist system of states and accepts its likely persistence and the difficulties this poses for human and world justice, but it simultaneously suggests the possibility of historical progress through the development of international norms and institutions.

Epistemologically, like Kantian idealism and tragic realism, the international society perspective assumes the availability of standards of moral and political judgement and makes a clear distinction between the two. As noted above, Bull's notion of justice is a Kantian one in which justice appears as a categorical and universal standard. However, insofar as Bull acknowledges the priority of order over justice as a value in international society he comes closest to tragic realism's insistence that in an imperfect world the (natural) norms of politics as opposed to the (rational) norms of morality must govern that society. Although Bull introduces the notions of justice and order as if they were transhistorical categories and bases for judgement, he also recognizes the historical and cultural relativity of value systems, political and moral. In this respect there is a thread of epistemological relativism in Bull's analysis, with regard to normative claims about international society. This suggests his approach is closer to the sceptical variants of realism which put the notion of transcendent normative standards of judgement into question.

This incorporation of both idealist and realist elements is evident when it comes to the application of the international society perspective to the assessment of and prescription for the future of international politics. As noted above, a pessimistic reading of Bull lends itself to a realist endorsement of the inter-state status quo as the appropriate basis for optimal international order in the absence of a hierarchical authority to enforce justice. Bull is clear that the pursuit of human and world justice constitutes a threat to the available basis of international order. An optimistic reading would come much closer to a Wilsonian argument for the development of international norms and institutions to transform the world as it is in the light of ideals of justice. Thus both communitarian and liberal cosmopolitan ethical viewpoints may take inspiration from the rationalist standpoint. As Linklater puts it in his discussion of the international society approach as a distinctive theoretical tradition, it is fundamentally 'janus-faced' (Linklater, 1996a: 109). The question that remains, therefore, is whether this approach succeeds in liberating normative international theory from the logic of a choice between idealist/ cosmopolitan (moral, universal) and realist/communitarian (political, particular) alternatives. In many ways, it is clear that it does not. All we find is that the international society approach harbours the same choices within it which were previously served up as separate traditions – and it is not clear that the international society perspective provides any resources for transcending the terms in which the choices have to be made. Rather it seems as if we will be idealists one minute, realists the next. Moral cosmopolitans and pragmatic communitarians. One example of this can be found in the work of Vincent, whose work on human rights in the contemporary international order is heavily influenced by the international society perspective. In the following advice, Vincent suggests a composite approach to normative international theory:

> From the morality of states we keep the cautious awareness that political power is concentrated at the level of the state, and that any scheme for moral improvement has to find its way in this world of states. Considerations of prudence do not determine the moral agenda, but they do condition its treatment. From cosmopolitanist morality we keep the sense of direction. And from Realism we keep the suspicion of any purportedly universalist doctrine: it may be that there is a mere part of the whole lurking beneath the rhetoric. (Vincent, 1986: 124–5)

It may, however, be too hasty a judgement to reject the international society perspective as an approach that simply hedges its bets between realism and idealism. What is interesting and distinctive about this approach is the way it depends on the notion that normativity is inherent in and concretely instantiated in international society. This suggests an understanding of international politics which departs from realism and idealism in that it (at least potentially) challenges the distinction between reason and nature, ideal and real – and the idea of politics as caught between or reducible to one or other side of the dichotomy. In comparison to realism's characterization of the international as a kind of void governed by rules of pragmatic self-interest and idealism's characterization of the international as a kind of void which ought to be governed by the moral law, the notion of international society offers the possibility of thinking about international politics not as a void requiring real or ideal principles of order, but as a self-developing order within which norms (not necessarily compatible with each other) are implicit and institutionalized. Logically speaking, this is a starting point which does not base itself on dichotomy and the idea of prioritizing one or other side of a given duality. Rather, it bases itself on the assumption that reality and ideality are always already indistinguishable. The problem is that although the idea of international society potentially undermines the terms of both realism and idealism as a normative approach to international politics, the meaning of the *via media* continues to be expressed in terms of a mixed realist/idealist vocabulary. This means that the nature of international society is described in terms which, as with Vincent's advice above, suggest a composite entity. International society is understood as the coexistence or addition of various institutions or norms which are grasped as separate rather than as intrinsically related. Depending on the focus of discussion, therefore, a rationalist analysis may take on a more or less realist or idealist dimension. The tendency in work which draws on the international society perspective, as already noted, is either to reduce the norms of international order to the realm of heteronomy and a realist understanding of the state system (nature – realism) or to find in them the seeds of the moral law and the universal community of mankind (reason – idealism).

A similar pattern to that apparent in the relation between rationalism and idealism/realism is reproduced in the relation between international society perspectives and debate in international ethics. The concept of 'society' is in radical contrast to the notion of community. Society is a broad term applied to the range and interaction of institutional structure and individual and collective agency which constitutes and reproduces artificial (social as opposed to natural) order; it is inherently both dynamic and diverse. In comparison to cosmopolitanism's static account of the normative in terms of an ideal community governed by universal principle and communitarianism's equally static account of the normative in terms of communal culture, international society suggests that the normative is concrete, complex and self-differentiating. However, when it comes to the articulation of international society as an alternative normative approach, commentators invariably fall into the language of international ethics and the choice between or accommodation of cosmopolitan and communitarian options – or lapse out of it altogether into the language of realism and the state system. The social degenerates into either the universal community of humankind on the one hand or the thick particularistic cultures of specific states on the other – or alternatively, the system. This can again be seen in the work of those such as Vincent, who continue to treat the normative as either a separate and accessible set of moral rules given by an eternal rational order or as the product of a specific culture as well as continuing to nod to the insights of sceptical realism. In the first case, international society becomes quasi cosmopolitan (in aspiration); in the second, it becomes quasi communitarian; in the third, it becomes anarchy. The first two options come together in the optimistic version of rationalism which understands history in terms of an immanent development towards a common international culture (kingdom of ends). This latter synthesis is apparent in Frost's argument discussed in the previous chapter and in Linklater's work to be considered below (Frost, 1996; Linklater, 1998).

Rationalism presents itself as the middle way, but the middle is a peculiarly difficult place to be, so often is it defined in terms of mixture or accommodation, with no vocabulary of its own. It can only be a way that offers a genuine alternative to realism and idealism/cosmopolitanism and communitarianism if it conceptualizes the international qualitatively differently. This is not something which rationalism has succeeded in doing, but it does at least alert us to the possibility of radically rethinking the terms on which mainstream normative international theory is premised. I have argued that rationalism, when it uses the term international society, is trying to conceive something which it, quite literally, does not have the resources to think. The perspectives we are now going on to consider begin with the assumption that not a 'middle way' but an alternative way is what normative international theory needs, one which puts the idea of 'normative theory' of the international as such into question. International society perspectives attempt to re-think the nature of international politics in terms that resist reduction to either realism or idealism. The perspectives we are now going on to consider go further in that for them the reconceptualization of the nature of normative international theory itself, and the relation of theory to its object, is seen as essential to breaking away from the conceptual constraints of orthodoxy.

From Marxism to critical theory

In the previous section, Wight's categorization of international theory into realist, rationalist and revolutionist variants was mentioned. As a category, revolutionism encompassed both inherently moralistic approaches, which assumed the validity of moral standards in the judgement of international politics and revolutionary approaches which presumed the possibility of not only judging international politics in terms of moral standards but also creating an international order which fulfilled the demands of justice. Wight includes both Kant and Marx under the label 'revolutionism' in spite of the radical differences between them (Wight, 1991: 40–7). In recent attempts to re-think international relations theory usually termed 'critical theory', Kant and Marx are again brought together through an engagement with Habermas's work.[3] In order to assess the contribution of critical theory to re-thinking realist/idealist terms of reference in international theory, it is necessary to examine the distinctively Marxist element in this synthesis.

In the construction of canonic international theory which has characterized twentieth century work on international politics, Marxism occupies an interesting position as, as it were, the 'other' other of realism, rationalism and idealism as we have discussed them so far. This is partly for the obvious reason that the ideological struggles of the twentieth century have not predisposed the mainstream international relations academy to take Marxism seriously – something which has been reinforced by the end of the Cold War. More importantly, however, aspects of the conceptual framework of Marxism are very much at odds with mainstream alternatives, particularly realism. Marxist scholarship has therefore always operated on the margins of work on international relations in the post-war period. Nevertheless, in spite of the fact that, as is frequently pointed out, Marx and Engels wrote relatively little on international politics in general, Marxism has inspired work on international politics from Lenin's analysis of imperialism to contemporary world systems theory.[4] What follows is an attempt to pick out general features of Marxist international theory in terms of its ontological, epistemological and prescriptive elements. We will then go on to examine how this tradition of thought has been incorporated into critical theory.

The ontological presumptions of Marxism have been and continue to be subject to considerable debate. However, what is relatively uncontentious is that, unlike realism and idealism discussed above, Marxism does not premise its theory on specific assumptions about the goodness or badness, rationality or irrationality of human individuals. In particular Marxism rejects the dualistic metaphysic of idealism and tragic realism in which humans are caught between natural and ideal determination. In place of this Marxism presents an account of human individuals, societies and states as the ever changing product of complex determination, essentially to be understood in terms of the struggle to produce and reproduce the means of human existence (Marx and Engels, 1970: 42–52).[5] Marx's work can be read in terms of crude economic determinism or in much more sophisticated terms, but whichever interpretation one adopts, what is constant is the assumption that normativity (in the sense of values, ideals, principles of judgement and prescription) is not some-thing absent from or qualitatively distinct from real material existence. The best known exemplification of this, according to Marx's analysis, is that in the modern period of capitalism, the multiple alienation and immiseration of the proletariat provides the objective basis for a struggle for a new world order in which those conditions will be abolished. This brings us, of course, to Marx's most famous claim, that there is a devel-opmental logic to history. This is a claim reminiscent of Kant's philo-sophy of history but with the difference that whereas Kant identifies the moral law on the one hand and nature (providence) on the other as the motors of historical development towards perpetual peace, Marx puts economics, ideology and human agency at the forefront of historical change.[6]

There are several significant aspects to Marx's account of what inter-national politics are. Whereas both realism and idealism base their accounts on a particular understanding of individual and state right and the relation between them, Marx treats these concepts as being them-selves secondary products of more fundamental relations of production. Politics, for Marx, cannot be understood as a discrete autonomous realm either in the case of domestic or international politics. In traditional realist/idealist vocabulary this means that neither strategic interests (nature) nor individual or collective rights (reason) have any kind of autonomous status in Marx's ontology (which is not to say that they do not have considerable actual and ideological power). The main focus of Marxist analysis of state and inter-state politics therefore is the ways in which factions within states and states themselves represent and enact economic interests which, under capitalism, essentially relate to class position. This means that Marx does not operate with an essential distinction between state and inter-state politics. More importantly, it means that he introduces the idea of both the international and, under capitalism, global economy as the crucial category for understanding politics in general. Capitalism, not the inter-state system, international society or the moral law is the most significant reference point in under-standing and prescribing for the stuff of international relations. It is important to note, also, that this means that the stage of international politics is occupied in Marxist accounts by a range of actors which have very little visibility in realism, idealism or rationalism. In addition, classical Marxism assumed that the class based organization character-istic of the politics emerging within industrializing states in the nine-teenth century was in principle a global phenomenon. Neither the bourgeois nor the proletarian was essentially linked to a homeland. The socialist revolution, it is implied, will therefore usher in a global order in which states have disappeared and notions of right, individual or collective, are unnecessary (Linklater, 1996b: 121–5).

The epistemological assumptions of Marxism again differentiate it in certain respects from the other perspectives examined so far. There are elements of Marxism which link it to sceptical realism, in that Marxism insists on the historical conditioning of all claims, whether of a factual or normative kind. The notion that certain kinds of conceptual frameworks suit certain kinds of interests is also one which is common to Marxism and sceptical realism (Carr the most obviously sceptical realist in terms of historical relativism was clearly influenced by Marxist philosophy of history). However, whereas sceptical realism treats strategic interests as contingent, Marxism suggests that certain interests carry the weight of history behind them and their normative goals can therefore be seen as objectively progressive. Marxist theory, therefore, attempts to synthesize the particular and universal in the standpoint of the proletariat. The proletariat's insights into the truths of history are both historically conditioned and true. Marxism presents itself as a liberatory science – a concept oxymoronic according to traditional understandings of freedom and science (Linklater, 1990: 45–53).

Marxist diagnosis of and prescription for international politics follows from its ontological and epistemological assumptions. The more optimistic strain of Marxist analysis which flourished in the nineteenth and early twentieth centuries believed in and pursued the idea of world revolution and the necessity of overthrowing capitalism and the bourgeois state. In this mode, it is clear why Wight places Marxism alongside Kant in his revolutionist category – there is a strong belief in the possibility of progress in world history – indeed in an end of history. The experiences of the latter part of this century have done much to blunt this optimism in theory. Contemporary work which draws on Marxist inspiration is frequently heavily pessimistic in tone seeing in economic globalization the fulfilment of the interests of capital over against those of labour (Smith, 1994; Linklater, 1996b; Brown, 1997a: 186–206).

It is clear from the above exposition that there are elements of Marxism as a theoretical approach which distinguish it radically from previously considered perspectives. In particular, Marxist ontology, both in terms of its metaphysical presumptions and its account of history and international politics, introduces very different conceptions of the international realm from either realism or idealism. However, when it comes to the epistemological and prescriptive elements of the theory there continue to be strong echoes of familiar debates between realism and idealism. At the crux of the Marxist account is a notion of theory as both historically conditioned and true and the identification of the proletarian class as the universal subject of history. Marxism has struggled with the question of how to account for these theoretical positions without lapsing into idealism (in which the proletariat has special access to the moral law and the abolition of capitalism acquires the position of an ought to be) or realism (in which the proletariat represents a particular interest and the end of history is the product of natural determination) (Linklater, 1990: 34–54). In the development of normative international theory it has been the conceptual affinities between Marxism and realism which have been perceived as most problematic by the school of critical theory which is heavily influenced by Marxism (Linklater, 1990: 21–7). In contrast, it is the conceptual affinities between Marxism and idealism which have been perceived as most problematic by postmodernist international theory (Ashley and Walker, 1990). Both these schools take issue with the prioritization of class relations as the key to the nature and potential of international politics. The different traditions in feminist international theory are differently sympathetic to Marxism, but are also united in rejecting prioritization of class relations in the analysis of the international (Spike Peterson, 1992; Sylvester, 1994). Nevertheless, all these new anti-orthodox approaches draw to a greater or less extent on the resources and insights offered by Marxism, as will become evident below.

Marxism has had a lot of theoretical offshoots in the study of international relations, though it has acquired significant status in relation to orthodoxy mainly in the fields of international political economy and development studies (Brown, 1997a: 186–206). In addition, as noted above, it has also been strongly influential on the development of critical international theory which presents itself as a fundamental challenge to and transcendence of the realist and idealist paradigms.[7] Critical international theory acknowledges Marxism as one of its key influences but is also strongly critical of aspects of Marxist theorizing. Linklater, one of the leading exponents of contemporary critical international theory, summarizes its critique of Marxism as follows:

> This project denies that class power is the fundamental form of social exclusion or that production is the key determinant of society and history. (Linklater, 1996c: 280)

As we shall see, what critical theory takes from Marxism are certain of its ontological and epistemological assumptions and particularly the idea of the link between analysis and liberation along with the possibility of progress in history.

In the same article as that quoted above, Linklater claims that critical theory overcomes 'the flawed dichotomy between realism and idealism which has lent a peculiar structure to so much debate within the field' (1996c: 280). In a different context, Hoffman makes a similar claim on critical theory's behalf in relation to the debates in international ethics, in which he argues that critical theory finds a way beyond the utopianism of abstract and a-historical standards of judgement and the pragmatic acceptance of the status quo (Hoffman, 1993: 199). We will now look briefly at two prominent examples of contemporary critical theorists, Cox and Linklater, in order to assess the adequacy of critical theory's challenge to orthodoxy. These two theorists represent two distinguishable traditions of critical theory, one (Cox) which stays rather closer to traditional Marxist analysis and the other (Linklater) which is more obviously influenced by Habermas's fusion of Marx and Kant. It should be noted that because of the perceived dominance of realism as an approach to the understanding of international politics, critical theory has tended to focus on realism rather than idealism in articulating its position. I will follow the pattern of tracing the ontological, epistemological and prescriptive elements of critical theory's analysis.

Cox's work is well known for its eclectic use of a variety of theoretical traditions, although his most prominent theoretical debts are to the Marxist historicist tradition in social science (Cox and Sinclair, 1996; Mittelman, 1998). It is Cox's historicism which is the key to the way in which he traces and challenges the limits of realism (particularly neo-realism) in both ontological and epistemological senses. Thus, at a deep level, Cox follows Marx in rejecting the primary metaphysical status of either the human individual or the state as well as the dualism which places a moral order over and above the actual world order. Like Marx as well, Cox understands history as a dynamic process in which historical conditions produce the possibilities of revolutionary change – which will be carried through, if at all, by the struggles of the oppressed and excluded in the current world order. However, Cox is considerably more cautious than classical Marxism about the idea of an inevitable direction to historical development.

The main critical target of Cox's work is neorealism. He criticizes its characterization of its object of analysis for its a-historical perspective in which the limits of a particular present are treated not as historical constructions, which come about through a complex interaction between states and sub-state and trans-state forces, but as unquestionable eternal verities (Cox, 1996a: 63–5). In making this critique of neorealist thinking, Cox sees himself as calling for a new realism in international theory, one which genuinely reflects the factors structuring international politics. He draws attention to a range of conditions of possibility for international politics which go beyond the state system, including economic, cultural and ideological factors (Mittelman, 1998: 67–73). As in Marxist analysis, he argues for the range of agencies in the realm of international politics to be recognized as including a variety of collectives in addition to states as well as individual human actors. His claim is that if the object of study for scholars of international politics is not seen to include these conditions of possibility and range of agencies, but deals with inter-state relations in isolation, then it cannot go beyond work that reproduces and reinforces the 'common-sense' of the age because it takes for granted a framework of analysis, without questioning the conditioning of that framework itself (Cox, 1996b: 85–123; 1996c: 124–43). This kind of theorizing he labels 'problem-solving theory' (Cox, 1996b: 88). It is a kind of theorizing, he argues, which presents itself in classically positivist terms as simply reflecting a given reality, whereas in practice it is part of the reproduction of that reality and works in the service of those whose interests are served by that reproduction. That process of reproduction confirms patterns of inclusion and exclusion and positions agents differentially in terms of power and in terms of their objective interest in the perpetuation or challenging of the current world order and the perception of its justice or injustice. Here again, Cox follows Marxism in insisting on the ontological inseparability of fact and value; this clearly has consequences for Cox's epistemological position (Mittelman, 1998: 73–9).

Cox identifies modes of social scientific investigation and normative theorizing as part and parcel of the historical development which delivers a particular articulation of the pattern of state power, productive forces and world order. Rather than being a neutral and guaranteed route to the truth, therefore, the methodological approach characteristic of neorealism in particular (which presents itself as scientific) actually reflects a series of assumptions about politics, power, human nature and knowledge which are historically conditioned. Cox's arguments about history and knowledge establish a strong link between description and prescription in all social science. Not only do all theories include value-laden assumptions, all theories are also actively perpetuating or challenging particular relations of power. This means that international theory is not only about politics, it also is itself political (Cox, 1996b: 87; 1996c: 140–1). Cox introduces the distinction deriving from Gramsci between hegemonic and counter-hegemonic discourses to capture the way in which theory is political. Certain kinds of explanation are seen to derive from and reinforce the norms embedded in either hegemonic or counter-hegemonic discourses. For example, neorealism is argued to be a theoretical framework which arose out of the bi-polar world of the Cold War and worked to perpetuate the hegemonic practices of Cold War politics. An alternative social scientific theory, such as that of world systems theory, which identifies exploitative relations across the global economy, might exemplify a counter-hegemonic discourse, which promotes and sustains the interests of the marginalized populations of the current world order (Smith, 1994: 148; Brown, 1997a: 188–93).

Cox's claim that social scientific theory is inherently political extends to the claim that explicitly normative theory is also inherently political, a part of rather than a reflection on historical development. The identification of norms as within history, rather than located in a trans-historical moral law transmitted through the conscience of the historian, undermines the assumption common to both realism and idealism that the spheres of politics and morality are inherently distinct. In this argument, Cox is again following a traditional Marxist pattern with the similar implication that in terms of diagnosis and prescription, critical theory is essentially 'on the side' of the underdog, i.e., those whose objective interests are currently denied. In the case of critical theory, however, the prescriptive brief for what should be done is broader and more open-ended than Marxism in that oppression and correspondingly emancipation is understood in multiple terms as going beyond class to a multitude of other sites. This opening out of the scope of the purpose of critical theory is provided with a rather different kind of theoretical back-up in work such as that of Linklater and Hoffman, which distances critical theory rather more strongly from Marx than is the case with Cox.

Linklater's work has much in common with Cox. In *Beyond Realism and Marxism* (1990), Linklater also argues that the restriction of analysis in international relations to inter-state relations fails to recognize the role of sub- and trans-state political and economic forces in conditioning the possibilities of international politics (Linklater, 1990: 1–7). As with Cox's work, Linklater's argument is not designed to dismiss the insights of realism, but to identify their partiality and examine the role of what has been excluded in order to enhance explanation and understanding in the field. Like Cox again, Linklater seeks to bring history into the a-historical assumptions of traditional international relations theory (essentially systemic neorealism) and to challenge the claim to neutrality in its theoretical and methodological framework. In Linklater's case, however, there is a specific variant of the challenge to the real/ideal, inter-state/state distinctions which are constitutive of classical realism and idealism. Whereas Cox works with the notion of hegemonic and counter-hegemonic discourses, Linklater draws on a broader range of theories, including Habermas's discourse ethics and theory of historical development to identify the potential of the current world order to transcend the logic of the state system reflected by realism (Linklater, 1990: 163–4; 1992b: 35–6; 1998: 77–108).

One reason why Linklater's critical theory has a rather different complexion from that of Cox is that it has developed in the context of an ongoing conversation with all of the theoretical traditions captured by Wight's classification of traditions of international theory. Linklater engages with classical realism, neorealism, idealism (revolutionism) and rationalism, taking them all seriously and being particularly influenced by aspects of the latter two (Linklater, 1982, 1990, 1992b, 1998). In more recent work he has also engaged with alternative critical traditions, in particular, postmodernism (Linklater, 1992a, 1998). Like Cox, his work is eclectic; it seeks to encompass and synthesize a range of theoretical positions in order to transcend them. In recent attempts to characterize the nature of critical theory, Linklater has argued that it should be considered in terms of three dimensions: normative, sociological and praxeologoical (Linklater, 1992a, 1998: 14–45). In examining these three constituents of international theory, the ontological, epistemological and prescriptive elements of Linklater's theorizing can be discerned.

Linklater shares with Marxism and with Cox's critical theory the view that realist and neorealist claims to scientific impartiality are bogus. All theorizing is understood as normative in both its inseparability from evaluative assumptions and in its political effects. In particular the argument that certain aspects of world politics (state system, pursuit of national self-interest etc.) are immutable is understood as the false universalization of an abstraction from a contingent historical situation which has the effect of confirming certain patterns of inclusion and exclusion (Linklater, 1996c: 282–4). These are patterns of inclusion and exclusion which cannot be justified by reference to any general principles generated by either realism or idealism, whether those of nature (*realpolitik*) or those of reason (morality). As we saw earlier, Marxism relied on a particular historical story about the route to emancipation which identified standards of objective human interest by which current political arrangements could be judged and condemned and which would provide the mainspring for revolution. Cox detaches the Marxist position from its reliance on the class struggle as the only salient context for the experience of exploitation and oppression, but holds on to the general notion of the centrality of the value of emancipation across the range of sites of exclusion and oppression. In his exposition of the normative aspect of critical theory, Linklater homes in on the ideal of emancipation and addresses the question of what it means and how it can be defended as the prime orientation of critical theoretical work (Linklater, 1996c: 279–80). In doing this he addresses the criticism regularly made by realists and by postmodernists that critical theory is simply a lapse back into idealism, premised on underivable axiomatic principles which aspire to the status of the moral law but actually give universal validity to the particular moral code implicit in Western modernity (Jahn, 1998).

Linklater's first line of defence against the argument that he is reproducing an idealist position is that critical theory relies not on critique in terms of a-historical standards but on immanent critique. In other words the standards by which international politics can be judged emerge from the tensions and contradictions implicit in domestic and international politics itself (Linklater, 1999: 45–56). His second line of defence is that the universal ideals upheld by critical theory are universal in an inclusive rather than an exclusive sense. In this respect he differentiates critical theory from Marxism and its commitment to a single species-wide ideal end of history. Instead Linklater argues that critical theory involves commitment to the opening up of the possibility of dialogue to diverse agencies and ideals (Linklater, 1996c: 284–90; 1998: 77–108). For this reason he stresses the procedural character of the normative thrust of critical theory. It does not claim to settle issues of the good life but only to maximize participation in and minimize unjust exclusion from the debate. Both of these defences draw strongly on Habermas's work and the notion of discourse ethics (Linklater, 1998: 87–100). The notion of immanent critique derives from Habermas's argument that the principles for the critique of modernity are implicit within its lifeworld. The procedural character of the normative ideal of critical theory is also derived from Habermas's famous reference to an ideal speech situation in which the norms of communication are undistorted by power.[8]

> Collaboration across the frontiers to produce arrangements which are more universalistic, more sensitive to cultural differences and more committed to reducing social and economic inequalities than their predecessors is entailed by domination-free communication. A global narrative of universal emancipation which aims at this, the triple transformation of political community, is immanent within the dialogic ideal. The ethical foundations of political community in the post Westphalian era should revolve around these convictions. (Linklater, 1998: 106)

We will come back to the question of whether critical theory is a return to idealism after examining the sociological and praxeological aspects of the theory which Linklater identifies.

Both sociological and praxeological domains of critical theory are understood by Linklater in terms of the normative orientation described above. The purpose of critical sociology therefore is to understand in Adorno's and Horkheimer's phrase the 'dialectic of enlightenment' in relation to international politics in order to assess the possibilities of the positive evolution of modernity. This means in effect analysing and assessing the forces at work in the contemporary world which work towards or away from the ideals set out in critical theory's normative commitments. Here the influence of both Habermas and his account of the evolution of modernity and of the rationalist work on international society is present in Linklater's work (Habermas, 1984, 1987; Bull, 1995). Whilst being wary of Marxist or Kantian historical stories that identify only one direction to history, there is a philosophy of history at work in orienting the kind of work in which, according to Linklater, critical sociology would engage. This is made evident in the critical praxeology which Linklater argues must be linked to the normative and sociological dimensions of critical theory. According to Linklater, critical praxeology works on the Kantian precept of treating history as if it were inherently progressive. Critical praxeology actively seeks to extend the positive political potential of the world as it is: 'Realizing the promise of the post-Westphalian era is the essence of the unfinished project of modernity' (Linklater, 1998: 220). For Linklater, the modern institution of citizenship provides a particularly good example of a resource for critical practice (Linklater, 1998: 179–212; 1999: 54–6). Linklater claims that amongst the conditions of possibility of that which realism takes as eternally given (i.e., the modern state) is a universal notion of right which points beyond particular interest. Over time, through political struggle oriented by normative ideals, the notion of citizenship within the state has extended to include previously excluded groups (Linklater, 1999: 45–9). Critical praxeology is committed to a second extension in which the legitimacy of the distinction between citizen and foreigner is also challenged by the universal principles implicit in the modern state. Thus the presumptions of realist analysis have to be re-thought not only in terms of the ways in which they have been historically produced/constructed but also in terms of their capacity for self-transcendence, conceptually and in practice.

In the previous section we examined the international society perspective as an alternative approach to international politics distinct from idealism and realism. It was concluded that although the notion of international society itself suggested a different way of thinking about international politics, other than through the 'system of states'/'universal community of humankind' options, the conceptual framework of rationalism essentially simply oscillated between the familiar sides of the debate. When Linklater comments on the structuring and distorting influence of idealism/realism alternatives on debate in international political theory he is drawing attention to precisely this phenomenon

(Linklater, 1996c: 280). However, Linklater (and other critical theorists) make the bold claim that critical theory does manage to achieve what rationalism fails to deliver – a way through and beyond idealist and realist alternatives. To what extent is this actually the case?

The claim that critical international theory transcends old debates between idealism and realism rests most fundamentally on its historicist re-thinking of the relation between theory and its object, which owes a great deal to critical theory's Marxist roots. Unlike idealism and realism, critical theory takes history seriously, treating the state system as a historical product and the nature of scientific and ethical standards as historically shifting. The claim that critical theory transcends idealism rests principally on its (critical theory's) proclaimed refusal to attribute universal significance to historically particular standards of judgement. The claim that critical theory transcends realism (in particular, neo-realism) rests mainly on the plausibility of its rejection of the presumptions of dispassionate scientificity on the one hand and the essential immutability of world politics on the other. It is at this point, however, that a pattern of thinking in critical theory is discernible which works against its claim to have moved beyond the idealist/realist split. Both the objections to realism which have just been cited are tied to critical theory's claim that both theory and practice can be regressive or progressive. A major aspect of critical theory's critique of realism is that it identifies realist theory with reactionary politics, whereas critical theory is identified with progress. If certain historically produced standards (such as emancipation or democratic participation) are being identified as progressive, then they appear to operate as having a universal significance. Indeed, they appear to operate in the same way as Kantian or utilitarian principles might operate to orient judgement in international politics. This apparent departure from strict historicism is confirmed in the praxeological imperative for critical theory of working with what Hoffman refers to as an 'ironic cosmopolitanism' (Hoffman, 1993: 199). Whilst critical theorists are wary of identifying their principles of judgement with a transhistorical, universally applicable moral law, their theoretical practice relies on an as-if identification of this kind which is strongly reminiscent of Kant's idealist philosophy of history.

The response which critical theory makes to the charge that it repeats the idealist mistake of identifying historically particular standards of judgement with transcendentally universal ones is to redefine the concept of universality. It is claimed that the kind of ideal universalism involved in critical theory is inclusive and procedural rather than the imperialist imposition of Western values on the world as a whole. This argument relies jointly on the notion that such a universal can be genuinely non-exclusive and on the notion that there are a plurality of grounds for normative judgement embedded in different subject positions and ways of life. On the one hand, critical theory seeks to operate with a universal notion of 'moral irrelevance' in relation to exclusion; on the other hand, it is committed to recognizing the relativity of claims to what counts as morally relevant difference in the first place. In accepting an essentially communitarian argument about fundamental diversity of group value and interest, critical theory replays within itself the cosmopolitan/communitarian debate, without the means of resolving it.

> Rather than seeking to undermine cultural diversity or eliminate the particularisms of local identities or communities, the ironic cosmopolitanism of critical international theory provides a framework for addressing the tensions between these multiple identities: between universalism and particularism, inclusion and exclusion, self and other. (Hoffman, 1993: 199)

In critical theory's vision of international politics, the battle between reason and nature is reproduced in the idea of a dialectic of enlightenment in which the 'dark' side of modernity struggles with its positive other. The main difference between critical theory and idealism seems to be not that it has a different understanding of the significance of moral value, moral relevance or of the moral status of the individual, but that it is more 'realistic', in that it recognizes the constraints on progress involved in the conditions of international politics (including both the state system and capitalism). An optimistic version of critical theory is idealism or cosmopolitanism with evidence; a pessimistic version is closer to tragic realism, in which history is a perpetual battle between the forces of good and evil.

Critical theory builds on Marxist insights, which are filtered through Kantian ones. Critical theory is Marxist in its recognition of the fact that international politics are historically produced and in its willingness to recognize the significance of non-state factors, in particular the global political economy, in the process of production. It is also Marxist in its argument that the seeds of change lie in the tensions and contradictions implicit in history. However, these Marxist arguments are 'Kantianized' in several ways. First, in the abstraction of a good from a bad side of history to form a standard of judgement; secondly, in the idea of an 'as-if' reading of history to promote progress; thirdly, in the cosmopolitan assumption that the individual is the prime moral unit of reference. As with rationalism's capacity to think international society, so critical theory's capacity to think the unity of theory and practice, morality and politics is undermined by a vocabulary that always already operates dichotomously. For this reason it is not surprising that the arguments of critical theory have provoked responses from all quarters that essentially replay the realist/idealist and cosmopolitan/communitarian debates. In particular, as already mentioned, realists, communitarians and post-modernists have objected that critical theory remakes the old idealist mistakes of transposing the moral law onto the ground of international politics without respect for either the realities of world politics or moral diversity.

However, as with rationalism, it would be mistaken to judge critical theory as simply a repetition of previous theoretical positions. Largely because of its reliance on Marxist insights critical theory goes much further than previous perspectives in re-thinking the nature of inter-national theory in relation to its object. Whilst previous perspectives have restricted the realm of international politics to states and inter-state relations, Marxism and critical theory have recognized a much broader range of relevant actors and institutions in the international arena. Whilst previous perspectives have understood the practice of theory in abstrac-tion from politics, Marxism and critical theory insist that theory is political. However, the latter insight is one that both Marxism and critical theory have found it difficult to hold on to without privileging one type of theoretical politics over another in such a way as to threaten a relapse into the conceptual dichotomies which they have been attempting to transcend. The analysis of Marxism and critical theory offered here suggests that the key to moving definitively beyond realist/idealist and cosmopolitan/communitarian positions in normative international theory is to understand the relation between theory and its object in terms of identity rather than difference. The problem posed by Marxism and critical theory is how such an understanding is possible con-ceptually. Of all of the voices which have criticized Marxism and critical theory as re-workings of idealism, the postmodernists have been par-ticularly vociferous. Let us now go on to examine postmodern attempts to move beyond the realist/idealist conceptual frameworks.

Postmodernism

In comparison to other social sciences, the discipline of international relations has only recently been influenced by postmodernist theory. Nevertheless, postmodernism has become an increasingly important voice in debates about normative theory and the nature, desirability and possibility of critique and progress in international politics.[9] The post-modernist turn in international relations theory is highly eclectic in the sources upon which it draws, although readings of Derrida and Foucault have been particularly important. Derridean-influenced work puts its emphasis on interpreting the world as text and on the undecidability and instability of textual meaning. Both the institutions and practices which constitute aspects of international politics and the theoretical approaches to understanding and judging international relations are subject to deconstruction.[10] Foucauldian-influenced work puts its emphasis on the discursive constitution of both the institutions and practices that structure international politics and the theoretical approaches to it. These are analysed using Foucauldian techniques of archaeology and genealogy.[11] Postmodernists insist on the impossibility of disentangling questions of what is from discourses about what is. There is no pre-discursive reality, so discussion of international politics is necessarily discussion of the myriad ways in which it is textually and discursively produced and reproduced as an object/subject.[12]

Perhaps the best single example of the kind of claims implicit in postmodernist international relations theory is to be found in an article co-written by Ashley and Walker which concluded an edition of *International Studies Quarterly* devoted to critical or 'dissident' essays, 'Reading Dissidence/Writing the Discipline: Crisis and the Question of Sovereignty in International Studies' (1990). In the course of a highly complex argument, Ashley and Walker centre their critique of orthodox approaches to international relations theory on the concept of 'sover-eignty', understood in a dual sense as both the assertion of the unques-tionable primacy of state sovereignty in international politics and the assertion of sovereign claims to truth in theoretical practice (Ashley and Walker, 1990: 367–8; 376; 381–3). Their critique encompasses Marxism and critical theory as well as more mainstream theoretical approaches. Ashley and Walker's claim is that the established conceptual ordering of international relations theory is in crisis because its dominant categories, such as those of 'national interest' and 'state sovereignty', are, in the post-Cold War era, increasingly unable to account for the phenomena which have traditionally been identified as the focus of work within the discipline.

Ashley and Walker argue that theorizing in response to this discip-linary crisis is possible either in a register of desire or a register of freedom (Ashley and Walker, 1990: 379–81). The register of desire encompasses any theoretical approach which lays claim to have fixed the boundaries of explanation and judgement. The problem with this kind of theorizing, according to postmodernism, is twofold: first, it is argued that these kinds of boundaries are always in practice open to deconstruction; secondly, it is argued that asserting any stable ground for analysing and criticizing the theoretical and practical status quo necessarily has authoritative and exclusionary implications. The established paradigms of realism, rationalism and idealism are clearly in a register of desire, since they presume given standards for both analysis and prescription, whether in terms of deep assumptions about human nature and the moral law or the ultimate importance of state or individual sovereignty. In addition, however, it is also argued that critical theory is in that same register. Postmodernists accuse critical theorists such as Cox and Linklater of relying on sovereign assumptions about history and criteria of judgement which collapse critical theory back into Marxism or idealism. In contrast, postmodernists are reluctant to suggest that there are any stable criteria by which one version of the international can be judged better than another, either in the sense of better representing some pre-discursive reality or morally better. Theorizing in the register of freedom celebrates the instability of discursively constructed boundaries:

> It does not try to hold on to some imagined totalizing standpoint – in crisis but a rarefied ideal – that would regulate discourse regarding what must be done. Instead, as the name implies, it celebrates a space of freedom – freedom for thought, for political action in reply to hazards and dangers, for the exploration of new modes of ethical conduct detached from the presumption of a transcendental standpoint – that opens up when, in crisis, this ideal is deprived of practical force. (Ashley and Walker, 1990: 381)

Ashley and Walker also claim that the critical work which is effecting this disciplinary crisis 'resonates' with dissident movements in the practice of international politics (e.g., feminist, ecological and peace movements) (Ashley and Walker, 1990: 377). Thus, the theoretical trangressions of a conceptual order in international relations theory are being mirrored by practical transgressions of the global political order in international politics and vice versa.

It was evident in the discussion of Marxism and critical theory above that the distinction between ontology and epistemology is increasingly difficult to sustain once a clear distinction between theory and politics is abandoned. To classify postmodernist international theory in terms of ontological, epistemological and prescriptive elements is even more problematic, since much postmodernist work is concerned to subvert categories of ontology, epistemology and prescription as traditionally understood (in general and in relation to international politics in particular). Nevertheless, it provides one way into a comparison between postmodernist theory and the range of traditions of which it is critical. At first glance, postmodernism shares many features with the ontological assumptions of critical theory. Like Cox and Linklater, postmodernists do not take for granted the nature of the object of study reproduced by realist international theory, which is crucially defined by the idea of the centrality of sovereign states and, in Foucault's terms, a 'juridical' conception of power as owned and exercised by states over against other states in a context of anarchy.[13] This means that the boundary between domestic and international politics is terminally blurred by a postmodernist approach, entailing wholesale re-thinking of what is relevant to both the definition and explanation of international politics. Underlying this apparent similarity, however, is a deep difference in the claims made by postmodernists about humanity and history from those of critical theory. In critical theory, the category of the human individual is retained and given pre-eminent normative weight and history is understood in terms of a dialectic between more or less progressive forces (assessed in terms of an ideal of individual freedom). For postmodernism these claims are fundamentally problematic because, as discursive products, both notions of humanity and of history are inherently unstable and therefore open to challenge and deconstruction. The use of such categories must be in permanent inverted commas, otherwise they signify a return to traditional slanging matches between realism and idealism.

Although clearly putting metaphysical presumptions of various kinds into question, postmodernists have been particularly concerned to challenge the epistemological focus of international theory. They do this both in relation to the claims made by orthodox theory for the significance of method in the generation of descriptive truths about international politics, and in relation to the claims made about the inherent goodness or badness of the world and how it is to be assessed/measured. Concern with the latter has frequently focused on the issue of 'critique' – what critique means and how it can be possible. Again, there is an apparent overlap with the claims of critical theory here: both approaches argue that the practice of theorizing cannot be separated from the strategic relations of power which traditional theory would locate solely in its object. Theory is again identified as political and as having effects. As already discussed, Cox and Linklater challenge the distinction realism and idealism draw between reason and nature, universal and particular, both by pointing to the normative agendas implicit in the study of international relations nurtured by hegemonic interests and by arguing for an alternative mode of theorizing oriented by alternative normative values. However, postmodernism is dubious about critical theory's claims to be able to distinguish good and bad effects in theoretical practice and thereby claim validity for certain sorts of theoretical work as opposed to others. This doubt must clearly extend to the status of postmodernism's own claims, so that the epistemological critique of postmodernism returns us to its metaphysical scepticism and the importance of inverted commas.

Nevertheless, in spite of this rejection of the idea of standards of justice and emancipation, Ashley and Walker claim that their theorizing is in a 'register of freedom' as opposed to a 'register of desire'. This register of freedom is identified with a Foucauldian notion of an imperative to constantly transgress the boundaries of given limitation (in theory and practice) rather than with any substantive ideal of a world without oppression. The prescriptive element of postmodernist theory is therefore one which puts emphasis on the instability of established categories and the importance of challenging any sovereign claims of theory. The connection invoked between the practice of postmodernist theory and the political struggles of marginalized international actors relies on the notion that both practise a politics of transgression. This prescriptive element of postmodernist theory has been developed in the work of Campbell, which draws strongly on a Derrideanized reading of Levinas, into an ethical imperative to recognize responsibility to the other (Campbell, 1998b: 181).

The postmodernist turn in international relations theory has not gone undebated within the discipline. Broadly speaking, there are two directions of criticism within the international relations literature. The first comes from mainstream theory (within the parameters of realism, idealism, rationalism) and usually involves an attack both on the abandonment of the idea of the specificity of the international sphere in relation to domestic politics and on the abandonment of traditional conceptions of social scientific work as an attempt to represent the truth (or, in the case of normative theory, the good) in contradistinction to power (Hockaday, 1987; Keohane, 1988). The second direction of criticism is best represented by critical theory, but is also common to idealist and cosmopolitan theory. According to this line of criticism, the assertion as to the inseparability of knowledge, truth and power ensures that the postmodernist theorist's claim to identify theoretical practice with a project of freedom (the political struggles of the oppressed) is unsustainable (Hoffman, 1988; Krishna, 1993). The latter critique echoes a line of criticism of postmodernism which has been articulated in liberal, critical and feminist political theory in general (Taylor, 1984; Fraser, 1989; Habermas, 1990b; McNay, 1992). What is at the heart of this latter critique is the argument that 'truth' and 'freedom' lose their meaning as a point of reference for progress if they are always implicated in exclusionary projects and relations of power. Within international relations theory this has led to postmodernist theory in general being accused of an implicit return to realism, in which the truth that the international is always already power politics is simply reflected and reasserted in more complex and sophisticated ways.

The accusation that postmodernism is a reinvention of realism (commonly made by critical theorists) mirrors the accusation that critical theory is a reinvention of idealism (commonly made by postmodernists). We saw in the previous section that the defence put up by critical theory against the latter accusation demonstrated a tendency to relapse into the dichotomous vocabulary which critical theory was attempting to transcend. So that critical theory came to be suspended between the familiar Scylla of universalism on the one hand and the equally familiar Charybidis of particularism on the other. A similar pattern is discernible in postmodernism's defence against the former accusation. One response is to call upon the notion of theorizing in the register of freedom mentioned above. But the way in which this is expressed in Ashley and Walker's argument is in the language of a categorical imperative and through an identification with the ideal of resistance to all forms of exclusion (Ashley and Walker, 1990: 381; Ashley, 1996: 253; see also, Campbell, 1998a: 513; 1998b: 198). It is difficult to understand the idea of theorizing in the register of freedom without invoking a notion of theoretical privilege which has very strong affinities with the commitment of critical theory to emancipatory ideals. Thus postmodernism's claim to have transcended realism appears to rely on the residual presence of highly traditional understandings of the distinctions between real and ideal, politics and morality. An alternative response made by postmodernism to the charge of realism is to stress its normative engagement but to argue that it rests on plural rather than monolithic understandings of the good. However, it is difficult to distinguish this theoretical move from the commmunitarian position which grounds judgement of moral value in specific contexts. In this respect not only does the debate between postmodernism and critical theory threaten to return us to the debate between cosmopolitanism and communitarianism, but, as with critical theory itself, the debate is echoed and played out within postmodernism itself.

Of all the perspectives examined so far, postmodernism seems to pose the most radical challenge to the setting up of normative international theory in terms of the conceptual parameters provided by idealism and realism. As with Marxism and critical theory, postmodernism is premised on the understanding that there is a relation of identity between theorizing and the object of theory. Moreover, postmodernism claims to go further than Marxism and critical theory in abandoning any reliance on the objective logic of history or on the epistemic privilege of the theorist which might re-insert the traditional wedge between theory and politics. Postmodernist theory calls for a radical re-thinking of how we think. As with critical theory, the key to how this can be done lies in post-modernism's refusal to separate morality and politics in international relations in terms of the old schema of reason versus nature, ideal versus real or universal versus particular. However, as we have also seen, this thinking of the identity of morality and politics displays a tendency to reproduce both idealism and realism in inverted commas. As with critical theorists, postmodernists apply to the notion of the identity of theory and politics a notion of good politics and bad politics. Postmodernism, there-fore, reproduces the move, characteristic of critical theory, of identifying its theorizing with good political practice (theorizing in the register of freedom); or alternatively reproduces the insight of sceptical realism, that theorizing in terms of universal standards of right is a guise for the pursuit of a particular interest (theorizing in the register of desire). Too often it seems that the debate between critical theory and postmodernism simply repeats the earlier debate between idealism and realism, with as little result and as much frustration (Hoffman, 1987, 1988; Rengger, 1988; Hutchings, 1992; Ashley, 1996; Linklater, 1996c; Jahn, 1998).

Feminism

Feminist international relations theory is an even more recent devel-opment within the discipline of international relations than critical and postmodernist theory and is more difficult to characterize in general. This is because feminist theory encompasses a wide range of perspec-tives, not all of which are mutually compatible. Feminist approaches include theories influenced by liberalism and Marxism as well as approaches which take their inspiration from critical and postmodernist theory.[14] The common theme which connects diverse theoretical positions under the label of 'feminism' is the claim that paying attention to the ways in which international politics and international theory are 'gendered' has a productive impact on how international politics are to be understood and judged. Feminists, like other critical and post-modernist theorists, question the existing ontological and epistemologi-cal assumptions of international relations theory and are also deeply concerned with the critique of the existing world order and the possibility of progress in world politics. The work of critics such as Elshtain and Enloe has drawn attention to the ways in which gendered divisions of labour and constructions of femininity and masculinity underly many of the practices in contexts from diplomacy to the military which are central to the maintenance of existing inter-state relations (Elshtain, 1987; Enloe, 1989). The work of Tickner and Spike Peterson has challenged the realist claim to explanatory neutrality by pointing out the gendered assumptions that help to construct the building blocks of realist analysis and methodology (Tickner, 1991; Spike Peterson, 1992). At the same time, theorists such as Ruddick have challenged idealist, cosmopolitan and communitarian as well as realist responses to the ethics of war and international intervention (Ruddick, 1990). Explicit or implicit in all of this work is an identification with the interests of those oppressed by gendered relations of power in international politics (not necessarily women only). In this respect there are clearly elective affinities between feminist work and the other perspectives considered in this chapter which claim that theory is politics and that good theory and good politics are tied to the interests of the excluded, exploited and oppressed. In order to assess the contribution of feminist theorizing to the project of transcending conceptual orthodoxy I will examine an example of feminist theorizing which does not rely on perspectives such as Marxism, critical theory and postmodernism which have already been analysed. This is the distinctively feminist normative international theory developed by Ruddick.

In her book *Maternal Thinking*, Ruddick develops an argument which can be seen as following through the implications of what Gilligan refers to as an 'ethic of care'. It involves a critique of traditional just war thinking – in both utilitarian and Kantian variants – as well as a positive characterization of how a different kind of moral judgement and political practice is possible in relation to war. It also involves a rejection of realist arguments as to the tragic inevitability or structural necessity of war and communitarian claims to the special ethical status of the collective group or nation. There are essentially two stages to Ruddick's argument. In the first stage she offers a phenomenology of what she terms 'maternal thinking', in the second stage she adapts Hartsock's notion of 'feminist standpoint ' and reads off the implications of using maternal thinking as the feminist standpoint for making judgements about the ethics of war and the appropriate feminist response to war.

'Maternal thinking', according to Ruddick, 'is a discipline in attentive love', a discipline which is rooted in the demands of a particular relation of care, that between mother and child, and which reflects a particular range of metaphysical attitudes, cognitive capacities and virtues (Ruddick, 1990: 123). Ruddick is careful to insist that she is neither equating mothers with biological mothers, nor presuming that actual mothers are all good at maternal thinking. In addition, although Ruddick's examples of maternal practice are largely drawn from the USA, she implies that the demands of preservation, nurturance and training, although they take culturally specific forms, are not culturally specific as such, so that there is a relevance in what she is discussing to that which transcends her own social and political context. This implication is confirmed by Ruddick's use of the notion of 'feminist standpoint' when she comes to, as it were, apply the consequences of maternal thinking to the consideration of intra and inter-state violence (Ruddick, 1990: 129–35).

The idea of a feminist standpoint derives from Hartsock's appropriation of Marx's analysis of capitalism as being based on the standpoint (serving the objective interests of) of the oppressed class. According to Hartsock, the exploitative character of capitalist relations of production becomes clear when understood from the vantage point of the proletariat. Similarly, the patriarchal character of relations of reproduction as well as production under capitalism is revealed from the standpoint of the women who bear the brunt of those relations (Hartsock, 1987). Building on this notion, Ruddick argues that maternal thinking, located as it is in the marginalized and denigrated sphere of caring labour, provides a standpoint from which the absurdity of both strategic military and just war thinking becomes evident. Although Ruddick does not follow Hartsock in maintaining that the feminist standpoint provides a demonstrably universally valid ground for truth, she is making a claim for the potential of maternal thinking to illuminate the meaning of war from a critical perspective (Ruddick, 1990: 135).

> When maternal thinking takes upon itself the critical perspective of a feminist standpoint, it reveals a contradiction between mothering and war. Mothering begins in birth and promises life; military thinking justifies organized, deliberate deaths. A mother preserves the bodies, nurtures the psychic growth, and disciplines the conscience of children; although the military trains it soldiers to survive the situations it puts them in, it also deliberately endangers their bodies, minds and consciences in the name of victory and abstract causes. (Ruddick, 1990: 135)

For Ruddick, both militarism (whether justified in terms of realism, contractarianism or communitarianism) and cosmopolitanism share a commitment to the expendability of concrete lives in abstract causes to which maternal thinking is inherently opposed. Ruddick claims this means that the implication of maternal thinking is not just the rejection of war but the active embracing of peace politics, a fight against war which draws on the acknowledgement of responsibility and relationship and the specificity of need and obligations which are inherent in a proper understanding of the labour of caring (Ruddick, 1990: 141–59).

> The analytic fictions of just war theory require a closure of moral issues final enough to justify killing and 'enemies' abstract enough to be killable. In learning to welcome their own and their children's changes, mothers become accustomed to open-ended, concrete reflection on intricate and unpredictable spirits. Maternal attentive love, restrained and clear sighted, is ill adapted to intrusive, let alone murderous judgements of others' lives. (Ruddick, 1990: 150)

Ruddick's theory rests on certain broad ontological and epistemological assumptions. At the ontological level, it is clear that the categories of individual, state, morality, politics and history which are crucial to previously considered mainstream and critical traditions are altered by a perspective that considers all these categories to be gendered. In effect we are introduced to a different kind of dualism in which the logic of domestic relations in the restricted sense of the domestic or private sphere is set against the logic of the public sphere of both state and inter-state relations, although with the acknowledgement that in practice the former has tended to support and reinforce the latter. Ruddick places realism and idealism, cosmopolitanism and communitarianism all firmly in the realm of the logic of public 'masculinist' theory and practice. Although it is clear that Ruddick does put an ontological priority on the human individual, this priority is based not on right, but on relation – in comparison to it, the rights of states are irrelevant and meaningless. For Ruddick then, the realm of international politics is primarily a realm of human relationship, not of human or state rights or an international state system.

The epistemological assumptions involved in Ruddick's argument are of a more familiar kind, since she argues, along with idealism, cosmopolitanism, communitarianism, Marxism and critical theory, for the notion of a standpoint from which critical judgements of international politics can be made. In contrast to these other approaches, however, it is neither a standard provided by the moral law nor by the particular collective of class or nation – instead it is the standpoint of maternal thinking. This standpoint is inherently prescriptive and involves a commitment to the practical and political struggle against violence and for peace. It is therefore, as with critical theory and postmodernism, based on the notion of the inseparability of theory and politics. Ruddick assumes that theory is the outcome of concrete practices and can never be neutral in its engagement with the world.

Ruddick's work provides one particularly influential example of feminist thinking about war and typifies an argument common in feminist literature in the 1980s, that women and/or feminists have a particular and peculiar relation to the moral assessment of war and to peace politics (Cohn, 1989; Harris and King, 1989; Warren and Cady, 1994). From the beginning, however, the work of Ruddick and of feminist theorists such as Gilligan and Hartsock who privilege the ethic of care or the labour of care as a starting point for moral judgement, has come under criticism from other feminist theorists whose work is informed by the insights of postmodernism and critical theory. Two related criticisms have been particularly common: first, the criticism that such work essentializes the standpoint of women, assuming sameness between women according to a particular model of the kind of work women are held, typically, to do (the postmodernist charge); secondly, the criticism, that the emphasis on concrete, particular relations and responsibilities as the context for moral judgement provides a ground for judgement which is inadequately generalizable and prevents the possibility of critical engagement beyond narrow, parochial levels of social interaction (the charge of critical theory). The first objection is parallel to the charge of identifying the particular with the universal which, as we saw earlier, communitarians laid against cosmopolitans and postmodernists against critical theorists. It is an objection with particularly acute resonances in the context of feminist politics both within multicultural states (for instance the charges as to the white and middle class dominance of the feminist movement in the USA) and between states (for example, in arguments between Western and Third World feminists about the ethics and politics of indigenous cultural practices, nationalism, population control and aid policy).[15] This criticism is one to which thinkers like Ruddick are sensitive and to which they have attempted to respond, generally by arguing for the strategic usefulness of the idea of a feminist standpoint as opposed to making claims for its absolute status. In becoming more tentative in the claims made for a feminist standpoint, however, theorists such as Ruddick, who argue for the contextualist location of maternal thinking in a specific practice, appear to fall into the hands of the other side of the coin of criticism (which cosmopolitanism and critical theory have standardly levelled against communitarianism and postmodernism), which is that an ethic of care offers only a parochial account of the conditions of judgement and therefore disables the possibility of critique across different particular contexts (Benhabib, 1992: 187). Once more, therefore, the articulation of a new approach to normative international theory which challenges the conceptual ordering underlying the choice between idealism and realism, cosmopolitanism and communitarianism threatens to come full circle back to the terms of the choices it was attempting to transcend.

Conclusion

In the first two chapters of this book, underneath the theoretical stalemates of idealism versus realism and cosmopolitanism versus communitarianism, a trace of a certain logic was discerned. According to this logic, what was called for in the theoretical approaches resting on entrenched conceptual dualisms was actually to think the unthinkable. In other words, to think the identity of reason and nature, ideality and reality, universal and particular and, consequently, to re-think the standard oppositions between morality and politics, state and inter-state relations. The problem was that the orthodox approaches to normative international theory were locked into a vocabulary which made such a task impossible. At the beginning of this chapter it was argued that this was also the case with rationalist perspectives, which sought a middle way between the conceptual oppositions without a conceptual apparatus through which that middle way could be articulated.

The discussion of more radical interventions in normative international theory has confirmed that theoretical approaches which seek to find an alternative to realist/idealist and cosmopolitan/communitarian dichotomies are marked by the aspiration to think the multiple terms of these dichotomies together, rather than apart. The analysis of critical theory, postmodernism and feminism has also confirmed that this aspiration is not easy to fulfil. All three of these approaches challenge orthodoxy through a rejection of the standard distinctions between morality and politics, state and inter-state relations and, most importantly, theory and politics. Problems arise, however, when these different theories come to account for their own theoretical practice and, in doing so, fall back into a choice between universalism and particularism which replays old debates. It would be completely wrong to suggest that critical theory, postmodernism and feminism simply fail in their theoretical projects. In particular, the identification of theory itself as political radically destabilizes conventional thinking about explanation as well as normative judgement in international politics. However, it seems that an account of this identification which does not rely on a privileged insight into what counts as good or bad theory/politics is necessary if argument in normative international relations theory is to move definitively beyond the boundaries set by idealism and realism, cosmopolitanism and communitarianism. It is with this task that the following chapter is concerned.

Notes

1 I do not pretend that the set of critical approaches considered in this chapter is exhaustive. There are other approaches, most notably the writings of theorists such as Onuf, Kratochwil and Wendt (sometimes labelled 'constructivist'), which undermine traditional dichotomies by stressing the constructed and rule-governed nature of different aspects of international order (Kratochwil, 1989; Onuf, 1989; Wendt, 1992, 1995).

2 See Bull and Watson (1984) for an example of work in this school of thought. Its most well-known proponents include Wight (1991), Bull (1995), Vincent (1974, 1986) and Watson (1992). Roberson (1998) provides a very useful set of critical essays on the international society approach. The journal *Review of International Studies* (Cambridge University Press) provides a forum for ongoing debate within this school of thought.

3 The terminology in international relations theory used for referring to recent critical perspectives can be somewhat confusing. The terms 'critical theory' and 'post-positivism' are sometimes used as generic terms to cover Marxist, Habermasian, postmodernist and feminist approaches. More usually, however, 'critical theory' is the label applied to perspectives derived from Frankfurt School critical theory, which is significantly influenced by Marxism (Hoffman, 1987, 1988; Rengger, 1988; Brown, 1994c). In this book, I always use critical theory (singular) in the latter sense and use the plural to refer to the full range of non-orthodox perspectives.

4 Three useful overviews of Marxist work on international relations are Brown (1992b), Smith (1994) and Linklater (1996b), see also Linklater (1990), Burnham (1998).

5 I am using Marx as shorthand for Marx and Engels where appropriate here. Key texts on which the characterization of classical Marxism given here are based include: *The Communist Manifesto* (1998); *The German Ideology* (1970); 'On the Jewish Question' and 'A Contribution to the Critique of Hegel's Philosophy of Right. Introduction' both in *Early Writings* (1975); and *Capital Vol I* (1976).

6   The two thinkers are not entirely different, Kant does after all give a role to material self-interest in his account of history, but on Kant's account the workings of nature (providence) are essentially blind (working through people rather than being worked by people) and there is certainly no concept of exploitation or class struggle involved in his account (Kant, 1991a: 108–14; Marx and Engels, 1998: 14–23).

7   Cox and Linklater are probably the best known critical theorists currently working in international relations theory (Cox and Sinclair, 1996; Linklater, 1990, 1998). For an overview of critical theory see: Hoffman (1987, 1993); Brown (1994c); Devetak (1996a); see also responses to Linklater (1998) in *Review of International Studies* (1999).

8   Habermas's version of discourse ethics has been articulated in several different works, see Habermas (1979, 1984, 1987, 1990a, 1996). The essential idea behind discourse ethics is the notion that the practice of successful communication itself relies on a series of implicit norms which can be unpacked to yield the ideal conditions under which arguments over normative issues should be carried out and resolved, see Benhabib and Dallmyr (1990).

9   Overviews of postmodernist work in international relations theory can be found in: Brown (1994c); Devetak (1996b); Ashley (1996). Works significantly influenced by postmodernist theory include Der Derian (1987); Ashley (1988); Der Derian and Shapiro (1989); Ashley and Walker (1990); Walker (1993); Campbell and Dillon (1993); Campbell (1998b); see also Campbell (1998a). In classifying postmodernist work in international relations theory as either Derridean or Foucauldian, I am oversimplifying the range of sources on which such work draws. Very often postmodernist theorists draw on both Derrida and Foucault (e.g., Campbell, 1998a, 1998b) and Nietzsche, Irigaray, Kristeva, Baudrillard, Deleuze and Levinas are also significant influences. However, the distinction between Derridean and Foucauldian theory does, in my view, capture a significant difference between work which is more focused on synchronic deconstruction of the discourses of international relations (Derridean) and work which is more historically, genealogically oriented (Foucauldian). Foucauldian genealogy is examined in more detail in Chapter 4 below.

10 Examples of Derridean-influenced work include: Ashley (1988); Der Derian and Shapiro (1989); Campbell (1998a, 1998b). In Campbell's case, Derridean deconstruction is read as an ethical project, a response to the fundamental demand to enact our responsibility to the other (Campbell, 1998b: 85).

11 Bartelson (1995) provides an example of Foucauldian analysis; Foucault is also a particularly significant influence in the work of Walker (1993). For a discussion of Foucauldian influenced international theory see Hutchings (1997).

12 This is evident in the work of Der Derian (1987) on diplomacy and Bartelson (1995) on sovereignty cited above. Both theorists draw attention to the discursive construction of diplomacy and sovereignty which have come, in

more mainstream analysis, to be treated as independent objects of investigation. Ashley and Walker (1990) likewise draw attention to the intimate
connection between the international relations academy's vision of world
politics and the politics of academic international relations itself.

13 Foucault formulates the contrast between 'juridical' and 'disciplinary' power
in his book *Discipline and Punish* (1977). The former refers to power exercised
over individuals (typically by the state and law), the latter to power which
produces self-policing individuals in modern society. The distinction is
illustrated by the contrast between public and extreme physical punishment
of criminals as opposed to the disciplinary regime of modern penal systems
– the famous contrast between the execution of the attempted regicide
Damiens and Bentham's Panoptican (Foucault, 1977: 3–6; 200–2). See
discussion of Foucault in Chapter 4.

14 Overviews of feminist international relations theory, which bring home the
variety of perspectives which come under the 'feminist' heading, include:
Grant and Newland (1991); Hutchings (1994b); Sylvester (1996); Steans
(1998). Key texts include: Elshtain (1987); Enloe (1989); Tickner (1992); Spike
Peterson (1992); Sylvester (1994); Pettman (1996).

15 There is a huge literature in and around all these issues. See Nicholson
(1990); Hirsch and Fox-Keller (1990); Gunew (1991); Grant and Newland
(1991); Mohanty, Russo and Torres (1991); Marchand and Papart (1995).

4

The Politics of International Theory

Introduction

In the first two chapters, we saw that schools of thought about normative issues in international politics were underlain by conceptual oppositions which had specific implications for how international politics, the nature and status of international normative theory and the relation between the normative theorist and the object of theory were thought and understood. The conceptual oppositions were between reason and nature, ideality and reality, universal and particular, and they dominated fundamental presumptions about the nature of morality and politics. The effect of these grounding oppositions in international theory was that the international was conceived primarily as a contested ground between the claims of the opposed alternatives which could not be understood without reference to each other. In more concrete terms, this conceptual armoury underlies the predominant view of a basic distinction between international and state politics and between international politics and morality. The response to this dual alienation issued in two theoretical

possibilities for conceptualizing international politics: either international politics was to be conceived as already as it ought to be, the
perpetual confirmation of the rightness of natural determination; or
international politics was to be conceived as being not as it ought to be,
with the imperative that it be re-conceived/legislated in terms of reason
(moral law, historical progress). As far as the nature and status of
normative theory was concerned, in debates between realists and
idealists, cosmopolitans and communitarians it shuttled between the
status of universal and absolute truth and particular and relative strategy
or 'way of life'. As far as the relation of the normative theorist to the
object of theorizing was concerned, the theorist was considered to be in
the position of 'doctor', diagnosing and prescribing for a condition from
which the theorist was abstracted.

As we saw in the previous chapter, a variety of theoretical work has
sought to tackle the inadequacies of orthodox conceptualizations. It was
argued that although this new work was premised on re-conceiving the
model of international politics in ways which defied the traditional
oppositions, nevertheless the understanding of the nature and status of
normative theory and the conception of the relation between theorist and
theorized tended to remain caught up in those oppositions, thus perpetually threatening the return to idealist/realist alternatives (or their
replaying in cosmopolitan/communitarian debates). Critical theory,
postmodernism and feminism standardly assume that international
politics is neither qualitatively distinct from state politics nor alien from
morality. However, although there is a high level of awareness of the
theoretical impasses involved in presumptions of the various dualisms,
elements of these new theorizations remain caught in older arguments
about the absolute or relative status of normative claims and their universal
or particular scope of application. There remains a tendency to hold on to
the notion of the theorist as moral doctor (critic and judge) – even where
this seems to be most deeply challenged (such as in postmodernist
approaches). The notion that theory is political, which is common to critical
theory, postmodernism and feminist international theory, remains linked
to ways of distinguishing between good theory and bad theory, good
politics and bad politics which replay the familiar oppositions in sophisticated ways. There seems to be genuine difficulty in challenging the
conceptual 'common sense' of reason/nature, ideality/reality, universal/
particular alternatives in the study of international politics. In this chapter
it will be argued that these oppositions will remain entrenched without a
more fundamental re-thinking of some of the most dearly held pretensions
of normative theory. To change the way of thinking in normative international theory requires not only that one does not view international

politics in essential distinction from domestic politics or from morality, it also requires the abandonment of prevailing notions of normative truth (whether understood as the abstract universal of moral law or the concrete universal of the particular nation-state) and the idea of the theorist as moral doctor. Instead, theorists must recognize themselves as patients and participants in the processes they seek to understand and judge. In this chapter I will be presenting an argument for a re-thinking of normative international theory of the kind to which the new critical theories considered in the previous chapter are aspiring. In order to do this, I will be calling upon the philosophical resources offered by two thinkers who are usually presumed to be opposed: Hegel and Foucault. In the theoretical practices of Hegelian phenomenology on the one hand and Foucauldian genealogy on the other I will argue that a great deal of help can be found for ways forward in normative international theory.

This chapter will begin by examining the reasons why the turn to Hegel might well seem to be the antithesis of the aspiration of the critical theories considered in the previous chapter. I will go on to examine some examples of the use of Hegel in international theory which appear to bear out the unsuitability of a turn to Hegel to resolve the problems which contemporary critical theories of international relations have set themselves to overcome. However, I will argue that there is a way of reading Hegel's work that does assist theoretical engagement with the project of thinking the international in terms other than those of the conceptual oppositions mentioned above. I will go on to argue that the implications of certain Hegelian conceptual moves have been more recently articulated in Foucault's genealogical work and that we can therefore use these theorists together to reconceptualize normative theory in the international sphere. In conclusion, I will explain and elaborate on the features of the Hegelian–Foucauldian approach to normative international theory and how it promises to move theorizing beyond the repetition of old debates, both in terms of how it allows the international to be conceived (the theory of politics) and in how it understands the nature of theorizing itself and the relation between theorist and theoretical object (the politics of theory).

The case against Hegel

To turn to Hegel at this stage in the argument initially seems odd, if only because he has already figured as a canonic presence in the discussion of normative international theory. As such, his position is somewhat paradoxical, since he is acknowledged as a key figure in realism and communitarianism (due to his apparent endorsement of the nation-state as the source of right and the necessity of war) as well as an influence on aspects of idealism and critical theory (via Marx and the philosophy of history). Going back to Hegel seems to be a return straight to the conceptual oppositions which contemporary critical international relations theories seek to challenge. Moreover I have already suggested, in Chapter 2, that the turn to Hegel in the ethics of international relations of theorists such as Frost is unproductive of theoretical progress. I would therefore like to begin, as it were, with the case for the prosecution – the reasons why returning to Hegel seems such a bad idea. Below are two major charges commonly made against Hegel's political thought: first, Hegel abandons the normative element in political and international theory, he identifies what is with what is right (the actual with the rational) and encourages passive acceptance of the status quo. Secondly, Hegel subsumes particular reality (individual subjects) under universal ideality (spirit) in his political theory. His account of both domestic and international politics is dictated by his identification of the state with the universal, rational Idea. From these two general charges follow a variety of particular ones which are clearly in conflict with the aspirations of contemporary critical approaches to normative international theory. These include the charges that Hegel assumes a unified (eurocentic) direction to world historical development, that he is a statist thinker who glorifies war, and that he is a patriarchal thinker.[1] It is not difficult to find textual support in Hegel's work for the above charges and they are normally substantiated by reference to his main work in political philosophy *Elements of the Philosophy of Right* (1991a). In this text Hegel examines and traces the modern concept of legal and political right from notions of natural and individual right through the social institutions of family and civil society to state right and international law. The interpretation of Hegel's work is a notoriously difficult matter, but it is claims such as the following that have been seen as condemning Hegel as both archetypal idealist and archetypal realist:

> . . . since philosophy is *exploration of the rational*, it is for that very reason the *comprehension of the present and the actual*, not the setting up of a world beyond which exists God knows where . . . (Hegel, 1991a: 20)

> The state is the actuality of the ethical Idea – the ethical spirit as substantial will, *manifest* and clear to itself, which thinks and knows itself and implements what it knows in so far as it knows it. (Hegel, 1991a: 275)

On the one hand Hegel appears as the archetypal realist in that he seems to accept that the ideal is identical with actually existing political arrangements and to condemn the introduction of alternative standards of judgement as absurd, wishful thinking; on the other hand he appears as the archetypal idealist in that he suggests that politics and history are governed by an ideal end. In either case, Hegel appears as a monolithic thinker, the philosopher in the God-like position of possessing the key to absolute truth. There seems to be no room left for difference or the accommodation of a plurality of perspectives and truths in his analyis.

The charge that Hegel assumes a unilinear direction to history is supported by the closing passages of *Elements of the Philosophy of Right* in which Hegel discusses historical development in terms of the progress of spirit through different forms of ethical life to the ultimate 'Germanic' phase (Hegel, 1991a: 372–80). Further support can also be gained from his *Lectures on the Philosphy of History* and many of his other works for the notion that through the 'cunning of reason', history is propelled by the absolute idea to an ultimate end which coincides with Hegel's own time and place (Hegel, 1975: 89).[2] The charge that Hegel is a statist thinker follows from his identification of the state with the 'actuality of the ethical Idea' and can be further substantiated by reference back to the final passages of *Elements of the Philosophy of Right* in which Hegel follows Kant's *Metaphysics of Morals Part 1* in moving from the discussion of the state to the realm of inter-state relations but with an apparently much less optimistic reading of the possibilities of perpetual peace (Hegel, 1991a: 368). Hegel states explicitly that the notion of right as inherent in states provides a context in which war is the default position of the international sphere, offering a proto-realist analysis (Hegel, 1991a: 369). In other political writings as well as *Elements of the Philosophy of Right*, Hegel supplements this realist analysis of international relations with claims about the nation (people) and war which prefigure communitarian arguments about the ethical significance of community and nationalist arguments about the superiority and inferiority of different peoples (Hegel, 1991a: 372–80).[3] Unsurprisingly, contemporary critical theories find little to attract them in a philosophy which embraces an inevitable 'grand narrative' without, apparently, so much as a gesture towards the dialectic of enlightenment. In addition, the charge that Hegel is a patriarchal thinker is very easily substantiated by reference to Hegel's discussions of women and gender in his *Philosophy of Nature* (1970: 411–14), *Phenomenology of Spirit* (1977: 266–89) and again in *Elements of the Philosophy of Right* (Hegel, 1991a: 200–8). All of Hegel's references to women and gender confirm the relegation of women to the natural and/or private sphere.[4] This clearly poses a problem for feminist

international theory, but also for critical and postmodernist theories
which deny the justification of the exclusion of women from either the
state or international political spheres.

This prima facie unsuitability of Hegel's work as a basis for re-thinking
normative international theory from the point of view of contemporary
critical perspectives is further borne out by the example of those theorists
who have attempted to base a new international theory on Hegelian
premises. The work of Frost has already been discussed in Chapter 2
(Frost, 1996). According to Frost, the impasse between cosmopolitan and
communitarian ethical positions in international relations can be overcome by a turn to Hegel which acknowledges the importance of the
instantiation of respect for autonomy within the modern state and the
modern state system. Frost draws on Hegel's argument for the dependence of spheres of individual right, family and civil society on the state.
In particular, the idea of a mutually constitutive relation between individual and state right for Frost legitimates the principles of the current
international order, its settled norms from respect for state sovereignty to
respect for human rights. This argument is also made by Brown, who in
an article 'The Ethics of Political Restructuring in Europe' (Brown, 1994b)
also turns to Hegel's *Elements of the Philosophy of Right* to underpin the
claim that the state is an ethical institution with a constitutive role in
relation to the individual.

> From the perspective of constitutive theory, human beings do not come into
> the world as free individuals – they are constituted as such by the operation of
> ethical institutions at the level of the family, civil society and the state. It is this
> basic position that provides criteria by which the processes of political change
> and reconstruction current in the modern world can be judged. (Brown, 1994b:
> 176)

Both Frost and Brown suggest that the modern liberal state remains
the optimum mode of political organization, supported from within by the
'ethical institutions' of family and civil society and from without by an
international system which institutionalizes state sovereignty. In both
cases, Hegel is presented as providing criteria by which political arrangements can be judged as well as an ideal for the state and the international
system. In both cases also, Hegel is presented as the 'middle way'
between communitarian and cosmopolitan insights:

> Constitutive theory incorporates some of the positions of other communitarian
> approaches – such as the pragmatic value to be attached to a sense of

community when major and disruptive projects are planned by a society – while rejecting others – such as the proposition that states should always be based on nations. Constitutive theory shares the commitment to human rights and duties, of many cosmopolitans, while denying that these values can be realized other than in a properly constituted state. (Brown, 1994b: 182–3)

From the perspective of critical theorists, postmodernists and feminists, the arguments of Frost and Brown, in so far as they essentially endorse the principles of the contemporary state and international status quo, confirm the dangers of turning to Hegel as a resource for normative international theory. Here we find evidence to support the charges made above that Hegel is statist, patriarchal and endorses the modern inter-state system, treating the particular outcome of the values of the West as the universal verdict of history.

A rather different use of Hegel in contemporary international theory can be found in Krombach's book *Hegelian Reflections on the Idea of Nuclear War* (1991). In this book Krombach turns not to the *Elements of the Philosophy of Right* but to Hegel's philosophical logic as a means of comprehending the nature of international politics in a nuclear age. According to Krombach, the logic of history necessarily develops via the dialectical relation of a system of states. Inherent in the dialectical possibilities of inter-state relations is the possibility of both war and peace, these are necessary consequences of the way states are and the way in which they relate to one another. In turn, war and peace, in different ways, reinforce and structure the particular states that make up the state system (Krombach, 1991: 82). The invention of nuclear weapons is likewise a necessary consequence of the dialectic of inter-state relations. However, with nuclear weapons a radically different possibility is introduced into the system of states, i.e. the possibility of the complete annihilation of the historical dialetic itself. Previously the negative power of war had been recuperable in a new set of inter-state relations; there was always a future, now this is no longer the case. Krombach argues that the only proper philosophical response to the nuclear age is to redouble efforts to understand the present in relation to the past, and thus to acknowledge our global responsibility for that present in all its potential. His analysis seems to offer very little hope.

If Frost and Brown present an idealist Hegel, in so far as they claim he identifies standards by which international politics can be judged and towards which international politics, if necessary, should be steered, Krombach reads Hegel in the opposite direction, as an unremitting and pessimistic realist. From the point of view of critical theorists, postmodernists and feminists, this Hegelianism is equally unpalatable. The state system is given the sanction of reason and the status of an end of history by being presented as the identity of the rational and the actual in the contemporary world. In terms of the project of critical theories of international relations, to re-think international politics in Hegelian terms as an escape from the old dichotomies appears to be both absurd and paradoxical. However, even in relation to the charges listed above and the uses of Hegel offered by Frost, Brown and Krombach there are some clues as to why it might be useful to look more closely at Hegel's thought. These clues are to do with the markedly different, indeed opposing ways in which Hegel's political philosophy can be read. In the interpretations given so far, Hegel is both a realist and communitarian and an idealist and cosmopolitan – the fact that he can, apparently, be both is suggestive of the mutually dependent conceptual apparatus on which these opposing positions rest. If Hegel's work makes these dependencies explicit then it might be useful to look more closely at his arguments to see whether he does more than simply alternate between opposing approaches. If the familiar conceptual oppositions are thought together in his philosophy, then it might both explain how he can be read in such radically different ways and also help in the constitution of new ways of thinking.

Revisiting Hegel

It would be impossible to offer a full account of Hegel's philosophy in the space available here. However, in order to make the case for revisiting Hegel as a possible resource for rethinking the terms of normative international theory it is necessary to look more closely at some key Hegelian arguments. I will concentrate on those which are central to the charges made against Hegel above. They are, on the one hand, Hegel's abandonment of prescription as the primary purpose of political theory, from which his apparent endorsement of the status quo, from the necessity of war to the consignment of women to the domestic sphere, follows. They are, on the other hand, Hegel's identification of the state with the actuality of the ethical Idea, from which claims about his uni-linear philosophy of history and statism follow. In both cases what is at stake is simultaneously Hegel's conception of politics within and between states in the modern era and his conception of that conception, i.e., of his own practice as a political theorist. Having explored these aspects of

Hegel's thought it will be possible to return to the question of whether his insights might yet prove useful in the project of reconstituting normative international theory.

Elements of the Philosophy of Right is a complex text with a complex history of interpretation. It was written on the assumption that it would be read according to Hegel's previously articulated philosophical system in the *Phenomenology of Spirit*, the *Science of Logic* (1969) and the *Encyclopaedia of the Philosophical Sciences* (1970, 1971, 1991b). In practice, however, its claims have frequently been read in abstraction from and in defiance of Hegel's own prefaratory advice. For a long time in Anglo-American scholarship, Hegel's political philosophy was dismissed as an apology for Prussian absolutism or a key source for nationalist and fascist political thinking.[5] This interpretation has been discredited in recent years and the current trend in Hegel scholarship is (as with Frost and Brown) to enrol Hegel's political theory into the liberal tradition of political thought (with communitarian modifications), with its support for a constitutional state and complementary endorsement of both individual and state sovereignty (Smith, 1989). The debate between right and left interpretations of Hegel's political sympathies does not concern us here, however, because ultimately both kinds of reading miss out on what is, in my view, the most crucial aspect of Hegel's political thought. This is that the argument of *Elements of the Philosophy of Right* is reducible neither to an empirical description of actual states and inter-state relations nor to a prescriptive account of ideal political arrangements. The text is more accurately understood as a phenomenology.

What does it mean to claim that Hegel's major work in political philosophy is a phenomenology? In crude terms it means that Hegel's political theory is claimed to consist in the analysis of the form of the ethical life of his time, an analysis which is carried out immanently, without reference to an independently articulated method or to transcendent criteria of judgement (Hegel, 1977: 46–57).[6] The term 'ethical life' encompasses the realms of law and private morality as well as social, economic and political life in the private and public spheres. In order to understand how Hegel's project is possible and what its implications for political theorizing are, however, it is necessary to go back to Hegel's account of philosophical science and absolute knowledge in the *Phenomenology of Spirit* and the rest of his philosophical system. The words 'science' and 'absolute' conjure up the idea of an omniscient being by whom the truth is grasped in a way which stands eternally, over and above the evanescence of political life. However, the God-like connotations of the position of the speculative philosopher are somewhat misleading when it comes to Hegel's use of these terms.

The argument of the *Phenomenology of Spirit* seeks to demonstrate (and the argument of *Elements of the Philosophy of Right* presumes) that there is always a relation between knowledge (theoretical claims about the world) and ethical life. Any self-conscious being, including philosophical scientists, remains caught within that relation rather than being able to transcend it. Hegel uses the term 'relative identity' to express this relation in order to capture the idea that this is not a purely contingent relation between fundamentally disconnected beings. Theorists are not simply connected to the world which they investigate, they are that world. This is not an absolute identity, however, but a relative and partial one. No one individual will find themselves wholly within, and no one individual exhausts, the possibilities of contemporary ethical life. A large proportion of the argument of the first five chapters of the *Phenomenology of Spirit* is concerned with problems raised by attempts to account for knowledge claims (both descriptive and prescriptive) by reference solely to the experience of individual conscious or self-conscious being in abstraction from the complex context of its mediation. Hegel makes clear that any such account will fail as long as it does not take account of the condition of 'spirit'. The term 'spirit' is notoriously difficult to interpret in Hegel's work; the reader is introduced to the idea in the famous account of the 'struggle for recognition' in the *Phenomenology of Spirit*, as 'this absolute substance which is the unity of the different independent self-consciousnesses which, in their opposition, enjoy perfect freedom and independence: "I" that is "We" and "We" that is "I"' (Hegel, 1977: 110).[7] In this initial definition both the 'I' and the 'We' appear abstractly in the psychological story of the essentially social nature of individual self-consciousness. However, as the argument of the *Phenomenology* progresses, it becomes apparent that no 'I' exists in abstract relation to any other 'I' and that any experience of both 'I' and 'We' is conditioned and mediated by (but also conditions and mediates) the given context of ethical life, which includes legal, economic, social and political institutions, values and customs. The interrelation between given ethical life (which is experienced as objective and alien by self-conscious being) and the 'I's and 'We's of self-conscious being is one of 'relative identity'; both are aspects of spirit, but neither is reducible to the other. This means that attempts to comprehend or analyse either aspect of spirit are conceptualized in terms of a form of self-understanding in which there is no possibility of finding a point beyond spirit from which to think. Spirit is what is constructed by and constructs individual self-conscious being; it is ethical life, it is also the reflection and comprehension of ethical life in art, religion and philosophy.

In the *Phenomenology of Spirit*, Hegel traces the development of spirit towards what he terms 'absolute knowledge'. The progress towards absolute knowledge in the *Phenomenology of Spirit* does not signify a journey towards transcendent truth but towards the recognition of spirit as self-determination (however complexly mediated) and therefore as the ever-changing condition of all knowledge and all truth. The knowledge of spirit as self-determination is absolute in that it is a universal claim about ethical life, all individual and collective action in the world and all practical and theoretical claims (whether we like it or not there is no pure passive reflection for the social scientist or philosopher). It is, however, also an entirely contingent claim, dependent on specific historical developments for its articulation. This knowledge, Hegel argues, is one that has been articulated in the modern, post-revolutionary world in a way in which it could not have been before (precisely because of the shapes that spirit has taken – only in modern ethical life is the concept of spirit as self-determination explicitly institutionalized in the idea of revolution and the founding of constitutional states), but it is as much the truth of classical Greek ethical life as of modern Europe.[8] It is not knowledge in the sense of a substantive or finished claim or body of claims which exists a-historically. It is much more like a formal, structural insight into the nature of human existence and human thought. Absolute knowledge is not what is contained in the final chapter of the *Phenomenology*, it (absolute knowledge) refers to the way in which the exposition of the *Phenomenology* itself has guided the observing consciousness of the reader into comprehending the history of consciousness as its own complex and multi-faceted act and fate (Hegel, 1977: 56–7). Absolute knowledge is not the prize waiting for us at the end of history, it is the recognition that spirit is the only end of history there is.

In the Preface to the *Phenomenology*, Hegel refers to the true as a Bacchanalian revel, 'in which no member is not drunk; yet because each member collapses as soon as he drops out, the revel is just as much transparent and simple repose' (Hegel, 1977: 27). The simultaneous presence of movement and rest in Hegel's metaphor is designed to express the two levels at which the argument of the *Phenomenology* works. First, the level of dynamism and change in the development of spirit. Secondly, the level of recollection, in which the reader comprehends the past as being in a sense always the same – that is, always the self-determination of spirit (Hegel, 1977: 28). The exposition of the *Phenomenology* shifts between these levels, but what the metaphor suggests is that the two levels should be thought together. This metaphor comes as near as is possible to providing a summary of Hegel's philosophy. It captures the paradoxical identity of immanence and transcendence both in practice (individual self-conscious beings are products of the self-determination of spirit but also complicit in that production) and in the ways in which it is comprehended or thought (the theorist is a child of his/her time, yet may also grasp the truth of that time). Thus not only are particular social, legal and political forms examples of self-determinations of spirit, but so also are the ways in which they are understood and judged. In one sense, Hegel is clearly suggesting that modern shapes of spirit allow/encourage a self-understanding of spirit which is transcendentally true (absolute knowledge as defined above). However, absolute knowledge does not and cannot give any insight into how a particular shape of spirit determines itself or how it should be evaluated. This is why *Elements of the Philosophy of Right* cannot take a prescriptive form if it is to remain true to Hegel's system.

There are two consequences which follow from the above reading of Hegel's identification of spirit as self-determination and knowledge as an aspect of, as well as recognition of, that self-determination. First, Hegel's conception of philosophical science has to be understood as constructed through the mediations of ethical life. Rather than the philosopher standing outside of ethical life on transcendent grounds of judgement, the Hegelian speculative philosopher is always within ethical life and possesses no key to either truth or goodness. Secondly, Hegel's conceptions of history and politics have to be understood as fundamentally open, rather than closed off either by absolute knowledge or an end of history. In the Preface to the *Phenomenology*, Hegel says 'truth is not a minted coin that can be given and pocketed ready made' (Hegel, 1977: 22). When Hegel begins *Elements of the Philosophy of Right* with the claim that his is an essentially descriptive task, to comprehend 'what is', then he does not refer to a process of passive reflection – the simple pocketing of the coin of truth, but to an active engagement with what is itself the active process through which spirit reproduces itself in the form of modern ethical life. Of course this raises the question, then, of the status of the claims that Hegel is making in *Elements of the Philosophy of Right*. If these are not claims made from a transcendent ground beyond history then what do they tell us and can they have any normative weight? At this point it would be useful to take another look at the specific claims Hegel makes in his political philosophy.

If Hegel's *Elements of the Philosophy of Right* is a phenomenology in the sense explained above, then its primary purpose is to explore and expound contemporary political life in terms of the principles of its self-understanding (the idea of right) articulated in the legal and political institutions, practices and theoretical reflections of its day. Therefore his argument shifts between the consideration of concrete institutions and practices and abstract arguments as to their legitimation offered in contemporary legal, moral and political philosophy. It is for this reason that the normative thrust of Hegel's arguments is so confusing since it is never clear whether or not he is endorsing either the concrete political arrangements or the principles by which they are being justified which are the subject matter of his analysis. This is evident, for example, in his treatment of the relation between family, civil society and the state and the relegation of women to the private sphere. Rather than closing off the realm of the family from that of the public sphere, Hegel's exposition of the form of ethical life which instantiates a complex division of labour and institutionalizes private property and individual right precisely demonstrates how civil society and the state constitute and are constituted by specific familial relations as well as being in tension with them. There are no neat boundaries drawn between the different spheres, the family produces property owners and citizens only because of the way it is constructed through legal relations; these relations are, however, constantly both subverted and supported by relations of love and vice versa. When Hegel refers to womankind as the 'everlasting irony' in the life of the community in the *Phenomenology of Spirit* and reproduces this account in *Elements of the Philosophy of Right*, it is not an expulsion of gender from the story of spirit but a recognition of the gendered construction of the private sphere as a constant challenge to the extreme particularism of civil society and to the supposedly neutral, abstract authority of law (Hegel, 1977: 288). This is not to make a claim that Hegel offers a feminist analysis. Nevertheless, he is demonstrating an ethical interdependency and tension between pre-modern and modern social relations – the paradox of what Pateman refers to as the 'sexual contract' – the experience of which is clearly compatible with a variety of prescriptive positions and which has been vital in the articulation of feminist political theory (Pateman, 1988; Shanley and Pateman, 1991).

In *Elements of the Philosophy of Right* Hegel moves from the examination of the concept of the state to the world of inter-state relations and world history. As has been noted already, if Hegel is understood as offering a prescription for contemporary international politics then his comments on external sovereignty, international law, war and peace will be interpreted as offering an account of how the problems posed by international relations should be regulated. The result of such a reading is confusing, since Hegel's prescriptions can be variously interpreted as both pro- and anti-Kantian (Walt, 1989; Smith, 1989: 156–64). If, alternatively, *Elements of the Philosophy of Right* is understood as an empirical description of the international politics of Hegel's time, then it is simply a passive reflection of the nature of inter-state relations in early nineteenth century Europe. In contrast to both of these possibilities, although related to both, is the phenomenological reading, in which Hegel's analysis is understood as following through the necessary implications for inter-state relations of institutionalized conceptualizations of the modern state as self-determining, autonomous and individual.

> *Internal sovereignty* is this ideality in so far as the moments of the spirit and of its actuality, the state, have *developed* in their *necessity* and *subsist* as *members* of the state. But the spirit, which in its freedom is *infinitely negative* reference *to itself*, is just as essentially *being-for-itself* which has *incorporated* the subsistent differences *into itself* and is accordingly exclusive. (Hegel, 1991a: 359)

In moving from the domestic to the international sphere in the closing passages of *Elements of the Philosophy of Right*, Hegel is following the logic of a concept of right which gives primary validity to domestic legislation as the ground of the legitimacy of the state. If right is grounded in and operates within states, then states gain an absolute status which demands recognition. Hegel is quite clear that as long as states are conceptualized as individual, autonomous entities, motivated by their own interest and with an absolute right to determine their own affairs, perpetual peace, as anything other than the staving off of war, will remain wishful thinking. Hegel also points out, however, that even in the relation of war, the mutual recognition of states points beyond their absolute claim to right:

> The fact that states reciprocally recognize each other as such remains, *even in war* – as the condition of rightlessness, force and contingency – a *bond* whereby they retain their validity for each other in their being in and for themselves, so that even in wartime, the determination of war is that of something which ought to come to an end. (Hegel, 1991a: 370)

Contra Frost and Brown, this should not to be read as a claim that the right kind of states will engage in peaceful mutual recognition. Instead it should be understood as the claim that the necessity of both war and peace, which is grasped separately as natural on the one hand and rational on the other in the thinking of political philosophers such as Kant, are both equally grounded in the ways in which political right was institutionalized and articulated in Hegel's day.

Much of the latter part of Hegel's argument in *Elements of the Philosophy of Right* can be read as a commentary on Kant's international political theory and philosophy of history. According to Hegel, Kant's thought offers crucial insights into the complexities of contemporary ethical life but fails to grasp those insights as themselves aspects of spirit's self-determination. Instead, for Kant, the identity of the rational and the actual in ethical life is understood in terms of the dual trans-historical existence of actual (nature) and possible (reason) worlds. In Kant's reading of history, the essential meaninglessness of history is given meaning through the philosopher's identification of an end of history, and his interpetation of history as progress. We have a choice between contingency, force and chance on the one hand and philo-sophical rationalization on the other. Hegel's argument demonstrates that these are not alternatives, but equally products of the same presup-positions which keep rational and actual apart. When Kant attempts to follow through the necessary distinction between nature and reason in his thought in the context of his philosophy of history, their distinction is inevitably brought into question. Either the finite and contingent (natural determination) is infinitized into the eternal truth of history (realism); or the infinite and necessary (reason) is posited as the end of history (idealism). The gap between natural and rational is not sustained by the thought that thinks it, any more than it is sustained by the complex institutions and practices of inter-state politics.

Even if one accepts this reading of Hegel as tracing and exposing the complexities and fissures of the self-determination and self-understanding of the ethical life of his time through the analysis of both concepts and institutions, it is still unclear what he means by the notion of the identity of the rational and the actual in international politics and history.

> The present has cast off its barbarism and unjust [*unrechtliche*] arbitrariness, and truth has cast off its otherworldliness and contingent force, so that the true reconciliation, which reveals the *state* as the image and actuality of reason, has become objective. (Hegel, 1991a: 380)

It is difficult to understand claims such as the 'true reconciliation, which reveals the state as the image and actuality of reason, has become objective' as anything other than the identification of the modern state and state system with a Kantian kingdom of ends. However, if it is understood that Hegel's premise is that reason (the conceptual self-understanding of spirit) is itself an aspect of (and inseparable from) the practical, institutional self-determination of spirit, then this is merely a reminder that reason is always historically located and has no tran-scendent ground. The special claim made for the idea of the state of Hegel's time and place is that, as a constitutional state, it rests on the recognition in principle of what, for Hegel, is the truth of spirit's self-determination. This is not a trans-historical ideal, in the sense of an ought-to-be which gives an overall normative meaning to history. The normative judgement of the constitutional state examined in Hegel's

Elements of the Philosophy of Right depends not on the necessary nature of spirit, which in itself generates no determinate normative judgements, but on the contingent and shifting, mutually mediating and mutually transcending relations between self-conscious beings and the givens of ethical life. With Hegel there is no escape either into the abstract moralism which condemns the world without engaging with it, or into the equally abstract realism which transforms contingency into eternal truth. The purpose of political theory, therefore, is not to provide an alien meaning to existence but to make explicit what is already implicit in the different mediations of rationality and actuality which the 'I's and 'We's of spirit inhabit and construct.

There are readings of Hegel's political philosophy which, in spite of his own claims to the contrary, would categorize it as straightforwardly evaluative and even prescriptive in the account that is given of modern ethical life. It is possible to read the idea of 'ethical life' itself as a kind of moral ideal, harking back to the perfect harmony of individual/social relations within the Greek polis. In line with the interpretation of Hegel given above, I would reject such readings and see Hegel's account as an attempt to comprehend the nature of the specifically Western modern self-determination of spirit. It is clearly the case that ethical life in the *Elements of the Philosophy of Right* is not harmonious. Rather, Hegel demonstrates how modern ethical life is constituted through a pattern of relative identities in which there are constant tensions between the different spheres of ethical life and between the individual and the private, economic, social and legal relations in which she/he is caught. It is a fairly common understanding of the task of the political theorist as being to attempt to articulate the ground of political judgement and action. For Hegel, however, this task takes on a different meaning from that which is commonly understood. For Hegel the ground of political judgement and action is not identifiable with any transcendental location, but only with the dynamism of the actual complexity of spirit's self-determination. However, to suggest that Hegel is able to grasp this complexity impartially or as a whole would be to grant Hegel a God-like position which is directly contrary to the presumptions of his own phenomenological project. It is not and could not be the case that Hegel presents a complete and impartial account of his contemporary ethical life, since no one self-consciousness could inhabit simultaneously all the multifarious determinations of spirit. Although description rather than prescription is Hegel's primary aim, he does take up normative stances and imply specific prescriptions in the course of his account of the modern state and the principles of right institutionalized within it, and these inevitably reflect Hegel's own relative identity with his time and place.

There is, however, a crucial difference between the evaluative and prescriptive aspects of Hegel's analysis and standard accounts of normative judgement. On Hegel's account of his own project the evaluative and prescriptive elements in his analysis have always to take the form of hypothetical rather than categorical norms. At each turn in his argument, Hegel demonstrates how the endorsement of certain kinds of principles and institutions depends on presuppositions which are embedded within the historical development of a form of ethical life and have complex and even contradictory consequences. Phenomenology, therefore, does not outlaw prescription; instead, in insisting on accounting for evaluative and prescriptive judgements it opens up the grounds and implications of such judgements in all their contingency and ambiguity, and this must include the judgements of the phenomenologist him- or herself. I would argue that Hegel's philosophy of right (like other political theories such as Kant's, even when they understand themselves more ambitiously) explains and implies things to the reader only in so far as readers recognize themselves in the account. Recognize themselves, that is, not as a matter of subjective preference but in terms of their own 'relative identity' with the ethical life within which they participate. Normative judgement is not the gift of the theorist to the reader; unless it is something already or potentially shared then it has no meaning. At the heart of Hegel's work is an acknowledgement of the impossibility of theoretical legislation. In the end it is the adequacy of the theoretical articulation of a particular shape of spirit, as judged by those participating in and constructing it which generates the meaning and effect of his theoretical work. Explanation and normative judgement in relation to particular aspects of ethical life remain possible, but they make sense only in terms of a project of self-understanding which is also an open-ended project of self-determination.

From the point of view of theories of international relations such as critical theory, postmodernism and feminism the key problem with using Hegel is that his political theory culminates in the claim that the modern European nation-state is the 'actuality of the ethical idea'. Whether or not Hegel is seeking to endorse the principles of state sovereignty and international law which are inseparable from the evolution of the modern state, for contemporary critical theories a Hegelian analysis necessarily fails to do justice to the range and complexity of actors and institutions which make up the context and content of international politics in the late twentieth century. The 'self' of spirit's self-determination in Hegel's analysis is shorthand for the complex and conflictual interrelation of individuals, collectivities and institutions which make up ethical life. However, even if the Hegelian exposition of the self-determination and self-understanding of spirit allows for complexity, tension and conflicts, it nevertheless suggests that ethical life can be grasped in the modern state and state system in terms of a self-understanding which is peculiar to early nineteenth century Europe. It is precisely this emphasis in orthodox international theory which contemporary critical theories are concerned to challenge and subvert. This is both because such theories oppose giving priority to the state and state system in the analysis of international politics and because such theories are suspicious of a eurocentric or Western bias in normative theoretical presumptions.

There are two responses which can be made to critics who accuse Hegel of being state-centric and eurocentric in his analysis. First, in direct defence of Hegel, it can be noted that Hegel's exposition of modern ethical life in *Elements of the Philosophy of Right* does not only treat the state as a condition of possibility for domestic and international politics, but also demonstrates how sub-state and trans-state factors condition (and threaten) the possibility of the state. As I suggested above in terms of Hegel's analysis of the place of the family within the modern state, Hegel opens up the understanding of the significance of gender and class in the shaping of ethical life. He also exposes the paradoxical nature of the modern state as both autonomous and dependent. Moreover, to the extent that the principles underlying the European state system of Hegel's day continue to structure and influence contemporary state and international law and institutions then his analysis remains of at least partial relevance. However, this kind of defence misses the point of the phenomenological reading of Hegelian political theory which has been presented in this section. The second response to Hegel's critics is to acknowledge that, on very good Hegelian grounds, Hegel's analysis is both radically outmoded and necessarily partial.

Although Hegel did acknowledge the role of international factors conditioning the state in ethical life, he paid very little attention to them in comparison to internal conditions of possibility. The tensions between internal and external sovereignty, which Hegel acknowledges in principle in his discussion of European inter-state relations, have become much more obviously acute in international politics in the past 150 years. Moreover, Hegel's analysis is radically outmoded in relation to a variety of global and transnational developments which have taken place since he wrote. In particular, Hegel's assumptions of the economic self-sufficiency of states and the lack of international institutions and non-state international actors clearly misrepresents the contemporary situation. In terms of Hegel's own argument, however, this is just what might be expected given that his own time and his own, partial, philosophical comprehension of that time did not exhaust the possibilities of change – whether progressive or otherwise. A contemporary Hegelian approach to understanding and judging international politics inhabits a very different formation of spirit – one which, to the extent that it is different, will provide a different set of resources for that understanding and judgement.

The outmodedness of the Hegelian analysis of international politics may be explicable in terms of a changing international context, but this in no way responds to the charge, also made by critics, that the analysis is biased towards the values of Western culture and institutions. There is no question that Hegel's analysis, as he acknowledges, is rooted in an attempt to understand the particular experiences of Western Europe in the aftermath of the French Revolution. There is also no doubt that the effect of Hegel's analysis is to privilege the explicit articulation of spirit as self-determination which, according to his phenomenology, is the defining mark of post-revolutionary ethical life (including politics), art, religion and philosophy. However, as has been noted above, the absolute claim which Hegel makes, i.e., that spirit is, always has been and always will be, self-determination is both ethically (prescriptively) indeterminate and contingently conditioned. On the one hand the absolute claim is compatible with any and every shape that spirit might take. On the other, the absolute claim is equally the acknowledgement of the relativity of any given theoretical articulation and the dependence of its meaning on how others are able to identify that articulation with their own self-understanding. The values which Hegel explores and criticizes in *Elements of the Philosophy of Right* are Western values, dependent on Western culture and institutions, whether they have resonance beyond that context depends on the degree of openness and closure between different forms of spirit. For this reason, the ethical limitations and possibilities of international ethical life, on an Hegelian account, cannot be settled in principle in advance, nor are they likely to be exhausted by any one theorist's account, however impressive, of spirit's self-understanding.

I have argued above that Hegelian phenomenology, and the conceptions of spirit and ethical life on which it relies, offers a powerful alternative to the ontological and epistemological assumptions which inform standard approaches to normative international theory. I want now to move on to suggest that a similar kind of understanding of the nature and status of normative theory and the relation of theorist to object of theory underlies Foucault's very different approach to political theorizing.

Foucault and the nature of political theory

Bringing the thought of Hegel and Foucault together seems initially as bizarre as returning to Hegel as a resource for contemporary normative international theory. Foucault as an archaeologist of knowledge is a theorist of discontinuity in the history of consciousness. For him, the very phrase 'history of consciousness' would be a suspect one, yet this is what Hegel's *Phenomenology of Spirit* purports to be. Foucault as a genealogist operates with the conception of power/knowledge, which seems worlds away from the transcendent connotations of Hegel's 'absolute knowledge'. Foucault as an ethicist focuses on the care of the self rather than the realm of state and inter-state right which is Hegel's concern in his political philosophy. Moreover, Foucault's explicit references to Hegel, although ambiguous in places (notably in the tribute to Hyppolite in 'The Order of Discourse', Foucault, 1981: 74–6) tend towards the position in *The Order of Things*, in which Hegel is part of the soon to be transcended 'anthropological' epistemic turn. In 'Truth and Power' Foucault asserts dismissively, '*Dialectic* is a way of evading the always open and hazardous reality of conflict to a Hegelian skeleton' (Foucault, 1984: 56–7). This is not to claim that Foucault is entirely wrong in his assessment of the distance between his and Hegel's theorizing. However, there are areas of thinking in which the two philosophers are much closer in their ideas than the standard classification of their work into modernist (Hegel) and postmodernist (Foucault) camps suggests. I will demonstrate this point through an examination of Foucault's genealogical work and of the complex relation of power, knowledge and truth it involves.

Two of the characteristics of genealogy which differentiate it from more conventional historical enquiry are as follows: first, genealogy is not the search for truth (either as origin or scientific explanation) but rather constitutes an exploration of the discursive conditions which make regimes of truth possible and of the effects of power inseparable from those discursive conditions (Foucault, 1980: 83–4; 131–3). Secondly, genealogy is history which sets out not to make the past familiar, but to make the present strange, this is exemplified most clearly in Foucault's *History of Sexuality*, Volume 1, and his challenge to the 'repressive hypothesis' (Foucault, 1990: 8–13). Foucault's histories are always geared to questions about how and why 'we' in the present come to take the limits of 'our' existence for granted (Foucault, 1977: 31; 1988: 262). These two characteristics suggest that there are two dimensions to the critical implications of genealogy. The first dimension challenges claims to truth which presume the separability of power, knowledge and truth through the demonstration of their perpetual entanglement. The second dimension, in drawing attention to the constructed, contingent and political nature of regimes of truth, opens up the possibility of alternative regimes, whether in the sense of subjugated knowledges or radically new constructions.

It is in the texts *Discipline and Punish* (1977), *History of Sexuality*, Volume 1 (1990) and the writings and interviews collected under the title *Power/Knowledge* (1980), that Foucault's most explicit discussions of the relationship between power and knowledge are to be found. The argument of *Discipline and Punish* makes, as a crucial part of its account of the birth of the prison, a series of claims about the nature of power as 'disciplinary'. These claims are set against what Foucault terms traditional 'juridical' conceptions of power (Foucault, 1977: 194). The difference between the two conceptions of power is exemplified in the famous contrast Foucault draws between the public and spectacular punishment of the attempted regicide Damiens, as opposed to the treatment of prisoners within the Panoptican. Juridical power belongs to and is exercised by a sovereign body to repress and control its subjects. Disciplinary power, on the other hand, belongs to nobody and is productive rather than repressive in its effects. According to *Discipline and Punish*, the construction of the sovereign individual, which is both the premise and the accomplishment of the Panopticon, is inseparable from the development of the human sciences. In this text, the discourses of human behaviour which helped to inspire and account for changes in the penal system in the nineteenth century are most frequently presented as effects and channels of disciplinary power (Foucault, 1977: 194, 204, 305). Thus, Foucault's argument appears to be that power produces discourses of knowledge, which in turn produce regimes of truth, criteria through which to discriminate between true and false or normal and deviant. This argument is carried through into *History of Sexuality*, Volume 1. In this text, Foucault again stresses the necessary relation of power to knowledge and the ways in which psychiatric and psychological sciences carry through effects of power (Foucault, 1990: 98–100). However, in this text it is clear that the relationship of power to knowledge and, therefore, to truth is more complex than that suggested in *Discipline and Punish*. Although Foucault continues to claim that, as he puts it, there is no exteriority between techniques of knowledge and strategies of power (Foucault, 1990: 98), this does not mean that discourses of knowledge and regimes truth are always secondary or subordinate to power (Foucault, 1990: 100–1).

One of the most frequent complaints made about Foucault's account of disciplinary power is that it seems to leave nothing outside of power for the purposes of explanation or normative judgement. If Foucault is read in this way then the traditional enlightenment opposition of knowledge and truth to power appears to be rendered meaningless. This is a reading which is encouraged by aspects of the arguments of *Discipline and Punish* and the first volume of *History of Sexuality*. Both texts debunk the pretensions of nineteenth century penal reformers and twentieth century psychiatrists to be involved in a project of the liberation of the true/ genuine subject from repressive power or the power of repression. However, as Foucault himself repeatedly asserts, this reading rests on a misunderstanding. In commenting on his conception of power, Foucault stresses that 'power' always stands as a shorthand for 'power relations' in his work and that relations of power are inherently immanent, tactical and strategic rather than in any sense transcendent (Foucault, 1982: 217; 1988: 103–6; 1990: 94–6). In contrast to physical determination, Foucault argues, power involves the possibility of resistance, and although it is inseparable from knowledge, truth and freedom the latter are not simply reducible to power (Foucault, 1982: 217–18; 1988: 106; 1990: 98). As Foucault sees it, to pose the conceptual choice as that between defining power in opposition to knowledge, truth and freedom and defining power as sovereign over knowledge, truth and freedom is to succumb to the 'intellectual blackmail' of being for or against enlightenment (Foucault, 1984: 45). Instead, Foucault requires that the genealogist recognize, first, that relations of power presuppose freedom and, secondly, that discourses of knowledge and regimes of truth are in perpetual interplay with, but not simply identical to, relations of power.

Foucault describes the perpetual interplay between relations of power and strategies of resistance in 'The Subject and Power' (Foucault, 1982: 221, 225); this discussion raises the question of how the distinction between power and freedom can be drawn. Foucault clearly rejects the idea that there can be any universal criteria of judgement which would settle this question. Relations of power and strategies of resistance are always specifically located and the recognition of what counts as either power or freedom depends on the particular context. However, the question still remains for actors in specific contexts as to what would count for them as practices of liberation. In the discussion of some specific examples of resistant practice in 'The Subject and Power', Foucault concludes that central to these struggles (examples include the women's movement, movements for children's rights, the anti-psychiatry movement) is the attack on the form of power which makes individuals subject (1982: 211–12). This form of power encompasses both external control of individuals and their internal self-governance (1982: 212). Participants in these resistances ask the question of who they are and refuse the definitions and relations through which the question has previously been answered. A little later in the same essay, Foucault draws a contrast between two kinds of philosophy: the universalist philosophy of Descartes, which asks about the nature of the 'I' as an unhistorical subject; and the specific analysis of ourselves and our present which he ascribes to Kant's reflections on enlightenment (1982: 216). In parallel with the political movements of resistance he has already discussed, Foucault maps out the practice of critical philosophy:

> Maybe the target nowadays is not to discover what we are, but to refuse what we are. We have to imagine and to build up what we could be to get rid of this kind of political 'double bind', which is the simultaneous individualization and totalization of modern power structures. (Foucault, 1982: 216)

The account of the relation between power and freedom as one of mutual dependence has implications for Foucault's other claim, that is, that discourses of knowledge and regimes of truth are in perpetual interplay with relations of power, although not reducible to them. What Foucault's account of critical philosophy suggests is that knowledge and truth may well be complicit with power, but that they may also be part of the strategic forces of resistance, opening up new possibilities for thought and being. This helps to make sense of one account Foucault gives of genealogy as a practice of local criticism which is involved in the 'insurrection of subjugated knowledges' (Foucault, 1980: 81). According to this account, genealogy, through painstaking research, recovers not only the discursive conditions of dominant regimes of truth thereby displaying the fragility of globalizing theory, but also reveals knowledge and truth which has been suppressed and which provides a ground for critique of dominant theory.

Through the exposure of the essentially political nature of claims to truth, particularly within the human sciences (Foucault, 1988: 106), genealogy traces the interrelations of power, knowledge and truth. Through the revelation of power relations as tactical struggles in which dominant discourses are sustained through an encounter and subjugation of alternative discourses, genealogy opens up the way to thinking differently about those dominant discourses (Foucault, 1980: 81–2; 1982: 216). As with power and freedom, however, it is clear that what counts as a subjugating as opposed to a subjugated discourse is dependent on context. As a theoretical practice, genealogy is slippery and its effects are undecidable in advance. The genealogist is no more immune to relations of power than any other kind of theorist and there can be no guarantee that the genealogist speaks on behalf of the oppressed.

I carefully guard against making the law. Rather, I concern myself with determining problems, unleashing them, revealing them within the framework of such complexity as to shut the mouths of prophets and legislators: all of those who speak for others and above others. (Foucault, 1991: 159)

Hegel versus Foucault

There are profound differences in the accounts of theory, politics and history put forward by Hegel and Foucault. First, unlike Foucault, Hegel does not conceive of ethical life as discourses of knowledge or relations of power best captured by a vocabulary of tactics and strategy. Secondly, in contrast to Foucault, Hegel's political theory still has the king's head in place, in that it deals with law, the state and inter-state relations rather than with micro-level relations of power. Thirdly, although Hegel acknowledges the significance of theory in spirit's self-determination he does not identify the theorist's role as necessarily linked to either the sustaining or subverting of dominant relations of power, whereas Foucault self-consciously aligns his theoretical practice with an idea of critique and a commitment to resistance.

Yet, in spite of these differences, Foucault's refusal, as a genealogist, to be a theoretical legislator presents strong echoes of Hegel's refusal, as phenomenologist and speculative philosopher, to set down what ought to be the case in the *Elements of the Philosophy of Right* (Hegel, 1991a: 21). What is it that underlies the resistance to prescription in such different theoretical approaches? Put crudely, I would suggest that both Foucault and Hegel understand ethical life (or relations of power and resistance) and the practice of theory as an aspect of that life as both absolute and relative: absolute in the sense that all aspects of political existence, including attempts to understand and judge that existence, are constructed and conditioned; relative in the sense that ethical life (or relations of power and resistance) is always a contingent structure of possibilities, possibilities which are in principle incapable of exhaustion. In other words, Hegel and Foucault share an insight into the logic of ethical life (or relations of power and resistance) as one which defies distinctions between nature (real, particular, relative, immanent) and reason (ideal, universal, absolute and transcendent). The implications drawn from this insight, however, are radically different and potentially opposed. For Hegel, political theory becomes the ongoing task of articulating the self-understanding of spirit; for Foucault, political theory becomes part of the tactical struggles between power and resistance, a perpetual targeting of taken-for-granted limitation. In both cases the different ways in which the theorists build on their central theoretical insight illustrates the complementary strengths and weaknesses of their approaches.

Where Foucault conceives of both theory and politics in terms of a fight or a game, Hegel conceives of theory and politics in much broader terms as processes which are open-ended, not only in direction and outcome but in the means by which they are conducted. Foucault's focus on micro levels of power gives the object of his analysis a specificity and particularity which enables the theorist to identify with and intervene on behalf of the forces of resistance rather than of power. Although the theorist can never be sure either of the accuracy of his analysis or of the outcome of his theoretical intervention, he can nevertheless orient his theoretical practice in terms of an idea of freedom (the meaning of which will always be specifically contextualized). No such option is available to the Hegelian theorist. Hegelian theory, like Foucauldian theory, grasps theory as both effected by and effecting its theoretical object through a relation with the reader which cannot be legislated in advance. Nevertheless, the Hegelian theorist is obliged to reject even the orientation towards transcendence and closure which is implicit in the Foucauldian commitment to the critique of given limitation. The task of the Hegelian theorist is primarily one of comprehension, a task which is one of both reflection and judgement. The aim is to articulate an understanding of the ethical life in which the theorist participates. Inevitably, this articulation will be partial and normatively inflected, but the politics of that articulation cannot be settled in advance since it depends on the relation with and response to that theoretical articulation by the reader. The responsibility of the Hegelian theorist is not towards discourses of resistance but towards the truth understood as an adequate self-understanding of the contemporary self-determinations of spirit. To the extent that both theorist and reader are equally implicated in ethical life, then their political responsibility is shared, and the theorist does not have a privileged theoretical position.

The main strengths of Hegelian analysis lie in the richness of the concepts of spirit and ethical life, which have a substantive breadth and depth exceeding the much thinner Foucauldian notions of discourse and power relations. The idea of spirit encompasses collective and institutional as well as individual agency and does not prejudge the extent to which these will be experienced by different 'I's and 'We's as compatible or in tension. Hegelian phenomenology covers juridical as well as disciplinary power and the openness of ethical possibilities within both. This means that Hegelian analysis does not fall into the Foucauldian pattern of privileging a theoretical orientation towards freedom as the critique of given limitation; it does not always condemn what is in terms of what might be. However, the weakness of Hegelian analysis is that the political dimension of self-understanding becomes underemphasized and too little attention is paid to the evaluative/prescriptive dimension and effects of power which follow from the claims to truth being made by the theorist. When stressing that he is not concerned with what *ought* to be the case at the beginning of *Elements of the Philosophy of Right*, Hegel is being disingenuous in the light of his own understanding of the relation between spirit and its self-understanding. It is here that Foucauldian genealogy has its greatest strength, since it emphasizes not simply the contingency and partiality but also the exclusivity of all claims to truth. The recognitive relation between theorist, object of theory and reader is a complex and active one. The best way of grasping this interrelation, one which is premised on the rejection of the conceptual oppositions traditionally deployed in the understanding and judgement of politics is that provided by combining the insights of Hegel's phenomenology with those of Foucauldian genealogy.

At the beginning of this chapter it was claimed that orthodox approaches to normative international theory were limited by their reliance on a series of conceptual oppositions (reason/nature, ideal/real, universal/particular) which confined them to variations on a standard theme. The play of these oppositions in idealist, realist, cosmopolitan and communitarian thought was by no means static; each perspective replayed the pattern of oppositions in a different way depending on the sleight of hand of the theorist positioning the stuff of international politics within the existing conceptual scheme. Nevertheless, the fate of international politics was essentially restricted to two possible normative conclusions: either it was necessarily that which it ought not to be, or it would necessarily (through the workings of reason or nature) become that which it ought to be. It has also been claimed that the mainspring of recent critical theories of international politics (critical theory, postmodernism, feminism) was the perceived need to escape from these conceptual shackles and re-think the ways in which international politics, the nature of normative international theory and the relation between theorist and object of theory were conceptualized. The readings of Hegel and Foucault given above are intended to point the way towards such a re-thinking. Hegel and Foucault do not only disrupt the conceptual oppositions at the level of conceptualizing politics, they also disrupt them in their account of their own theoretical practice. For neither thinker is politics understood as an absence, subject to competing claims of reason and nature. Instead, for both, politics is essentially a logic of self-constitution and self-transcendence, which can only be grasped immanently. The meaning of politics cannot therefore be fixed in terms of the identification of an ideal model of politics, whether this is understood in terms of reason or of nature. The only absolute for both Hegel and Foucault is that everything is relative. This is, of course, why for many normative theorists, the path taken by Hegel and Foucault is a dangerous one. If political theory is understood in terms of phenomenology and genealogy then this seems to imply an impoverishment of theoretical work. Instead of the theorist being the moral doctor, diagnosing and prescribing for the ills of the world, the theorist shares in the disease and has no access to a cure. The point of Hegel's and Foucault's anti-prescriptive theorizing, however, is that all theorizing is caught within politics, whether this is explicitly articulated or not. A great deal of Hegel's and Foucault's work is precisely devoted to demonstrating that the legislative claims of mainstream moral and political theory are not borne out when their origins, concepts and effects are examined – a point which is also repeatedly made by critical, postmodernist and feminist international theory.

Conclusion

In the approach to international normative theory inspired by the Hegelian and Foucauldian insights explored in this chapter the following assumptions will be essential. First, the institutional structures of international politics are not eternally given and will always be subject to change. The state and state system cannot be understood in distinction from both internal and external conditions of possibility (conceptual, structural and practical), which are not necessarily mutually consistent and which vary and shift over time in a way which cannot be predicted in the long term and which certainly does not accord with any pre-legislated pattern. Secondly, the international political theorist relates to both reader and the object of theorizing as flesh of their flesh. This does not mean that the theorist is the same as either reader or theoretical object, but that the premise of the analysis is that theorist, reader and object are all implicated in (in Hegelian terms are relatively identical with) international ethical life. Thirdly, international political theory is concerned with truth and judgement. However, neither truth claims nor normative judgements are anchored in the trans-historical roots of either reason or nature. Instead they are rooted in the theorist's own relative identity with the object of his or her analysis and validated solely in terms of the reader's recognition of that identity as in some sense the reader's own. This means that the multiple modes of relation to and complicity with the concepts, structures and practices of international politics are relevant to the adequacy and effects of theoretical claims. The theorist is not critic, legislator or doctor because the theorist's privilege, in so far as it exists, is immanent within international politics and not transcendent to it. This implies in turn that theoretical claims and judgements involve appeal and risk rather than recounting and certainty, and their validity is subject to the vicissitudes of political change. In summary, the kind of normative theorizing which emerges from the exposition of Hegel's and Foucault's ideas combines phenomenological adequacy with genealogical honesty in place of the fixed ontologies and authoritative epistemologies which have characterized mainstream normative international theory.

The argument of this book so far has been conducted at a high level of generality. I have attempted both to trace and critically assess orthodox and critical approaches to normative international theory and to provide a new basis for the latter in Hegelian phenomenology and Foucauldian genealogy. The discussion has moved a long way from paying attention to the issues which have provoked both the turn to the ethics of international relations and the challenges to orthodox theory discussed in previous chapters. These are issues such as global distributive justice, international human rights, the ethics of nationality and the possibility and desirability of cosmopolitan citizenship and democracy. In the following two chapters, I will illustrate the value of the approach to normative international theory discussed in this chapter through examination of two such focuses of normative theoretical debate: first, the ongoing debate over the international validity of rights to individual and collective self-determination; secondly, the ongoing debate over cosmopolitan citizenship and democracy.

Notes

1   It will become evident in the course of this chapter both that I do not agree with this reading of Hegel and that Hegel's work is open to a variety of interpretations. The key texts on which my reading of Hegel is based are: *Phenomenology of Spirit* (1977) and *Elements of the Philosophy of Right* (1991a).

For interpretations of the former text see: Kojève (1980); Rose (1981); Westphal (1979); Pinkard (1994); Forster (1998); Stewart (1998); for interpretations of the latter text see: Pelczynski (1984); Wood (1990); Dallmyr (1993); Hardimon (1994). Rose and Westphal are the commentators who come closest to my own reading. Houlgate (1991) provides a good introduction to Hegel's philosophy in general. Critical theory, postmodernism and feminist theory (in international relations but also in other contexts) tend to be heavily influenced by Marx's reading of Hegel, expounded most fully in his early unpublished commentary on *Elements of the Philosophy of Right* (Marx, 1975: 58–198). According to Marx, Hegel's work is significant for its insights into dialectical logic, but remains trapped in a purely idealist reading of history.

2 Discussions of the meaning to be attached to the idea of an 'end of history' in Hegel's work can be found in articles by Grier, Maurer and Harris (Stewart, 1996) and in Bubner (1991), Pompa (1991) and Hutchings (1991). In general, contemporary Hegel scholarship agrees that the Hegelian idea of an end of history does not mean that history effectively stops (see Kojève, 1980; Fukuyama, 1992) – see discussion in the following section.

3 Hegel does not write extensively about international relations. Recent discussion of Hegel's writings on war are divided amongst those who argue that Hegel acknowledges the necessity of war without glorifying it (e.g., Verene, 1971; Harris, 1980; Walt, 1989) and those who argue that Hegel saw war as a phenomenon that could be historically overcome (e.g., Smith, 1989: 156–64). For critical discussion of Hegel as statist or nationalist see articles by Ottmann, Knox, Kaufmann, Gregoire, Avineri (Stewart, 1996).

4 Debates about Hegel's philosophy and gender are ongoing and reflect the same kind of ambiguities as haunt readings of Hegel's political thought in general. Feminist philosophers are divided between seeing Hegel as a fundamentally patriarchal thinker and identifying aspects of his thought as useful for feminism. A series of articles reflecting diverse views has been collected by Jagentowicz Mills (1996).

5 The best known source for this reading was Popper's account of Hegel in his highly influential study *The Open Society and Its Enemies*, Volume II (1944–5). This kind of interpretation is long out of fashion in Hegel scholarship (see Stewart, 1996: Part 2, 53–128).

6 Hegel's conception of phenomenology is best explained in his Introduction to the *Phenomenology of Spirit* (1997: 46–57). In contemporary parlance the notion of 'immanent critique' often used by critical theorists probably comes closest to capturing the meaning. Phenomenology means literally the 'science of appearance', it is confined to and relies on the realm of experience. An excellent exposition of what is involved in the phenomenological investigation of consciousness in the *Phenomenology of Spirit* is provided by Westphal:

> The dilemma is sharp. Criticism calls for criteria, but any choice of criteria involves either dogmatism or faith, in either case the abrogation of criticism. How can there be criticism without presuppositions?

The answer is found by attending carefully to the object of our investigations – consciousness. As it turns out, "consciousness provides itself with it own criterion, and the investigation will be a comparison of consciousness with its own self". – This happy discovery is really simpler than Hegel makes it sound. Every mode of knowledge distinguishes itself from its object or truth. It has at least a general idea of its object, of what would fulfill its intention or verify its assertion, and this serves as the criterion by which all putative knowledge is measured. Thus the question about each form of consciousness is not whether it conforms to our expectations or Hegel's, but whether it satisfies its own demands. The self-understanding of natural science, for example, is significantly altered when reflection on the problem of induction or the paradoxes of confirmation reveals that it cannot live up to its previously professed promises. (Westphal, 1979: 15)

7   Probably the most famous section of the *Phenomenology of Spirit* following the influential reading of Kojève (Kojève, 1980: 35–51) is that dealing with the formation of individual self-consciousness (Hegel, 1977: 104–19). In this section of the text Hegel argues that human individual self-consciousness is fundamentally social, relying not on inner certainties but on recognition by and interaction with others. At this stage in the argument Hegel is discussing the most basic elements of self-conscious being, a discussion which is acknowledged to be inadequate unless it is extended to consider not simply the relation between human beings considered in isolation, but also that relation in the context of its construction and mediation by objective spirit (the world of social, economic, legal and political practices and institutions) which is both produced by and transcends subjective spirit (individual and collective self-conscious beings). The most recent example of social theory which uses Hegel's struggle for recognition as a founding principle is Honneth, although Honneth sees Hegel as betraying the insights generated by the *Phenomenology of Spirit* in his later work (Honneth, 1995).

8   Hegel's frequently reiterated claim that the time at which he was writing exemplified a new departure in both history and philosophy amounts essentially to the claim not that spirit had suddenly become self-determining when it had not been before, but to the claim that the idea of spirit's self-determination was now an insight that particular 'I's and 'We's of self-conscious being were explicitly articulating and institutionalizing, most obviously in the American and French revolutions. Of course, in the latter case in particular, Hegel argued that the notion of spirit's self-determination was misread in terms of a God-like ability to re-create the world which had disastrous consequences in the Terror (Hegel, 1977: 357–9).

PART THREE

FUTURE DIRECTIONS: DOING INTERNATIONAL POLITICAL THEORY

5

Self-Determination

Introduction

The notion of self-determination is central to normative debate in international theory. Realists, cosmopolitans, communitarians, critical theorists, postmodernists, feminists are all concerned with examining and promoting this ideal – although with radically different understandings of what it implies, from the principle of state sovereignty to the international political recognition of sexual difference. In this chapter I will be exploring the way in which the ideal of self-determination operates in a range of normative debates about individual and collective rights. Crucial to these debates are the issues of which 'self' is in question and what counts as self- as opposed to other-determination. For some normative theorists, the selves that should be self-determining in the international context are the selves of the individual human being, the nation and the state, and for yet others they include the gendered human being or the participants in new social movements, in Falk's phrase 'citizen pilgrims' (Falk, 1995: 211–12). Within each of these possibilities are concealed a host of further complex debates about why these particular entities are important and how their autonomy should be understood, accommo-dated and encouraged. Here both broad and specific policy issues become the object of normative judgement: Is there a right to nationality? Do nations have a right to be states? Should international intervention be permitted to enforce global moral norms? Should cultural difference be respected? Should free movement of people across state borders be permitted? The list is ongoing and seemingly inexhaustible.

In the first part of this chapter some of the ramifications of the idea of the human individual as the locus of self-determination will be con-sidered. It will become evident that the unresolvability of normative debates about international rights to self-determination in mainstream ethics of international politics bears out the argument of previous chapters that there is a tendency towards theoretical deadlock in this kind of normative international theory. However, it will also be argued that the nature of this theoretical deadlock has less to do with the substantive conclusions reached by the various normative approaches than with their grounding in what Steiner refers to as a 'first best' world characterized by an idealized fixed ontology and the associated claim of epistemological privilege for the theorist's insight into what self-determination means (O'Neill, 1992: 115–19; Steiner, 1992: 90). In the second part of the chapter it will be argued that the critical theories of international relations pre-viously discussed in Chapter 3, particularly feminism, go a considerable way to moving beyond this theoretical deadlock by challenging the idealized ontology through which concepts of individuals, nations and states are thought in more mainstream approaches. However, it will also be argued that the deconstruction of the archetypal subjects of self-determination in international politics cannot be fully accomplished whilst theorists remain haunted by an ideal of what self-determination means which drives a wedge between first (ideal) and second best (actual) worlds. In conclusion, it will be argued that the way to move forward in debate over international self-determination is to follow through the logic of the insights of critical theory, postmodernism and feminism more consistently. This means recasting normative theory and the assessment of normative judgement and prescription along the Hegelian/Foucauldian lines suggested in the Chapter 4.

The main implication of taking this theoretical turn is a recognition that debate over international rights is best understood and pursued in terms of the Hegelian concept of ethical life. According to this concept, neither international politics nor normative theory makes sense in terms of philosophical presuppositions which understand subjects of self-determination as self-contained entities or identify self-determination in opposition to other-determination. When arguing for or against different sorts of international rights and rights bearers, normative theorists are participating in international ethical life and articulating its variable potential. It is the context of international ethical life which powers the different schools of thought on such issues and determines what will count as an issue in the first place in theory and in practice. Which discourses are powerful enough to re-shape international ethical life cannot be determined in advance by reference to epistemic privilege or fixed accounts of rationally or naturally self-determining selves. The prevalence of one view over another is conditioned not by pure reason through rational demonstration nor by natural determination through contract or battle, nor even à la Rorty by sentiment through the quality of rhetoric, but by the extent to which the recipients of alternative rights discourses (a variety of individual and supra-individual agents) recognize those discourses as ones in which they share. It is the radically ambiguous institutional social, political and economic processes in which these discourses are embedded which will make the difference. Only in a world which resembled the 'first best' world of idealized theory could there be absolute vindication for any normative claim. In the absence of such a world normative claims will remain ambiguous, tentative, costly and unavoidable.

Which selves, what determination?

For many cosmopolitan international theorists the defining mark of *normative* international theory is that it is based on the ethical value of individual as opposed to that of supra-individual or collective selves. Cosmopolitan approaches of a liberal contractarian and Kantian kind do not simply put supreme value on the human individual but on the idea of individual self-determination or autonomy, though they do not understand it in the same way or with the same prescriptive implications. In the case of liberal contractarian approaches, the value attached to individual self-determination is based on the idea of individual natural right. Some versions of contractarianism, as noted in Chapter 2, link this notion of natural right to ideas of natural law and reason which, as with Kantianism, connect the value of human autonomy to some notion of higher moral capacities, or, for example, to a basic moral right to property. For other versions of contractarianism, natural right is a pre-moral attribute, simply the freedom to follow natural determination towards self-preservation in a state of nature. The latter version of contractarianism is different from the former and from Kantianism in that it presumes the necessity of the institutionalization of right in a political order, even though it legitimates that order in terms of the prior contract (an actual or hypothetical voluntary relinquishment of natural right). In liberal contractarianism, the meaning of national or state right is parasitic on the prior existence of individual right. This does not necessarily imply that collective right is not taken seriously. In Chapter 2 we saw that the idea of the morality of states could be justified in contractarian terms, when states are understood as the best or only way to secure individual rights. Contractarian arguments may underly both arguments for an international human rights regime which will secure certain individual rights and freedoms *and* arguments for strong state borders to protect the rights of insiders, particularly property rights, from any outside encroachment.[1]

In the case of Kantian approaches, the value to be attached to individual self-determination is expressed in the formulation of the categorical imperative which requires that persons should always be treated as ends in themselves and never solely as means to others' ends. The status of 'end-in-him/herself' derives in Kant's theory from the self's potential as a self-legislating being. The self is only truly valuable in so far as the self is judging and acting in accordance with the determinations of a pure will – rationally or morally. Self-determination for Kant, therefore, is understood in terms of a very specific kind of determination, not simply doing what one wills but what one should will (he is adamant for instance that capital punishment is justified and even required by the higher self of the individual who has transgressed the law against murder) (Kant, 1991b: 143–4). The implications of the imperative to respect humans as ends in themselves are prescriptively powerful – although different Kantian theorists differ over their precise nature. One clear implication, however, is that it must be impermissible to respect the rights of national or state collectives if these are using individuals purely as means to their ends. Thus there are many Kantian based arguments against killing or otherwise harming innocents in both war and peace. Some are more restrictive in their scope than others, confining demands for protection of human individuals against state or inter-state forces to so-called 'negative' rights against killing of innocents, torture, suppression of freedoms of thought and speech etc., while others are more extensive, demanding in addition 'positive' protection of individuals against hunger and poverty.[2] The crucial commonality between different types of Kantian theorizing, however, is that the rights of individuals are the litmus test of social and political arrangements. Nations and states are of instrumental as opposed to intrinsic value.

Kantianism and contractarianism along with utilitarianism and Marxism have formed the main theoretical resources for discussion about what should be the nature and extent of international human rights in the current international order (Beetham, 1995).[3] Common to all these debates has been the assumption that international rights were essentially attached to individuals. Metatheoretical debates, about what the basis for the idea of universal human rights might be, have been accompanied by substantive discussions as to which rights count as fundamental or secondary and how, if they exist, such universal rights should be institutionalized. In so far as the idea of international human rights has been recognized as having some validity, debate has been particularly preoccupied with the issue of negative (legal, civil, political) versus positive (material) rights, with Kantians, utilitarians and Marxists often more favourable to the latter than contractarians (Cranston, 1973; Nickel, 1987: 92–119; Vincent, 1992; Shue, 1996). Although (particularly in relation to the implementation of human rights regimes) the cosmopolitan idea of international human rights has been recognized to be in potential tension with the international context of a nation-state system, nevertheless this system has generally been taken for granted in cosmopolitan international theory (Vincent, 1992). The right to national self-determination, which is enshrined in the UN declaration of human rights, has only recently attracted much theoretical attention from Western academics. However, a debate has now opened up which directs critical attention to the privileging of human individuals in the international rights discourse of cosmopolitan theory and, in particular, the ethical priority given by Kantian and contractarian discourses to the notion of individual autonomy or self-determination. This is the debate over the right to nationality and the right of nations to self-determination or statehood. This debate has been fuelled by a combination of circumstances, including the consequences of the end of the Cold War and the resurgence of nationalist movements in Eastern Europe and the ex-Soviet Union as well as the experience of strong sub-state nationalist pressures within established Western states such as Canada and the UK. The obvious significance of nationalist politics in recent years in so many parts of the world has led to the questioning of the nation-state as a normatively desirable mode of political organization and thereby put into question the nature of the 'selves' which normative international theory seeks to empower or limit within the international arena (see Tamir, 1993; Miller, 1995; Caney et al., 1996; Gilbert, 1998).

Within mainstream normative international theory, by which I refer to the 'ethics of international relations' approaches considered in Chapter 2 (in which normative theory is thought of in terms of bringing moral principles to bear on politics), the debate engendered by a focus on the right to national self-determination is largely concerned with mapping the relative strength of principles of individual, national and state autonomy. An excellent example of this can be found in the collection of essays *National Rights, International Obligations* (Caney et al., 1996) in which a variety of theorists debate the following interrelated issues: the question of the moral legitimacy of rights to nationality; the issue of whether moral obligations are necessarily transnational, or whether special obligations can be owed to fellow nationals; and the problem of reconciling global norms with cultural diversity both within states and transnationally (Caney et al., 1996: 1). As far as the first issue is concerned the debate hinges on the question of whether the moral right to national self-determination is held by individuals or by nations. Much discussion, therefore, is devoted to the concept of nation. What kind of real or fictional entity is a nation and would any normative implications (such as a right to autonomy) follow from its existence? Unsurprisingly, given the vast number of conflicting definitions in social scientific and historical research into nations and nationalism, normative theorists find the concept of nation and related concepts of nationality and national identity hard to pin down (see George, Charvet, Tamir and Gilbert in Caney et al., 1996; Gilbert, 1998: 8–12). Some theorists argue that the concept of a nation is too radically indeterminate to have any fixed meaning. For those who accept that the concept has meaningful reference, the nation is generally assumed to be comprised of some or all of the elements of common language, territory, culture, tradition and collective self-identity in which members of the nation recognize themselves to be such. Of particular significance in definitions of the nation in normative theory is the element of national identity and the degree of its self-consciousness. Often the normative significance of nations and nationality depends on the extent to which individuals self-consciously identify with and value the nation (Tamir, 1993: 63–9).

Two types of cosmopolitan response to the question of what normative consequences, if any, are bound up with the concept of nationhood are prominent in *National Rights, International Obligations*. I refer to these alternatives as *liberal statism* (Charvet, 1996; Steiner, 1996; Caney, 1996) and *liberal nationalism* (MacCormick, 1996; Tamir, 1996). One response (*liberal statism*) argues for the normative irrelevance of nationality as a prior ground for right, on grounds that even supposing the existence of a nation is demonstrable, nothing of normative significance follows because rights to self-determination can only be held by individuals or states. Liberal statism is derived from liberal contractarianism. On this account collective right is state right because it can only be derived from actual or hypothetical voluntary contractual grounds and not from previously shared culture, language, territory or tradition as such (Charvet, 1996). According to this argument there are no problems with seeing obligations to fellow-contractors as taking priority over obligations to outsiders, since right is generated by contract itself and the individual natural rights which underly it. There is also a clear sense that the contractarian legitimation of right is universally valid, regardless of the existence of alternative cultural norms. As noted earlier, the liberal statist position is a paradoxical one since it simultaneously reinforces the normative significance of individual right and can be used to defend a strong distinction between rights of individuals within and without the contractually legitimized political order. This paradox is reflected in two opposing tendencies in reading off the normative implications of liberal statism on issues such as relation to internal cultural minorities within the state and immigration. On the one hand, for liberal statists, there are no grounds for respecting either global norms or culturally entrenched values unless they are in keeping with the political culture of contract. In principle, therefore, it seems that states could be justified in imposing contractual values on non-liberal minorities within the state or on outside communities, providing it was prudent to do so (i.e., did not risk the entrenchment of individual rights which grounds the state's authority in the first place). On the other hand, the demands of national and cultural minorities within existing states have drawn liberal statists back to the question of the conditions of possibility of contractual political order and led to arguments defending the right of a given group of individuals, perhaps identifying themselves as a nation, either to re-constitute their contract entirely through secession or to re-negotiate it with the majority community in terms of group rights (Charvet, 1996: 65). As with the Hobbesian residual right of individuals to self-defence, however, for liberal statists this carries no necessary implications for the majority community's existing rights – there is no automatic duty to respect the right to secession or to institutionalize groups' rights, though it might be prudent to do so. In relation to questions of trans-national migration, but particularly to emigration into established states, there is a powerful liberal statist argument for immigration policy to be determined solely in terms of the rights of insiders (Steiner, 1992: 90–2). Although this does not necessarily imply a policy of closed borders, there is no legitimate ground to protest against a commitment to closure on the part of states. However, liberal statist arguments, particularly those which are pre-mised on the ultimate significance of property right, have returned again to the conditions of possibility of contract and, in recent years, produced arguments for the opening up of state borders, since the individual's right to property is argued to be the fundamental ground of state right and when state rights block the individual's right to property (whether of an insider or outsider), it is state right which should give way (Steiner, 1992: 90–1).

> It is the sad fate of virtually every moral and political doctrine to be called upon to deliver judgements in given circumstances which, on its own basic principles, constitute a 'second best' situation. The result of such deliverances, more often than not, is some proposal that embarrasses those principles by advancing certain types of morally valid right at the expense of other types, whereas in a 'first-best' world all these rights would be compossible. (Steiner, 1992: 90)

The arguments of liberal statism on rights to self-determination in an international context draw attention to the consequences of a theoretical position which applies first best criteria to second best situations. Thus, in a perfect world, the possession of no individual rights would be at the expense of anyone else's and the mechanism of voluntary contract would govern all social and political relations. However, in an imper-fect world not only does liberal statism find itself having prescriptive implications which seem contrary to its fundamental principles but it also finds itself having to think about factors, such as national identity, for which it does not have adequate first best conceptual equipment.

According to critics, liberal statism fails to comprehend the fact that liberal individuals and liberal states are sustained by things other than natural right and rational self-interest. In Canovan's recent work on the concept of nationhood, she has pointed to the way in which the nation is the neglected but ever-present condition of the bringing together of universal principle and particularistic identity in liberal political theory and ideology (Canovan, 1996a, 1996b: 78–81). Canovan herself suggests that attempting to give explicit theoretical articulation for and legitima-tion to the role of nation and nationality as the mediator between indi-vidual and state, or as the resolution of conflicts between inclusionary and exclusionary elements of modern citizenship, is pragmatically unwise because the success of nationality as a mediating factor in modern politics is premised on its vagueness and ambiguity (Canovan, 1996b: 76). However, it is precisely this which is currently being attempted by the

liberal alternative to liberal statism in answering the question of justifying rights to national self-determination, the alternative of liberal
nationalism.

Liberal nationalists argue for the importance of national rights to self-
determination on grounds that nationality is constitutive of and therefore
matters to individuals. This approach is exemplified by the work of
theorists such as Tamir (1993, 1996) and MacCormick (1996) and owes
much to Lockean and Kantian liberal traditions in combination with some
distinctively communitarian claims. Like liberal statists, liberal nationalists accept the primacy of individual rights to self-determination as the
grounds for legitimacy of any given political order (MacCormick, 1996: 35–
8). However, for liberal nationalists, individual rights to self-determination
are inseparable, first from ideal models of self-determination which are, as
with Kant's analysis, grounded in moral principle, and secondly, from the
view that individuals are always embedded in specific, constitutive
cultural identities, one of which is national identity (Tamir, 1993: 33;
MacCormick, 1996: 42). Liberal nationalists, therefore, interpret Kantian
respect for individual autonomy to include respect for the national identity
element which is constitutive of any particular individual, which implies
the right to nationhood and nationality. However, the ideal element in
Kantian conceptions of individual autonomy acts as a counterweight to the
notion of absolute respect for nationality and links liberal nationalism to
the promotion not of nationality as such but of liberal nations, made up of
liberal individuals (Tamir, 1993: 42–8). A boundary between inside and
outside is drawn between national and non-national in liberal nationalism
but the difference between obligations to insiders as opposed to outsiders
is somewhere in between the inclusive and exclusive versions of liberal
statism, with neither individuals, nations nor states as such having
absolute rights to autonomy. Of all of these three, however, it is states
which emerge as having the least normative significance. Liberal nationalism links individual and national self-determination as mutually
ethically valuable whilst downplaying the moral significance of the
principle of state sovereignty. This is because at the heart of liberal nationalism is the idea of the ethical significance for the individual of cultural
identity. Individuals and cultural identities are entitled to respect because
of their intrinsically valuable nature. However, states are entitled to respect
only in virtue of the extent to which they protect individual rights and
cultural identities (Tamir, 1993: 142–67; MacCormick, 1996: 49). For liberal
nationalists, membership of a nation is somewhere between the voluntary
contracting into a particular polity and the involuntary membership of a
family. There are special obligations to fellow nationals, but these operate
under constraints of duties to respect the rights of individuals in general.

Liberal nationalism assumes the existence of universal global norms which include the principle of respect for national cultural difference – as long as that difference does not challenge the limits of liberal nationalism's tolerance which are marked by Kantian liberal principles of respect for individuals.

On questions such as the rights of cultural minorities within states, liberal nationalism tends to support, as might be expected, the rights of self-proclaimed national minorities to self-determination. However, this does not necessarily imply that liberal nationalism is committed to the principle that all nations must be states. It may equally favour the kind of political arrangement said to be emerging in the EU in which local national identities are protected under a trans-state framework (Tamir, 1993: 150–3; MacCormick, 1996: 50–1). Or, alternatively, to favour the path of multiculturalism in which existing states grant differential rights to such minority groups (Kymlicka, 1995). Whereas the fundamental principles of liberal statism work against the notion of any level of right between that of the individual and state authority, liberal nationalism is apparently perfectly amenable to the recognition of sub-state national group right, as an extension of traditional liberal principles of both liberty and toleration. However, as with liberal statism, there are tensions in the liberal nationalist position when it comes to defining what respect for rights to national self-determination within an existing multi-nation state or political order might mean. Liberal nationalists, as noted above, combine the idea of respect for individual cultural identity with respect for individual autonomy understood in a Kantian sense. For liberal nationalists, the individual right to national identity is linked to the notion that this is an identity which is at some level voluntary. This does not mean that this identity has its origin in contract or that individuals ever existed outside of their national identity. It means that national identity is something to which individuals (because they are also moral beings in a Kantian sense) are capable of having a critical relation. National identity is something which individuals can redefine or revise internally or, ultimately, it is something which individuals can come to reject and walk away from. There is therefore a necessary tension between liberal nationalism and the kinds of national identity which block the possibility of critique/change or exit. Thus when theorists such as Kymlicka provide a liberal model for the recognition of group rights they are forced to distinguish between collective rights giving rights of 'internal restriction' to a minority group – which means that that group can limit the liberties of its individual members – and collective rights of 'external protection' which protect the minority groups against majority decisions that would undermine the basis of their existence (Kymlicka, 1995: 35–44). The former are problematic for liberal nationalism, because they threaten the possibility of critique/ change and exit, the latter, Kymlicka argues, are perfectly compatible with liberal values. Clearly, however, it is very difficult to sustain the distinction between 'internal restrictions' and 'external protections' if, for instance, the survival of a particular form of community is premised on the exclusion of some individuals from education or decision-making or restrictive policies on emigration from a national homeland.

Liberal nationalist prescriptions in relation to issues of migration, particularly immigration into national communities, display similar tensions. In giving considerable weight to the idea of a national right to self-determination, liberal nationalists are particularly concerned with the protection of national cultural identity. Immigration, therefore, could in principle be restricted if it threatened the survival of national identity. However, national identity is important because it is important to individuals and individuals have a right to self-determination in accordance with but also in critical relation to the identities by which they are constituted. Liberal nationalists recognize, therefore, the normative power of arguments from both political and economic migrants, that they too have a right to self-determination. This leads Tamir, for instance, to argue that nations should only have the right to restrict immigration if they are exporting goods to enable less fortunate groups to be self-determining elsewhere. Liberal nationalism then becomes dependent on conditions of global distributive justice as well as other fundamental liberal values (Tamir, 1993: 61).

Like most attempts to combine distinct elements in a justificatory strategy, liberal nationalism is accused by its critics of collapsing back into one or other of the elements it seeks to combine. These critics come both from the liberal tradition itself and from communitarianism (see Chapter 2 above). Liberal contractarian and Kantian critics accuse liberal nationalism of going too far down the slippery slope of communitarian thinking and abandoning, or putting in jeopardy, the respect for individual rights on which liberal nationalism is supposed to be premised (Caney, 1996; Charvet, 1996). Liberal contractarians find the notion that national identity in itself carries normative consequences incompatible with the idea of individual right and the voluntary basis of political community (Charvet, 1996: 57). Kantians are concerned about the problem of discriminating between acceptable and non-acceptable national identities (Caney, 1996: 133–4). According to both liberal statists and Kantians, the compatibility claimed by liberal nationalists between liberalism and national identity is the product of wishful thinking, which does not take account of the gap between the ideal world of theory and the actual 'second best' world we inhabit. Alternatively, communitarians claim that the liberal nationalists' continued endorsement of the importance of choice and moral principle means that they have failed to grasp what nationality actually means and, in practice, are bound to revert back to either liberal statist or Kantian positions. For communitarians, the question of the right to national identity can only be answered in terms of an essentially collective as opposed to individual basis for the right to national self-determination (Walzer, 1981, 1992, 1994a, 1994b; Miller, 1995, 1999).

The two main variants of the liberal response to the question of the right to national self-determination are opposed, but also reflected, by two variants of a communitarian response. These reflect the two strands in communitarian thinking identified in the discussion of moral communitarianism in Chapter 2, which are frequently entangled together in specific communitarian arguments. On the one hand, *organic communitarianism* rests on an analogy between the Hobbesian natural rights of individuals and the natural rights of communities. On the other hand, *civic republican* communitarianism, following Rousseau, rests on the assertion of a link between the moral significance of the capacity for autonomy in individuals and collective democratic self-rule. In the former case, the right to national self-determination is grounded in a nation's prior natural right to survival. In the latter case, the right of national self-determination is not grounded in the prior right of a pre-existing communal entity but in a collectively generated 'general will', in which individuals are forged into a self-legislating body of citizens through the overcoming of their particular individual interests. The former position implies that nations, in so far as they are culturally cohesive determinate communities, should be states. The latter implies rather the opposite, suggesting that democratic states are the ideal mode of political order and that in order for them to be, they also need to be underpinned by nations. For both, however, a privileging of the rights of insiders over outsiders in the nation-state is justified. Walzer, as we have seen, makes a distinction between thick and thin moralities which grounds a norm of non-intervention (Walzer, 1994a). Miller makes a distinction between obligations of right to co-nationals and obligations of humanity to foreigners, with the latter clearly being weaker than the former (Miller, 1995: 73–80).

The prescriptive implications of both positions in relation to rights of national minorities and immigration are similar and apparently clear cut. In both cases, the obvious way in which to accommodate group difference is secession, since the nation-state depends on solidarities which will be weakened by deep splits between different national identities within a common citizenship. In both cases also, the right to grant membership of a national community is necessary to that community's survival and can rest only within that community and there are no externally generated rights of individuals to gain entry across borders (Walzer, 1981: 32). Nevertheless, as with liberal statism and liberal nationalism, when communitarianism is applied to issues such as toleration of cultural diversity or free movement of peoples in practice, its prescriptive implications are less clear cut than might have been expected. To begin with, the actual world in no way corresponds to either the organic or republican communitarian ideal – the world does not divide into self-contained cohesive communities or participatory democracies. This has rather different implications for the two types of communitarian argument. Organic communitarianism, like liberal statism, lacks conceptual equipment to deal with the actual interdependence and entanglement that characterizes existing communities. It therefore lends itself to the same kind of pragmatic compromise between first and second best worlds in which sources of right other than organic community gain instrumental defensibility. The recognition of the inherent significance for individuals of participating in national community leads, for instance, to Walzer's argument for the rights of individuals to asylum and the thin morality which supports the norm of non-intervention (Walzer, 1992, 1994a, 1994b). There are clearly prudential grounds for limiting national right in relation to other nations. There may also be prudential reasons for a nation to accept something less than full nation statehood, perhaps where no clear territorial partition is possible (Miller, 1995: 108–18). Or, alternatively, there may be prudential advantages to permeable borders between nation-states and individual rights of migration. The situation is rather different in the case of republican communitarianism, which, like liberal nationalism, does not value the community (individual) purely as such but in relation to a higher potential of the community (individual). Behind the 'higher' in both of these cases is a universal ideal of freedom as autonomy in the Kantian sense. In an analogous (but reversed) pattern to liberal nationalism, republican communitarians, by identifying collective self-determination with a higher form of will, beyond prudential self-interest, link rights to national self-determination to rights for individuals and states. In practice, the positions of republican communitarians and liberal nationalists merge into support for the liberal democratic political community and the simultaneous endorsement of individual and collective right, something which is achieved in the first best world of theory by the assumption that all political communities take on this form in conditions which enable mutual recognition and respect without remainder. Walzer moderates the rights of states to control membership in the light of universal principles (Walzer, 1981: 32). Miller, like Tamir, ends up endorsing the need for global distributive justice to underpin collective rights to self-determination (Miller, 1995: 105).

The exchange within and between liberal (cosmopolitan) and communitarian theories on the question of the right to national self-determination is a battle between ideals as to the priority to be given to the values of individual, national and state autonomy. The problem which all of these ideal accounts returns to is that of accommodating different autonomies, both horizontally (e.g., how are different individual autonomies made compatible with each other) and vertically (e.g., how is individual right made compatible with national or state right). A further battle of ideals is also played out between an understanding of autonomy in terms of determination by purely natural or purely rational will. This is reflected in the tensions between liberal statism and liberal nationalism in their understanding of the meaning of individual autonomy, and between organic and republican strands of communitarianism in the understanding of collective autonomy. Whichever idea is in question, it provides a standard against which the actual world is always found wanting. The noise of the battle obscures the extent to which all of these perspectives are making very similar arguments and running into similar problems. In relation to the first subject of battle both liberal and communitarian theories conceptualize the subjects of self-determination as determinately bounded, radically distinct entities. Intersubjective, inter-national and inter-state spheres are presented as empty space in which the different selves collide, horizontally and vertically, or must somehow be forced to fit in with one another. In the case of theories (liberal and communitarian) which understand self-determination in Hobbesian terms the accommodation of different rights is achieved through pragmatic self-interest. In the case of theories (liberal and communitarian) which understand self-determination in Kantian terms the accommodation of different rights is achieved through universal principle. In both cases, however, the second best world of international politics fails to live up to the first best world of theory and the fit between individual, nation and state which is achievable in principle proves unworkable in practice. Each of the theoretical approaches is therefore in a position to condemn the others on grounds of hypocrisy and inconsistency.

In the critical international theories previously discussed in Chapter 3, the different sorts of liberal and communitarian responses to the question of rights to national self-determination are criticized on the grounds that neither liberalism nor communitarianism has looked closely enough at the three subjects of self-determination with which they deal: the individual, the nation and the state. Until this is done, it is argued, there will be no basis for extending the discussion beyond an ideal mutual accommodation of these entities which restricts discussion of subjects such as multiculturalism or trans-national migration to a world of ought-to-be, or, alternatively, a violent forcing of these different elements into harmony through the imposition of either global norms or culturally specific values on the different subjects of self-determination in the international sphere.

Deconstructing selves and self-determination[4]

In this section, I will be examining ways in which critical theory, postmodernism and feminist theory approach the questions posed by the cosmopolitan/communitarian debates in the ethics of international relations: is there a moral right to national self-determination? Are moral obligations necessarily transnational or are there special obligations owed to fellow nationals? How can one reconcile global norms with cultural diversity? The meaningfulness of these questions and their answerability depends for critical theorists of the international on two key things: the ontological claims made about the being of individuals, nations and states and the epistemic status of normative claims about the meaning of self-determination. As was made clear in Chapter 3 above, critical theory, postmodernism and feminism present distinct, if over-lapping, ontological and epistemological positions, so each will be considered in turn. I will then return to the question of what prescriptive implications, if any, follow for issues such as the protection of rights to cultural identity or trans-national migration. It will be argued that critical theory, postmodernism and feminism are limited in their reconceptu-alization of the subjects of self-determination in the international context by the residual presence in their theorizing of the same idealized notion of self-determination which operates in the theories considered in the previous section. In conclusion, I will demonstrate how the most useful insights of these critical approaches can be taken further into the mode of normative theoretical engagement argued for in the previous chapter.

The ontology of critical theory challenges the notion of both nation and state as subjects of self-determination as they appear in liberal statist and communitarian thinking but holds strongly to a Kantian ideal of the autonomous individual human being (Hoffman, 1993; Linklater, 1998). For example, Linklater's ontological position is essentially a radicalization of the liberal nationalist argument given above. It is a radicalization because it goes much further than liberal nationalism in envisaging a post-Westphalian international political order and a move beyond both closed national identity and the principle of state sovereignty. This move is accomplished partly on the basis of rejecting the notion of the international as the empty spaces between nations and nation-states (Linklater, 1998: 34–45). For Linklater, there is such a thing as international society which both constitutes and is constituted by a variety of levels of political and economic order – there is therefore no clear cut inside/outside distinction where nations and states are concerned. However, Linklater's position is still identifiable with the liberal nationalist position, because at its heart is the Kantian ideal of respect for persons as ends in themselves, with the understanding that this respect must extend to the range of identities through which a person is constituted (gendered, ethnic, national, sexual and so on) (Linklater, 1998: 46–76). In Linklater's theory, as with liberal nationalism, the normative key is the capacity of individuals to engage critically with their world on the basis of moral norms. Unlike liberal nationalists, however, Linklater identifies this normative key as operating within actual institutions in a logic of self-transcendence – this is particularly evident in his account of the modern state. Where Canovan sees the fudge of nationality keeping the tensions between universality and particularity in place within the state, Linklater argues that the universal principles (such as the notion of universal human rights) work over time to transcend the nation-state linkage and enable the recognition of both particular identity and universal right in a new form of international political order (Linklater, 1998: 184–9; Linklater, 1999). Linklater argues that in developed Western states, notably Europe, this logic of transcendence is already far advanced and needs to be articulated both for the sake of further improvement in the Western context and as the basis for relation with other parts of the world in which this logic does not operate in the same way (Linklater, 1998: 218; 1999). Linklater's vision of the developing world of international politics is one in which there is a co-existence between more familiar pluralist and solidarist modes of international society and a new post-Westphalian order in which the fit between sovereignty, territoriality, nationality and citizenship which kept the Westphalian order in place no longer applies (Linklater, 1998: 60).

In keeping with the characteristic stance of critical theory, Linklater does not assume that the world will necessarily progress in terms of the normative key of the critical capacities of individuals. However, it is his conception of this key which explains the confidence with which he identifies what counts as progress. Here his reliance on Habermasian moral epistemology is crucial. According to Habermas, moral rightness is dependent on the agreement of moral norms in open, non-distorted dialogue between those affected by the implementation of the norm in question (Habermas, 1990a; Linklater, 1998: 87–93). Linklater's judgement of what counts as moral progress is those institutional changes which extend the inclusion of persons affected by norms in decision-making processes over those norms and minimize morally irrelevant exclusions. More than that, however, progress is those changes which maximize the possibility of non-distorted communication in the argument over norms – a situation in which the inherent critical capacities of human individuals, their ability to be swayed by the better argument, are able to flourish.

> How to develop new forms of citizenship and community which release the potential for wider universalities of discourse which is already immanent within the modern state and international society is the central praxeological question. (Linklater, 1998: 151)

If we return to the question of the right to national self-determination posed in the ethics of international relations, we find it answered, by Linklater, in instrumental terms which are again reminiscent of, but more radical than, liberal nationalism. Critical theory supports a right to national identity on the grounds of the right to individual autonomy, because national identities are constitutive of individuals. However, even more than with liberal nationalism, critical theory is critical of exclusive versions of national identity and is committed to opening up boundaries between communities. Moreover, critical theory gives equal weight to the range of identities constitutive of any particular individual and would not necessarily give normative priority to national identity. Linklater sees himself as building upon both cosmopolitan and communitarian insights to move beyond the idea of nations and states as the principal modes of political order.

> Far from being antithetical, communitarianism and cosmopolitanism provide complementary insights into the possibility of new forms of community and citizenship in the post-Westphalian era. They reveal that more complex associations of universality and difference can be developed by breaking the nexus between sovereignty, territoriality, nationality and citizenship and by promoting wider communities of discourse. (Linklater, 1998: 60)

As with liberal nationalism, the fundamental understanding of moral norms in critical theory is universalistic. However, where liberal nationalism appears to get caught in tensions between universal and particular which it cannot resolve except in an ideal world, critical theory resolves the tensions by stressing the immanent critical force which will push individuals within communities to transform them in line with greater openness. The possibility of legitimating special obligations to co-nationals or respecting cultural difference is always limited by the guiding force of the moral norms – and therefore the limits of toleration – implicit in modernity. This is evident in relation to the prescriptive implications of critical theory on topics such as the recognition of group rights and trans-national migration. In both cases, critical theory supports principles of recognition and openness, but always in the context of the extension of dialogic possibilities in the contemporary world order. This is acknowledged by Linklater in the argument that without the implicit acceptance of the logic of inclusion which is characteristic of modernity a post-Westphalian order is unlikely to develop. Relations between liberal and non-liberal political communities cannot therefore take the same form as relations between liberal communities whether within or between existing states or transnational organizations (Linklater, 1999).

It was noted above in Chapter 3 that critical theory aimed to synthesize the range of insights characteristic of realism and idealism, cosmopolitanism, communitarianism, international society and Marxism. In his most recent book, *The Transformation of Political Community* (1998), Linklater also lays claim to encompassing the insights of postmodernism and feminism. In relation to issues such as the right to national self-determination and compatibility of particular and universal moral obligations, universal norms and cultural diversity, critical theory accomplishes its synthesis through the linking together of an ontology of nations and states (which identifies them as dynamically evolving through a complex and inseparable set of internal and external determinations) with the notion of a logic of moral transcendence which is located in the higher rational capacities inherent in any individual human being. It is the latter element in the analysis which leads organic communitarian and postmodern critics to identify critical theory as another version of liberal cosmopolitanism which reproduces the logic of the realism/idealism debate. According to this critique, the problem with critical theory is that it is insufficiently ontologically and epistemologically radical in its analysis of the self of self-determination which is crucial to its emancipatory project, the human individual. For communitarians this is a matter of the underestimation of the inherently social nature of the self and the contextual determination of moral claims (Walzer, 1983, 1994a). For postmodernists it is a matter of the volatility of any ontological categorization and the unsustainability of any normative theoretical high ground (Walker, 1993, 1999; Jahn, 1998).

Postmodernism, like critical theory, challenges the idea that nations and states have any particular normative status or right to autonomy. In the case of critical theory, this challenge rests on an analysis of inter-national politics in which nations and states form elements of a complex totality which transcends them, a totality which includes, crucially, the moral capital immanent in modern universalism. In the case of post-modernism, this challenge rests on a similar reconceptualization of international politics in which boundaries between inside and outside are understood as fluid, permeable and capable of being transgressed. However, for postmodernism, first, the inside/outside boundaries which constitute the autonomous individual are included in the challenge and, secondly, the idea of moral capital inherent in modern universalism is rejected (Ashley and Walker, 1990; Walker, 1993; Ashley, 1996; Devetak, 1996b; Campbell, 1998a, 1998b; Dillon, 1998).

Postmodernism substitutes subject positions for subjects and multiple, discursively constructed identity/ies for given cultural identity/ies. In postmodernism there is no prior existing self, whether naturally, morally or culturally constituted, which exists to ground the right of self-determination. The ethic of postmodernism shifts discourses based on a linkage between rights and the given ontological categories of individuals, nations, states towards a discourse of process and achievement. However, even though identities of all kinds are treated as volatile constructions, it is the achievement of agency by identities which are disempowered by dominant forms of political identity which are given a normatively exemplary status in postmodernist theory (Ashley and Walker, 1990). The tendency of dominant strands of both normative and explanatory theory in international politics to treat certain identities as fixed and beyond question is seen to be not only ontologically mistaken but also normatively wrong (Campbell, 1998a: 513–14; 1998b: 163). In general, because of postmodernism's rejection of both Kantian and communitarian conceptions of the individual as well as their rejections of the necessity of the dominance of nations and states as modes of political organization, postmodernism valorizes the work of international actors which challenges any or all of these given limitations. The idea of self-determination understood as a categorical imperative to respect and acknowledge responsibility towards the 'other' operates as a regulative ideal in postmodernists' normative assessments of various kinds of political struggle in contemporary international politics (Campbell, 1998a: 513). This leads to a focus on, and implicit prescriptive endorse-ment of a politics and ethics of difference.

> Much of the postmodern turn can be understood as a series of attempts to reclaim or reconstruct or even to finally create some practical space for, say, a Kantian concern with the conditions of the possibility of knowledge or the meaning of autonomy in a world in which the secular guarantees of Reason and History can no longer console us for the death of God. It can also be

understood as a multi-faceted struggle to come to terms with the possibility of
a critical or emancipatory political practice given the extent to which the great
secular substitutes for God in modern political thought – Reason, History, the
sovereign state, the sovereign individual and the universal class – have
themselves come to seem so problematic. (Walker, 1993: 20)

Thus, for postmodernism the question of whether there is a right to
national self-determination makes no sense in general, because it assumes
a given content both to the category of nation and the category of
self-determination. Nevertheless, it is clear that in certain contexts,
postmodernists might well want to argue for the positive normative
significance of struggles for rights to nationhood or the sub-state recognition of national identity and indeed for any other aspect of identity
which has been constructed in opposition to the given, dominant limitations (Campbell, 1998a: 513). However, it is also clear that for postmodernists the judgement necessarily shifts once a particular mode of
political agency comes into a dominant position, either through its exclusion of other nascent identities externally or its limitation of its own
dynamic possibilities internally. This is nicely illustrated in some
postmodernist reaction to feminist theory and politics. Postmodernists
are sympathetic to feminist politics up to the point at which it relies on
fixed understandings of the categories of women or gender, then it
(feminism) becomes condemned for its imperialist imposition of
particular forms of gendered identity on all women (Walker, 1988: 151;
1991).

It should be apparent, therefore, that in one sense postmodernism
endorses the notion that all moral obligations are 'special'. Such obligations are always the product of specific and complex conditions. Nevertheless, in contrast to communitarianism (with which there appears
initially to be considerable prescriptive overlap), postmodernism's relativism is twinned with a positive endorsement of the general value of
difference and resistance over identity and government. It is this general
endorsement which underlies the nature of the contextual judgement
which postmodernist theorists make about actual political struggles. This
is why both multiculturalism within states and the rights of refugees and
migrants against states tend to be supported, or even given exemplary
status, by postmodernist theory. This is not simply because postmodernists such as Walker see this kind of politics as an aspect of the ontological realities of the emerging global order, but also because the
opening up of possibilities for alternative identities to flourish and the
opening up of state borders is in accord with the normative status given
to the transgression of limits by postmodernists in both theory and

practice. It is this generalized commitment to ongoing deconstruction and the enabling of difference as both theoretical practice and practical prescription that leads other schools of normative theory engaging with the question of rights to self-determination to see postmodernism as rendering normative debate in international relations meaningless. In fact, however, it is this commitment which makes postmodernism most easily recognisable as normative theory in a traditional sense, one which pits an ideal of eternal overcoming in a 'first best' world over against a second best world and always already finds the latter wanting (Campbell, 1998b: 219).

Feminist international theory, as noted above in Chapter 3, takes a variety of forms, and there is no single feminist response to traditional questions about rights to self-determination in an international context. As with liberal nationalists and critical theorists, however, feminism does not generally give inherent value to nations and states as autonomous entities. Both nations and states are valued only in so far as they empower or disempower those affected by gendered relations of power.[5] This suggests that feminism shares with liberal nationalism and critical theory a fundamental attachment to the concept of individual autonomy. However, feminists are also critical of the idea of individual self-determination underlying dominant liberal discourses, such as those of international human rights. This is because it is argued the notion of 'individual' or 'human' with which such discourses operate is blind to the significance of sexual difference or gendered identity (MacKinnon, 1993).

> ... the discourse and practice of international human rights retains a male-as-norm orientation that persists in treating women's rights as secondary.
>
> International human rights conventions specifically reject the principle of non-intervention when violation of rights occur [sic]. Yet systematic violence against women is treated as 'customary' or a 'private matter', and thus immune to international condemnation. (Spike Peterson, 1990: 305)

What does this criticism imply for feminist normative engagement with the concept of self-determination? It can be taken as an argument that the ideal of self-determination is the same for all human beings but that existing human rights regimes omit, or pay insufficient attention to, specific ways in which women's rights need to be protected in a patriarchal world (*liberal feminism*). On this account the aim of feminist politics is to produce the conditions within which women can be sovereign individuals in a classically liberal contractarian or Kantian sense. It can also be taken as an argument for the need to develop a norm of specifically female self-determination, against which struggles for individual, national or state autonomy could be judged (*radical feminism*). It is this kind of view which underlies the notion of sex-differentiated citizenship rights and feminist challenges to rights of nations or states to exploit or oppress women (Elshtain, 1981; Pateman, 1988, 1992; MacKinnon, 1993). In much feminist theory, however, including Spike Peterson's work cited above, the argument against liberal rights discourses implies a more radical challenge to the concept of individual self-determination, one which calls into question the notion of individuals (generic or gendered) as either ideally or really the same kinds of independent entity as each other (*difference feminism*). The implication of this kind of feminist theoretical approach is to extend the undermining of inside/outside distinctions between different subjects of self-determination which characterizes critical theory and postmodernism to women as well as individuals, nations and states (Bock and James, 1992; Steans, 1998: 60–80).

These three different kinds of feminist theoretical response can be seen at work in arguments within feminism about the right to national self-determination and the sub-state recognition of cultural identity. For liberal feminists such rights are dependent on the extent to which equality of rights for women is institutionalized within any given political community. Liberal feminism therefore takes a similar normative position to liberal statism and liberal nationalism in judging collective right essentially in terms of individual right. Radical feminism charges liberal feminism with misunderstanding the essentially masculine nature of a supposedly generic model of autonomy. In its place, radical feminism sets gendered identity against generic concepts of individual self-determination and gives it normative priority over national and state right, so that neither established cultural value nor a community 'general will' are recognized as valid subjects of self-determination as such. Difference feminism has been developed as a response to both liberal and sexual difference feminisms by feminists who have identified themselves as simultaneously subject to gendered relations of power and excluded by mainstream feminist accounts of what women's right to self-determination means. In particular, difference feminism has objected to the notion of 'women as such' and, in ways which parallel communitarian and postmodernist arguments, argued that suggesting a fixed identity for all women conceals the cultural imperialism of white against non-white and Western against non-Western women (Mohanty et al., 1991; Marchand and Papart, 1995; Yuval-Davis, 1998). Difference feminism revives the possibility of the normative significance of nation and culture as subjects of self-determination. In some versions it essentially repeats communitarian and postmodernist conceptions and evaluations of cultural relativism. However, it can also be interpreted in a way which, in spite of the parallels, is subtly different from the arguments of communitarians and postmodernists. As against communitarianism, difference feminism treats inside/outside national/cultural boundaries as inherently permeable, so that whilst it assumes the possibility and value of identification of women with nation or community it also assumes the possibility and value of identification of women with other women across national/cultural boundaries. Commonality of condition is not a matter of either/or choices or a normative hierarchy of right – both overlaps and clashes between national and gendered selves as subjects of self-determination are an ongoing matter of contingency. As against postmodernism, difference feminism does not work on the presumption of an ideal of self-determination as the transgression of given limitation. Instead, the ideal is located within the fluid but also sticky possibilities available. Of all of the perspectives considered so far, difference feminism is the one that has paid most attention to the impossibility of disentangling self- from other-determination (and identity) in the quest for criteria by which to judge the value of different kinds of political struggle (Hutchings, 1999).

Normative judgement beyond deconstruction

Critical theory, postmodernism, radical and difference feminisms deconstruct the self-contained subjects of self-determination in cosmopolitan and communitarian ethics of international politics. In doing this they, as it were, confront the first best ideal world with the second best actuality in which there is no purity of individual or collective self or self-will. Self-determination is always also other-determination in a context in which the conditions of possibility of agency are necessarily heteronomous. For this reason, these kinds of critical approaches avoid the perpetual battle, characteristic of liberal and communitarian debates, to make different sorts of self-determination compatible which have already been defined in incompatible terms. However, it is still unclear what lessons follow for normative theorizing from the deconstructive work carried out by critical, postmodernist and feminist theorists. In particular, what are the implications for assessing claims made as to the rightness or wrongness of particular normative responses to questions of individual, national or state right? A standard response from more orthodox ethical perspectives to the approaches discussed above is to raise the question, if there is no place for the validation of judgement beyond the complexities of the second best world, then how do you validate the judgement that, for example, 'female circumcision is wrong' and persuade others of its truth. In what follows I attempt to articulate the kind of normative theoretical response which is derivable from these deconstructive approaches in relation to the ethical question of whether cultures that deny women individual rights to self-determination should be ethically condemned.

In terms of mainstream normative theory, the positions taken on this issue have generally approximated to familiar cosmopolitan and communitarian alternatives, with the former regarding 'traditional' cultures as fundamentally disrespectful of women's right to individual self-determination and the latter stressing that the nature and validity of women's rights depend on the overarching value system/s operative within their (women's) communities, communities which have an inherent right to be respected. The exchange between these ethical positions follows an equally familiar pattern, with universalist and particularist moral ontologies, objectivist and relativist moral epistemologies set against each other, but with the idea of self-determination crucial to both. From the point of view of critical international theories, for this argument to become something more than a slanging match between ethical universalism and ethical particularism three stages of theoretical work are necessary. The first stage involves the, by now familiar, process of putting into question the categories and assumptions through which the question as to the universal validity of claims for women's rights is posed. The second stage involves accounting for the prescriptive agendas of those who are putting, or responding to, the question. The third involves the utilization of resources examined in the previous stages to support a specific prescriptive position.

The first stage of analysis is not intended to settle the question of right and wrong but to establish the extent to which right and wrong is actually in question. The condemnation of community in the name of individual right relies on a world view in which both individuals and communities are conceptualized as self-contained units. As demonstrated in the previous section, such a world view relies on an untenable first best understanding of the nature of individuals and collectives which is necessarily therefore blind to the complexities of meaning of which the second best world is capable. The significance of the different ways of valuing and treating women for women in different contexts is not obvious once the radical disjunction between individual and collective self-determination is called into question. For instance, it may become apparent that abortion rights are necessarily linked to enforced female infanticide in some contexts and to enhanced life chances for women in others, or that the politics of female circumcision are fundamentally bound up with religious or nationalist affiliations which affect its priority as an issue for women in some contexts whereas it is a key site for emancipatory struggle in others. If, as I have argued, the question of what self-determination means cannot be settled in advance of what it is recognized to mean in the real, second best world, then a great deal must depend on assessing the extent to which certain meanings are or are not recognized and may or may not be compatible. This is not to say that ethical clashes in the understanding of the meaning and value of self-determination for women in the second best world will not emerge. But by taking seriously the impossibility of disentangling self- from other-determination at either an individual or collective level, normative analysis is much less likely to make the mistake of mapping ethical differences onto taken-for-granted distinctions between individual and community, which then enable the mutual demonization of incompatible ethical positions.

Deconstructing the terms in which the question of the condemnation of communities that do not respect the rights of women is put does not answer the question. Instead it suggests the prescriptive agenda of a variety of ways in which the question is asked and the inevitable implication of these agendas in how it is answered. Accounting for such agendas is the second stage of normative theoretical work implied by critical international theories. At this stage the task of the theorist is to articulate the fullest possible account of the meaning of self-determination implicit in the asking and answering of the question. This articulation must include both the grounds and implications of the claim being made. For those arguing, for instance, for a liberal position, the range of legal, social, political and economic conditions which both underpin and are implied by a liberal understanding of the meaning of individual self-determination must be made clear. But part of this clarification must also be to point up what is lost as well as what is gained from the identification of women as 'persons' and the internal tensions within liberal states between the recognition of women as persons and their positioning in relation to the public/private distinction. This exercise is not going to resolve the question of whether women are entitled to rights of abortion or rights over their own body in an absolute sense. But normative theory can make explicit how it already has been, can be or could be institutionalized and what may be lost or gained in the process.

The third stage of theoretical work implicit in critical normative approaches is required when the theorist moves beyond the deconstruction and analysis of given normative judgements to the formulation of his or her own version of questions and answers about rights to self-determination. However, it is the two previous stages of analysis which provide the resources and clarify the limitations of any such formulation and which provide the basis for the judgement of the validity of the prescriptive agenda being put forward. If a normative theorist judges, for instance, that women should have rights over their own bodies it is incumbent upon him or her to make explicit both the grounding of that judgement in his or her place in the second best world and the nature of the (desired) world in which such a prescription makes sense. There is no security of authority in normative judgement and it is always partial and exclusive. But to the extent that such judgement is open about its own conditionality and exclusivity it can form part of an ongoing argument and struggle towards the conditions of possibility of the recognition of the validity of that judgement by others. The truth of normative judgement does not rely on short cuts provided by access to epistemic authority; neither does it rely on argument or rhetoric alone. Rather, it relies on the capacity of others to identify with the premises that underpin and the promises that follow from any particular normative claim. When mainstream approaches to normative theory ask the critical theorist to respond to questions such as whether female circumcision is wrong, the critical theorist is obliged to answer that this depends on the world you inhabit and desire to inhabit. The task of demonstrating that a world should be constructed in which it is obvious that female circumcision is wrong itself depends on elements of that world being sufficiently in place for the claim to make sense to those who are listening. Without such elements, prescription must rely not on argument but on coercion.

It might be expected that by beginning with the mutual interconnection of the different possible subjects of self-determination in international politics, rather than their ideal insulation, critical international theories would avoid the displacement of their own criteria of judgement into the transcendent realm of what ought to be the case. However, the re-thinking of the subjects of self-determination (individual, nation and state) carried through by the critical theories does not necessarily imply the rejection of an ideal of self-determination which operates against the actual conditions of possibility of agency. In critical theory the ideal reappears expressed in terms of the Habermasian conditions of non-distorted communication, in postmodernism it reappears as the general imperative to deconstruct/reconstruct the given limits of political agency and identity, in some versions of feminism it reappears as sex-differentiated rights for women. In essence, the more or less residual presence of traditional ideals of self-determination in the normative judgements of critical theory, postmodernism and feminism reflects the survival of the idea of autonomous as opposed to heteronomous determination and categorical as opposed to hypothetical ethical imperatives. In critical theory's 'transcendence', postmodernism's 'transgression' and feminism's vision of women's self-determination, the same model of pure natural or rational self-creation which is crucial to liberalism's grounding of individual right and communitarian's grounding of collective right is to be found. It is this tendency towards theoretical purity which helps to fuel traditional realist charges as to the irrelevance and dangerous implications of normative judgement as such in the realm of international politics.

However, the tendency towards slippage back into the terms of old idealist/realist or cosmopolitan/communitarian debates is counteracted by the equally significant tendency in critical international theories towards a new kind of realism. According to this version of realism, a normative judgement is not unrealistic (utopian/idealistic) because it presents a vision of a different kind of world. It is only unrealistic (utopian/idealistic) if it fails to engage with the conditions of possibility of the new world in relation to the old by taking a short cut through an idealized ontology in which pure self-determination is possible and an idealized epistemology in which normative judgements are authorized by transcendent authority. According to this view, it is dangerous to treat any model of self-determination as a generic ideal, however formal, to provide criteria for judgements of right and wrong – not because such models may not be genuinely inspiring and meaningful ideals but because they invariably involve, but rarely acknowledge, specific cultural and political conditions of possibility by which they were enabled and in relation to which they make sense. This problematizes claims to the generalizability in principle of particular ideals and its also draws attention to the fact that attempts to realize such ideals will have radically different consequences in different contexts. But at the same time, it keeps in place recognition of the unavoidability of making normative claims and the difficulties surrounding their realization.

Conclusion

The making and defending of normative judgements about international politics is an everyday activity, certainly not confined to the realm of academic normative theory. The role of academic normative theory has been to provide systematic defences for and arguments against particular normative positions. How can normative theory operate if it continues with the shift towards thinking in terms of the second best world and its ethical potential only when thinking and making judgements about, for instance, rights to self-determination in the contemporary international context? I have argued that the problem with much existing normative international theory on the topic of self-determination is that it fails to encompass the complexity and conditionality of agency in international politics and that it is prone to give a transcendental significance to one or other aspect of the world's ethical potential and thereby lose contact with the world as it is and might be – confining normative debate to a world of ought-to-be. Traditionally, the clash between first and second best worlds has been seen as grounds for condemnation of the latter, but in a Hegelian/ Foucauldian approach to international ethics the opposite is the case. Here the presumption is that any normative prescription will be judged ultimately on its truth in the second best world. This is a truth grounded not in unassailable first principles but in the complex and multi-faceted experience of what Hegel terms spirit. Such a shift necessarily alters the conception of that of which normative theory is capable and changes the epistemic status (though not necessarily the degree of conviction) of the theorist's judgement. Following on from the argument of the previous chapter and the second and third sections of this chapter there are, I would argue, two aspects to the articulation of arguments for and against particular normative prescriptions which characterize this more modest kind of theoretical work: first, the phenomenology of the version of international ethical life on which any particular theoretical position relies (the first two stages of theoretical work described above); secondly, the genealogical assessment of the theorist's own ethical judgement (the third stage of theoretical work described above).

The phenomenology of international ethical life involves examination of the range of conditions which constitute the nature and possibility of agency in the current world order. This is partly a matter of the social scientific understanding of international politics. It is vital that normative theorists are explicit about and can explain their reliance on particular explanatory models – a reliance which is always in place but rarely acknowledged in mainstream ethics of international politics. According to second best normative theory, what matters is what is the case, therefore what is being claimed about what is the case must be available for evaluation as much as any claim for what ought to be the case. However, the phenomenology of international ethical life involves more than the acknowledgement of reliance on a particular ontology of international politics. The main purpose of phenomenological analysis is the assessment of the ethical potential inherent in the current inter- national order. The notion of 'ethical potential' has similarities to critical theory's concept of 'moral capital'. However, in the case of critical theory, this is understood as having a particular rational and uni- versalistic reference which is abstractly derivable even if also historically inherent. In the case of the phenomenology of ethical life, the point is to identify the range of values and principles institutionalized within different aspects of the international order and the ways in which they operate in mutual support or in tension with one another. International normative theory depends on insight into what kinds of institutions enable or disable (or have the potential to do both) the actualization of different patterns of recognition within and between different interna- tional political actors.

If we look back at the different approaches to the ethics of self- determination explored in this chapter, it is clear that there are funda- mental problems with the phenomenological adequacy of mainstream liberal and communitarian perspectives. In all of these cases, the 'self' of self-determination is identified with an ideal of both purity of self and purity of the form of determination of action which is taken to be genuinely autonomous. The problematic nature of these assumptions is apparent as soon as the solutions to ethical problems formulated in terms of the ideal world are applied to the second best reality. Three possible implications follow: either the normative ideals admit defeat in the face of the horrors of reality and confirm the irrelevance of norma- tive judgement to international politics; or the ideals yield paradoxical policy consequences which apparently subvert the ends which they were intended to produce; or the ideals are enforced, with benign intentions, in a world into which they do not fit – something which is clearly apparent in the waves of imposition of the nation-state system periodically experienced since Wilson's principles of self-determination were accepted as the ideological basis for global geo-political order. In contrast, the arguments of critical theories of international politics are much more sensitive to the complexity of the conditions of possi- bility for political agency in international politics and the radical difficulty of disentangling self- from other-determination. In relation to the identity of selves, critical theories recognize the mutual impli- cation of states, nations, individuals and a whole host of other agencies in the being of any one agent. Rather than seeking to distinguish between self- and other-determination, critical theories examine the ethical potential and sustainability of particular constellations of agency. The desirability of any articulation of political agency is then assessed in terms of the political projects of critical theories themselves, which brings us to the genealogical aspect of second best normative theorizing.

The genealogy of normative judgement is at one level an extension of the phenomenology of international ethical life since it is premised on the recognition of the implication of normative judgement within ethical life. One of the things that the theorist must do is to identify literally where their judgement is coming from, what are the concrete conditions of its possibility and what are its implications in terms of the acceptance or transformation of the realm of international politics. Hegelian/ Foucauldian normative theory is premised on the identity of theorist with object of theory, so the question of the conditions of the possibility of judgement cannot be answered in terms of derivation from tran- scendental ideals/principles but must involve reflection on the theorist's place in the second best world. The second aspect of the genealogy of judgement, however, is the clarification of what in Foucauldian terms would be referred to as its effects of power. To put it in crudely realist terms, what benefits and inclusions, costs and exclusions follow from any particular normative prescription and on what grounds are they identifed as costs and exclusions? One of the long cherished pretensions of normative theory, as Rorty pointed out (see Chapter 2 above), is that moral truth is somehow above and beyond politics. The Hegelian/ Foucauldian approach to normative theory is premised on the possibility of normative truth but without the sanitizing effect achieved by the translation of this truth to a higher, first best sphere. Normative truth is in the world, it is contested and, in the process of that contestation, it is likely to be experienced by some international actors as painful.

There is a lack of genealogical honesty in most of the normative approaches to international politics which have been considered. Liberals and communitarians do not place their ethical judgements in the contexts which give rise to them, or if they do it is only as a preliminary to authorizing them in the radically opposed ideal worlds of ethical universalism and ethical pluralism respectively.[6] This results in the odd consequence that liberals and communitarians sometimes want the same thing in terms of ethical values and principles of political organization but become permanently side-tracked by a debate about the different premises on which they have come to their conclusions (note the strong overlap between liberal nationalism and civic republican communitarianism). Moreover, neither liberals nor communitarians are fully honest about the effects of power to be generated by the realization of their ethical ideals which are necessarily exclusive in their impact. Liberal theories gloss over this by stressing the rationality and ultimate acceptability (or else the historical inevitability) of liberal values, which means that assessments as to their costliness by non-liberals must be fundamentally mistaken. They also do not address seriously the question of whether liberal polities necessarily rely on non-liberal conditions (Canovan, 1996a, 1996b). Communitarians gloss over the same issue by imagining a fit between actual people and a finite set of self-contained communities – a place for everyone and everyone in their place – so that problems surrounding the principle of national self-determination are just to do with the fact that we have not yet fitted the nations and the states properly together. Critical theorists, postmodernists and radical feminists are not immune from the same kind of problem. The greater phenomenological sophistication of their analysis of international ethical life is not necessarily matched by an appreciation of the effect of the conditions of possibility and exclusive implications of their theoretical judgement on its authoritative status. Critical theorists abstract their own judgement from history by identifying it with history and end up, like liberals, depoliticizing their analysis by associating their ideal with transcendental truth and progress in history. Postmodernists turn deconstruction from a phenomenological analysis located in the complex conditions of possibility of different types of international political actors to an abstract positing of the principle of deconstruction as a transcendent normative ideal. Radical feminists move from an appreciation of the gendered nature of traditional ideals of self-determination to the setting up of an alternative ideal of women's or feminine self-determination as a given basis for normative judgement. The result of this is that all critical theories, like mainstream normative theories, can become locked into debates over the authorization of normative judgements in an ideal world of pure selves and self-determination, in which case they end up repeating the logic of arguments between realists and idealists, cosmopolitans and communitarians. This need not necessarily follow and I have argued that, in many ways, critical international theories are developing a normative perspective which is both phenomenologically sophisticated and genealogically honest. In the following chapter, in the light of the above discussion, I will go on to examine a recent debate in normative international theory which is bound up with the significance given to self-determination by all of the approaches discussed in this chapter – the debate over the merits of democratic political cosmopolitanism.

Notes

1   In this tradition of thought, individual rights are conceived largely in 'nega-
    tive' terms of the protection of individuals against encroachments on their
    freedom by the state and law. Thus protection of bodily integrity and
    property right have a particularly high priority (Cranston, 1973). Mapel (1992)
    provides an overview of liberal contractarian thinking in international theory
    and certain examples are discussed below (Steiner, 1992; Charvet, 1996). See
    also the discussion of contractarianism in Chapter 2 above and Dower (1998:
    57–66). See O'Neill (1991, 1992) for a critical perspective on liberal contrac-
    tarianism from a liberal Kantian viewpoint.
2   For discussions of liberal Kantian arguments on human rights see: O'Neill
    (1989b, 1991); Renteln (1990); Donnelly (1989; 1993); Shue (1996).
3   The key difference between Kantian and contractarian approaches and those
    of utilitarianism and Marxism to issues of human rights is that the first two
    perspectives link the idea of rights to a strong notion of the intrinsic value of
    individual autonomy, whereas for the latter two the notion of rights is
    of instrumental value only in relation to broader general goals. In the case of
    Marxism, the whole notion of individual rights is a suspect one: rights dis-
    courses are, at best, a way of ameliorating conditions in an imperfect world
    that needs to be changed much more fundamentally (Brown, 1992b; Nielsen,
    1998).
4   I am using the term 'deconstruction' here in a non-Derridean, technical sense
    to signify the taking apart and reconstructing of the concepts of self and self-
    determination at work in the theoretical work considered under 'Which
    Selves, What Determination?' above.
5   The tensions between feminist politics and nationalist politics have been the
    subject of considerable debate in feminist literature: see Jad (1995); Walby
    (1996); Yuval-Davis (1997); Charles and Hintjens (1998). There is also a very
    considerable literature on feminism and citizenship rights (for an overview,
    see Hutchings, 1999).
6   This is a complaint frequently made about liberalism by communitarian
    critics. However, as was evident in the discussion of moral communitarian-
    ism in Chapter 2 and in the discussion in this chapter, in the international
    context communitarianism operates in an equally idealized world in which
    the boundaries of community are identifiable and in principle without cost
    (Walker, 1999).

6

Political Cosmopolitanism

Introduction

Cosmopolitanism has been under consideration as one of the approaches to normative international theory throughout this book. We have come across it in various guises, in Kantian, utilitarian, contractarian, Marxist and critical theoretical forms. In general, however, we have been examining moral cosmopolitanism as opposed to political. That is to say, the focus has been on cosmopolitanism as a framework for moral judgement rather than as a prescriptive framework for world order – although clearly the former has always had implications for the latter. There is no necessary connection between cosmopolitanism in its moral and political variants: moral cosmopolitans may endorse the state system, just as Hobbesian realists may argue for a world state (Dower, 1998: 17–26). Nevertheless, those arguing for political cosmopolitanism in one form or another very often invoke moral cosmopolitan premises in their theses. Moral cosmopolitanism refers in general to moral universalism, that is to any moral theory which presumes the universal validity and applicability of moral principles. Political cosmopolitanism here refers in general to any position which prescribes types of political practice and institution that operate over, above or across the boundaries of the nation-state and which are at least potentially global in their reach. Political cosmopolitanism is therefore, as I am using it here, a very general term; it does not necessarily entail the idea of a world state, indeed, as will become evident in the course of this chapter, most contemporary political cosmopolitans are very wary of the idea of a world state formulated according to the familiar principle of state sovereignty. In general, contemporary work on political cosmopolitanism is premised on the importance of democratizing the covert and undemocratic cosmopolitan decision-making which is already going on in the world (Falk, 1995: 47–8).

In the context of the Cold War and the dominance of sceptical and systemic realist analysis of international relations, political cosmopolitanism was virtually excluded as a topic of normative debate. The recent upsurge of normative international political theory on topics such as cosmopolitan democracy and law, world citizenship, critical social movements and global civil society has been provoked largely in reaction to certain perceived historical developments.[1] First, and most obviously, the end of the Cold War itself, in relation to which a variety of issues are significant. These include the ongoing claims made for the global triumph of liberal democracy, the experiences of international intervention or lack of it under UN auspices over the past ten years, plus the hopes and fears generated by the struggles for national self-determination, individual rights and democratization in Eastern Europe and the ex-Soviet Union in particular. All of this has encouraged the re-thinking (and questioning) of the meaning and viability of democracy and the nature of its link with the bounded nation-state (Archibugi and Held, 1995; Held, 1995, 1996). Secondly, economic and cultural globalization. These latter phenomena are the subject of intense debate as to their history and extent. Nevertheless, belief in the reality of economic and cultural globalization has been the mainspring for much argument both for and against the desirability of different kinds and degrees of political cosmopolitanism as, it is argued, the nation-state becomes increasingly unable to sustain its claim to sovereign power (Camilleri and Falk, 1992; Giddens, 1994; Falk, 1995; Bauman, 1998). Thirdly, the development of the European Union, in which many commentators see the growing instantiation of a form of political cosmopolitanism in which sovereignty is exported both below and above the level of the nation-state and genuinely transnational citizenship is enjoyed by citizens of member states (Meehan, 1993; Brown, 1994a; Kaldor, 1995). Fourthly, the increasing visibility of certain transnationally active critical social movements centred on human rights, ecology, women's rights and peace has directed attention both to policy issues with global dimensions and political practices which undermine, or simply ignore, the inside/ outside distinctions that confine politics proper to the sphere of the domestic state (Falk, 1995; Linklater, 1998; Walker, 1988).

The striking thing about all of the above developments is that there is no consensus in either explanatory or normative theory as to their extent, significance and meaning as new developments in international politics. In the case of post-Cold War political developments, there are conflicting views about the extent of actual democratization in large numbers of states and about the meaning of the resurgence in ethnic nationalism in many parts of the world. For some these are growing pains in an international order which now has the opportunity to genuinely embody ideals of self-determination within states and equal relations between them; for others, they are a confirmation of realist analyses of power politics and the dominance of self-interest in intra- and inter-state behaviour.[2] In the case of economic and cultural globalization, there are severe disagreements amongst analysts as to the reality and novelty of these phenomena. The thesis of economic globalization argues that there has been a qualitative shift from an international to a global economy, in which global economic processes operate (partly through the invention of new technologies) in ways unconstrained and unmediated by state power. The thesis of cultural globalization points to the revolution of information technology and the role of various media in the propagation of cultural messages which are, again, unconstrained and unmediated by cultures located within states or sub-state communities. It is extremely difficult to assess the extent to which globalization is actually occurring or what its implications are. Critics point to the continuing significance of certain key state actors in the global economy and to the restriction of the mass of economic global processes to certain parts and participants of and in that economy. They also point to the fact that signs taken as evidence of economic global- ization were equally in evidence at the end of the last century when the significance of certain state actors could not be in doubt. Both realists and liberal internationalists are dubious about claims made by global- ization theorists for the increasing redundancy of the state.[3] The same kind of disagreements characterize the analysis of the European Union and new social movements. In the case of the development of the EU, there are conflicting explanations for the growth of integration and its future in the context of EU enlargement (Kaldor, 1995: 86; Bankowski and Scott, 1996; Bellamy and Warleigh, 1998: 447). In the case of new social movements, again both their actual influence and their novelty are subject to question (Walker, 1988; Camilleri and Falk, 1992: 199–235). At all times, the notion that the state is ceasing to be the key mode of political organization is at issue.

It is clear, therefore, that none of the above historical developments, as they enter into debate over political cosmopolitanism, are an uncontested matter. The reading of history given is always already normatively inflected so that selected descriptive and prescriptive elements combine in arguments both for and against different forms of political cosmo-politanism as a desirable way forward from the old inter-state model of international politics. The prescriptive dimension of these pro and contra arguments, as will become apparent, owes a great deal to the debates over self-determination discussed in the previous chapter. Anti-cosmopolitan arguments, usually in addition to challenging the reading of history given by cosmopolitans, tend to take a statist or communitarian form (or some combination of the two) and hinge on the value of state agency or cultural autonomy – from this viewpoint, political cosmo-politanism is generally interpreted as covert imperialism (Toulmin, 1992; Zolo, 1997). Pro-cosmopolitan arguments lay stress on the increased need for control and accountability in international political and economic policy-making, and are generally inspired by the ideal of individual self-determination – from this viewpoint anti-cosmopolitanism supports what Falk refers to as geo-governance from above (controlled by elite political and economic actors) as opposed to humane governance from below (Falk, 1995: 14–16). Important to both pro and contra theoretical positions is the political ideal of democracy and what it means. The question around which much debate over political cosmopolitanism revolves is one of whether democracy (understood as some form of individual or collective self-determination) and cosmopolitanism are incompatible or whether the former depends on the latter in the post-Cold War world. In this chapter we will explore and assess three models of political cosmopolitanism which argue for the latter position. These models correspond to those identified by McGrew as the dominant con-temporary modes of political cosmopolitanism: liberal internationalism; cosmopolitan democracy and radical democratic pluralism (McGrew, 1997: 254).[4] It will become apparent that what is at stake in the differences between the models is less disagreement over readings of history (though those are there) and more disagreement about locating the source of democratic ethical potential, whether in the traditional forms of liberal or social democratic (socialist) democracy (emancipatory politics) or of radical democratic pluralism (life or identity politics).[5] The models will be examined and assessed in relation to ongoing debate within established pro- and anti-cosmopolitan positions in normative theory and in the light of the phenomenological and genealogical requirements generated by Hegelian/Foucauldian normative theory. The aim of the chapter is both to illuminate the ethical possibilities and dangers inherent in contemporary versions of political cosmopolitanism and illustrate the approach to international normative theory for which I have been arguing.

Modelling cosmopolitan democracy

Liberal internationalism

The revival of liberal internationalism as the preferred form of political cosmopolitanism amongst some commentators returns normative international theory to the idealist legacies of Kant, nineteenth century liberalism and the Wilsonian vision of a world of self-determining peoples whose relations with each other are regulated, on a consensual basis, through international institutions. Liberal internationalism relies on an analysis of contemporary world order in which conditions for international cooperation strengthen in line with the democratization and economic liberalization of states. In parallel with the history of liberalism within states, it can be taken to imply weaker and stronger political cosmopolitan visions. According to the weaker, libertarian vision, changes within the state are sufficient to ensure individual rights and more open and democratic inter-state dealings and the hidden hand of the free market precludes the necessity of anything other than regulatory cosmopolitan institutions (this position corresponds to liberal statism discussed in Chapter 5). According to the stronger, social democratic vision, the ideal of the free and equal participation of liberalized states in a new world order will have stronger implications for the construction of interventionist cosmopolitan institutions – along the lines of global constitutional protections of individual freedoms (this position corresponds to liberal nationalism discussed in Chapter 5). In both cases, however, it is the ethical potential of the state and of the market in relation to the individual which plays the crucial role.

The arguments for liberal internationalism have emerged most strikingly in the post-Cold War period in interpretations of Fukuyama's claim that the defeat of soviet socialism signalled the end of history and in the work of liberal democratic peace theorists. In the case of

Fukuyama, the key argument put forward in *The End of History and the Last Man* (1992; Williams et al., 1997) is that liberal democracy and free market capitalism satisfy between them the human desires which form the motor of historical development. The first desire is the human desire for recognition from others, which Fukuyama identifies with Kojève's interpretation of Hegel's work (Kojève, 1980; Fukuyama, 1992: 143–80) and the second desire is the desire for technological control over the material world, which then takes on a material logic of its own (Fukuyama, 1992: 71–97). Thus the ideological victory of liberalism and the globalization of capitalism together represent the limit of human achievement and the effective end of history. Fukuyama acknowledges that not all states have yet become post-historical states and he also suggests that there are tensions between the two categories of desire which liberal states may not be able to contain in the long term (Fukuyama, 1992: 328–99). He argues that the satisfaction of material desires and the absence of larger emancipatory goals which characterizes the 'end of history' may lead individuals to a state of nihilistic despair. However, even so, Fukuyama's reading of history in relation to its end draws strongly on Kant's vision of progress towards perpetual peace (Fukuyama, 1992: 276–84). The latter idea is taken up in liberal democratic peace theory, which argues on the basis of historical evidence that liberal democratic regimes do not go to war with one another and are able to regulate their relation with each other through mediation and arbitration (Doyle, 1993; Russett, 1993; M.E. Brown et al., 1996). The upshot of this latter argument is the (profoundly anti-realist) claim that the way to ensure peaceful inter-state relations and effective international institutions is by encouraging all states to become liberal democratic in form.

Fukuyama's and liberal democratic peace arguments chimed in strongly with the rhetoric emanating from the victorious parties to the Cold War, which reached its height in the 1990 Gulf War. The new liberal internationalist world order was envisaged as a form of weak democratic political cosmopolitanism to be underpinned by liberal democracy on the one hand and free market capitalism on the other. This is weak cosmopolitanism because although it envisages a greater role for international institutions in global governance and their increasing accountability to the people of the world at large, it continues to rely on the current premises of international law, which ground the legitimacy of those institutions in the consent of sovereign states, so that states continue to act as key mediators between internal populations and external relations. In this sense it stays very close to Kant's ideal of a confederation of republics. According to this perspective, the routes to increased political cosmopolitanism are the twinned policies of democratization and economic liberalization within existing states. Political cosmopolitanism in the liberal internationalist sense is only desirable within a context in which the participants in global governance are increasingly alike. In so far as states are increasingly alike political cosmopolitanism can be polyarchic in structure, with only limited need for, for instance, global democratic decision-making structures which directly represent non-state interests or actors. Thus liberal internationalism would support UN reform or a global human rights regime but would be less likely to endorse the idea of a global parliament. Liberal internationalism, as in its nineteenth century variants, recognizes the desirability of peace and the fact of greater economic interdependence as necessitating cooperation between international actors, state and non-state, but it envisages this happening through a reform of existing international law and institutions, with radical change confined to existing authoritarian and socialist or under-developed states.

Liberal internationalism clearly relies on a particular interpretation of historical developments as well as on certain explicit normative presumptions. It is premised on the claims that there are necessary (and empirically demonstrable) links between liberal democracy and pacificism and between economic globalization and incentives towards inter-state cooperation. These claims are obviously inflected by normative commitments to the values and rights implicit within both liberal democracy and the free market. Underlying liberal internationalism is a strong belief in the ultimate normative significance of individual self-determination to which basic human rights to liberty, security and property are crucial. Underlying it also is the conviction that liberalism (political and economic), democracy and the state form a viable, mutually consistent combination which will form the stable basis of political cosmopolitan progress in history (Bobbio, 1995: 17–41)

Cosmopolitan democracy

Cosmopolitan democracy refers to a form of political cosmopolitanism which both shares a considerable amount of ground with liberal internationalism and is premised on the critique of the nexus of liberalism, democracy and the state on which liberal internationalism depends. The two best known proponents of cosmopolitan democracy are Held and Habermas. Both thinkers share the view that the fundamental principle of democracy is a principle of autonomy and both identify it in recognizably liberal democratic terms as a principle of individual self-determination under constitutional law which protects the encroachment on those fundamental human rights which are the condition of possibility of individual self-determination in the first place (Held, 1995, 1996; Habermas, 1998). The difference between cosmopolitan democrats and liberal internationalists is not the ultimate values which they endorse but the conditions which each argues make the instantiation of those values possible. Thus, although oriented by fundamental liberal ideals, cosmopolitan democrats are critical of liberal democracy as in practice failing to live up to those ideals. This critique draws on both classical civic republican (Rousseauian) and Marxist criticisms of liberal democracy. The former argue that liberal representative government discourages active citizenship and tends effectively to deteriorate into elite rule with democracy degenerating from a mode of collective self-determination to a mode of the selection of rulers (Held, 1996: 36–9). The latter argue that the individual rights and freedoms enshrined in liberal democracy are a sham in a context where material inequality is rife (Held, 1996: 133–54). In addition to these familiar republican and Marxist complaints against liberal democracy, however, cosmopolitan democrats also argue against the liberal internationalist premise that the state remains the key to the development of political cosmopolitanism.

The idea of the state emerged in Europe as both the de facto recognition of and prescription for the understanding of political authority as possession of exclusive power in relation to a given territory. Externally this sovereignty depended on recognition by other sovereign powers; internally it depended on the capacity to control a given territory and its inhabitants, a capacity dependent usually on a mixture of what Niebuhr referred to as dominion and community (Niebuhr, 1959: 149; 265). According to cosmopolitan democrats, the generalization of the state as the key unit of political organization is a very recent phenomenon and the outcome of a very different range of processes than those which originally grounded the Westphalian system in post-medieval Europe. The external recognition of a particular territory as a state at the level of international law has not necessarily been accompanied either by that external recognition in practice or by its internal viability. The post-1945 period, in which the state system expanded significantly, has been characterized by direct, both military and non-military, consensual and non-consensual intervention in the affairs of weak states and by civil conflict and the break-up of states (Watson, 1998: 147–55). Only a very few, powerful states, can have been said to operate in approximation to the classical realist sense, as sovereign powers and even these are becoming more subject both to pressures of external intervention and internal secession. The principle of state sovereignty has never been a wholly accurate representation of the position of any given state, but it approximates less and less to the situation of the majority of states in the contemporary world. This is not to deny that states exist or to claim that they do not continue to play the part of international actors. However, the liberal internationalist vision depends on the status of states as equal sovereign powers – something which is manifestly not the case and seems unlikely to become so. For cosmopolitan democrats the disjunctures between the theory and actuality of state sovereignty are already too great for states themselves to be democratized without prior or parallel democratization at other global, trans-state and sub-state levels (Held, 1995: 279–80). Cosmopolitan democracy argues for a range of institutions below and above the level of the state to ensure individual protection and accountability in the light of economic globalization and the increased importance of global issues of human rights, peace and ecology which require global responses.

In his book *Democracy and the Global Order* (1995), the model of cosmopolitan democracy Held develops comes closer to the traditional view of political cosmopolitanism than that offered by liberal internationalism or radical pluralism, although proponents of cosmopolitan democracy are quick to repudiate the suggestion that their model resembles a world state in the traditional sense. The model of cosmopolitan democracy offered by Held involves a double democratization of both political and economic/civil society aspects of international organization and practice. Held elaborates on his model in some detail: at the political level he argues for cosmopolitan democratic law which will institutionalize individual and collective rights and establish the principle of democratic autonomy in decision-making. The principle of democratic autonomy means decisions are made essentially by those that are affected by them, so that sovereignty is dispersed rather than centralized. Where decisions have to be made at the global level, for instance with regard to ecological or military issues, global representative institutions will be created which are democratically accountable through elections and in response to critical public spheres in civil society (Held, 1995: 267–86). There are close links between Held's argument and those stemming from critical theory, particularly Habermas's work. Both Held and Habermas stress the importance of the democratization of civil society and the creation of a public sphere which will form a basis for the ongoing critique of institutional power. This has led to attention being paid to the possibility of an emergent cosmopolitan public sphere (Macmillan, 1998):

The cosmopolitan public sphere is not merely a structure but an ongoing process: the process by which emerging collective actors address the audience of world citizens and, in so doing, change the institutions that organize the publics into majorities. Cosmopolitan social critics and international collective actors may participate in the emergence of new publics, keeping democracy vital and its decision-making organizations flexible. (Bohman, 1997: 196)

At the level of civil society and economy, Held argues for limits on concentrations of ownership and control and the free market, for guaranteed basic social rights and for a multi-sectoral economy. He also argues for the maximization of possibilities of voluntary grass roots association within civil society. Held argues that his model does not resemble a world state because it involves no concentration of sovereignty; however, it does assume the necessity of certain areas of global decision-making and the importance of such decision-making being fully democratized.

In *Democracy and the Global Order*, Held charts the history of the development of the modern international order. At the heart of Held's argument is a normative ideal of democracy as grounded in respect for the principle of autonomy. As Held acknowledges, this is an essentially liberal model in that the importance of collective self-rule is derivable from the importance of individual self-rule. Held suggests that there are three essential conditions for democracy within states: democratic public law; a 'will to democracy' and a 'democratic culture'. What each of these conditions is based on is the recognition of the value of self-determination for all selves. In this context the notion of the nation-state as the 'we' of democratic self-determination has no privileged status at a normative level. The link between democracy and the nation-state is a contingent historical fact which no longer applies under conditions of globalization and the increasing disjuncture between the state's claim to sovereignty and the political actualities. The ideal of democratic self-determination requires the breaking of the link between democracy and the state. Held's argument, therefore, is based on similar values to those underlying liberal internationalism but is much more sceptical of the state and inter-state politics as the sole means for the realization of liberal principles. Here, Held shares the radical democrat's concern about geo-governance from above, in particular in relation to the global economy and the radical democrat's emphasis on the importance of citizen participation to democracy. However, Held rejects the radical democrat's wholehearted disillusion with law and macro level institutions as being capable of sustaining a genuinely democratic political culture.

Cosmopolitanism and democracy in conflict

Before going on to explore the third model of political cosmopolitanism, radical democratic pluralism, it is useful to examine the arguments stemming from mainstream anti-cosmopolitan normative perspectives, which can be applied to either or both of liberal internationalism and cosmopolitan democracy (Buzan et al., 1998). These arguments are already familiar, as they stem from realist and communitarian theories which have been examined in previous chapters. In general, the arguments point to tensions between democratic political cosmopolitanism and the ideals by which it is inspired, either at the level of principle or at the level of concrete institutionalization. I will examine arguments directed against liberal internationalism first. The critique of liberal internationalism focuses on claims made for the generalizability of liberal democracy, on the version of the 'domestic analogy' on which it relies and on the claims made for the political cosmopolitan effects of economic globalization.

For liberal internationalism, the values implicit in liberal democracy, in conjunction with the levels of prosperity and interdependence generated by the globalization of free market capitalism, are the enabling factors for political cosmopolitanism. The state is the forum within which liberal democracy and the free market develops and all states must have the potential to become liberal democratic and economically liberal states. Beetham identifies five components necessary to liberal democracy: civil and political freedoms; the rule of law; the institution of a representative legislative assembly; divisions between private and public spheres and between state and civil society and state neutrality between competing conceptions of the good (Beetham, 1993: 56–7). Anti-cosmopolitan critics of liberal internationalism note that none of these components can exist without the development of a highly specific type of legal and political culture and economy. The plausibility of liberal internationalist claims as to the generalizability of liberal democracy to states which do not share the peculiar history of Western Europe and its New World colonies depends on the genuine universalizability of liberal democratic legal and political culture in principle. Realist and communitarian arguments object that liberal democratic legal and political culture is relative to a particular history which cannot simply be assumed to be applicable to states that have a radically different history and culture (Parekh, 1992; Huntington, 1993, 1996; Bontekoe and Stepaniants, 1997; Zolo, 1997: 134–8; Lawson, 1998).

Classical realist arguments, along with various international society, communitarian arguments and existing international law, treat states on analogy with individuals as self-contained, purposive actors in the realm of international politics. Liberal internationalism makes a similar analogy but departs from realism in that the nature of the state and the nature of the person is given a more crucial role than the context in which they operate in determining the way in which they will act. This means that liberal internationalism is obliged to defend not only the individual/ state analogy but also a relationship between internal constitution and outward action. In this sense liberal internationalism is clearly a theoretical cousin of liberal nationalism (and civic republican communitarianism), discussed in the previous chapter, in which the interconnection between Kantian conceptions of individual autonomy and liberal constructions of nationality was also linked to tolerant and generous behaviour abroad. The individual/state analogy itself depends, as was argued in the previous chapter, on models of both individual and state autonomy which are questionable in general and in particular in the contemporary world where both individuals and states differ markedly from other individuals and states in their self-containment and their capacity for agency. However, even if we assume the possibility of state on a par with individual agency, realist critics in particular would raise the question of how plausible is the analogy between good people and good states? Is there is a necessary connection between liberal democracy within states and liberal democratic inter-state relations?

Evidence for the benefits of political liberalism within states for inter-state relations can be found both in liberal democratic peace theory and in the functioning of a range of cooperative political, strategic and economic international institutions set up by and for liberal democratic states – most notably in the case of the latter, the institutions of the European Union. According to liberal democratic peace theory, the fact that liberal democracies have not gone to war with one another in the modern period along with the fact that in the same period they have frequently gone to war with non-liberal regimes, substantiates the premise of liberal internationalism, i.e., that liberalism within all states is the key to a different world order. The strong claim is made that it is the normative underpinning of liberalism, not simply coincidences of state strategic or economic interest, which is the key ingredient. However, although the evidence for a liberal zone of peace is quite strong, this doesn't in itself answer the question of whether the link between liberalism as such and peace is contingent as opposed to necessary. According to realist critics, the number of established liberal states is relatively small and much of the evidence in liberal peace theory includes regimes which have little entitlement to that label. Secondly, within much of the period under consideration major powers have been locked into Cold War, inter-bloc rather than inter-state politics. Thirdly, there are a whole range of strategic arguments for the increasing ineffectivity of war as an instrument of political policy (M.E. Brown et al., 1996; Burchill, 1996a: 61–3). In many ways, the evidence provided by developments such as the European Union is stronger for the purposes of liberal internationalism – here a degree of political cosmopolitanism is clearly evolving (Meehan, 1993; Kaldor, 1995). However, the distinction between the inside and the outside of the EU, as well as the tensions between member states, can be taken as evidence both for the continuing importance of national-interest as the key determinant of inter-state action (in realist terms), but also as confirmation of the need for strong, bounded solidarities as the basis for any stable form of political order, including liberal democratic forms (in communitarian terms) (Brown, 1994a; Diez, 1997).

The third argument on which liberal internationalism depends concerns the mutual reinforcement of political and economic liberalism at the level of the state and through that at the level of inter-state relations. Do democratization and free market capitalism go hand in hand towards a liberal internationalist cosmopolitan order? The historic links between liberalism and capitalism are clear and most obvious in the overlap between the legal relations which need to be in place for capitalism and the market to operate and liberal understandings of individual right, including property right (Macpherson, 1962). However, it is far from clear exactly what is the nature of this relationship, whether it is one of mutual compatibility, mutual conditioning or the priority of the one over the other or, alternatively, one of tension – or some combination of any or all of these. Is capitalism compatible with other forms of polity? In recent years claims have been made that the traditional and hierarchical cultures and polities of South East Asia are perfectly capable of coexisting with the post-Fordist economy of late capitalism. If this is the case then the liberal internationalist bracketing of liberalism and capitalism becomes one possibility rather than an inevitability, even if the global reach of capitalism is admitted. Is liberal democracy a luxury that can be afforded only when sufficient levels of prosperity have been attained as is claimed by many underdeveloped states, suggesting that capitalism is the precondition of liberalism? Or, vice versa, is liberalism the crucial condition for successful capitalism and does this explain the collapse of the tiger economies and the struggles of the emergent free market economies in Eastern Europe and elsewhere.[6]

Some of the realist and communitarian arguments against liberal internationalism share common ground with those made by cosmopolitan democrats. The communitarian emphasis on the significance and

specificity of political culture is reflected in the civic republican element
of cosmopolitan democracy arguments – their insistence on the need for
a robust global civil society and for localized levels of sovereignty and
decision-making. The realist sensitivity to the massive inequalities of
power between states and the uneven effects of economic globalization is
reflected in Held's double democratization project, designed to curb the
acquisition of hegemonic political or economic power by any minority of
actors. However, this shared ground does not make communitarianism
and realism any more sympathetic to cosmopolitan democracy than
liberal internationalism, if anything – less. There are two main reasons
for this: first, realists do not subscribe to the analysis of economic
globalization or the disjuncture between economic and political control
which it implies. They continue to argue that the state remains the crucial
actor in the global political economy, whereas arguments such as Held's
rely on the claim to a high level of disjuncture between state and economic power (Thomson and Krasner, 1996; Clark, 1997, 1998). Secondly,
and more crucially, both realism and communitarianism are suspicious
of the ideal element at work in both liberal internationalism and cosmopolitan democracy. From the point of view of realists, this returns us to
the old realist/idealist debates and the realist's view not only that
universal political ideals (whether they are assumed to exist or not) are
difficult to substantiate in theory, but also that they are dangerous to
attempt to realize in practice, being linked to a profound political
myopia. From the point of view of communitarians, this returns us to the
cosmopolitan/communitarian debate and the communitarian assumption of radical cultural pluralism and the consequent rejection of the
notion of universal ethical or political values. For communitarians, this
means that political cosmopolitanism is always a kind of imperialism in
disguise – suppressing and excluding alternative communities in the
name of an ideal. Both realist and communitarian elements of anti-
cosmopolitanism are exemplified in the kind of argument offered by
Zolo (1997), in which liberal internationalism and cosmopolitan
democracy both emerge as being unrealistic, dangerous and culturally
imperialist.

Radical democratic pluralism

Radical democratic pluralism as a preferred form of political cosmopolitanism represents something of a cocktail of elements of postmodernist,

Marxist and civic republican democratic theory.[7] The focus of the radical vision of political cosmopolitanism is on forms of political agency and organization outside of the mechanisms of state and international law. Work on new social movements and global governance in the World Order Models Project by thinkers such as Falk and Walker has put forward arguments in favour of the strengthening of global civil society and the possibilities of transnational democratic intervention by grass roots political organizations (Walker, 1988; Falk, 1995). Work drawing on the experience of environmental political movements has stressed the significance of direct democratic participation and the problems of relying on conventional political and legal structures for the pursuit of globally significant issues (Lipschutz and Conca, 1994; Dryzek, 1995). Work drawing on the political struggles of national minorities and women has stressed the importance of local identities and local parti-cipation as the ground for democratic self-determination in a global context (Basu, 1995; Pettman, 1996; Charles and Hintjens, 1998). Radical pluralists reject the largely optimistic reading liberal internationalism gives of the spread of liberal democracy and free market capitalism on both empirical and normative grounds. They see the rhetoric of the new world order as disguising the increasing grip of geo-governance from above, in which globally crucial policy-making decisions reside in the hands of a few, unaccountable elite actors. In addition, radical pluralists agree with cosmopolitan democrats that the sovereign state is, by and large, increasingly less effective as a principle of political organization in the complexly interdependent world of economic and cultural global-ization. The reform of states as such, therefore, is an inadequate response to the need to make global governance more transparent and accountable in the contemporary world. According to this point of view the cosmo-politan politics of liberal internationalism relies on structures of inter-national cooperation which are increasingly redundant and inevitably corrupted by their domination by certain fixed hegemonic interests.

Clearly, many of the criticisms directed at liberal internationalism by radical democratic pluralism overlap with those offered by cosmopolitan democrats, realists and communitarians. At the same time, however, radical democratic pluralism is also critical of the other viewpoints. In the case of cosmopolitan democracy, even though radical pluralists share many of its presumptions, in particular the importance of political participation and the threats posed by economic globalization, they are dubious about models such as those of Held or Habermas. This doubt rests on two main grounds: first, a problem for radical pluralists is that they are dubious about the effects of juridical power (legal and institu-tional power as such), whereas cosmopolitan democracy clearly foresees a multiplication of law and institutions at a variety of levels. This distrust of juridical power is rooted in both principled objections to the definitive exclusion of any form of political agency at the constitutional level and in practical doubts as to the likely colonization of any such institutions by hegemonic interests (Dillon, 1998). Secondly, radical pluralism rejects the moral cosmopolitanism which is crucial to both liberal internationalism and cosmopolitan democracy both because it is impossible to ground authoritatively and because it glosses over and thereby depoliticizes its exclusion of other normative positions (Campbell, 1998a). These objections to cosmopolitan democracy ally radical pluralism with certain realist and communitarian arguments. However, radical pluralism is distinguishable from realism on grounds that it endorses the reading of the decreasing significance of states as global actors and on grounds that it gives normative priority to new resistant forms of politics in the context of globalization. It would distinguish itself from communitarianism in that it does not regard communities in terms of fixed identities as sources of normative value. Radical democratic cosmopolitanism rests on critical deconstructive arguments as to the cultural and gendered specificity of the liberal ideal of the sovereign individual (Jabri, 1998). However, it also rests on a deconstructive appreciation of the difficulty of distinguishing between self and other determination at the collective as well as the individual level. Community is always a political and ongoing achievement for radical pluralism, never a given source of value (Mouffe, 1993; Campbell, 1998a). Moreover, radical democratic pluralism does not value cultural identity as such, it distinguishes between reactive and resistant identities. Reactive identities are exemplified by ethnic nationalism and religious fundamentalism. Resistant identities are exemplified by critical social movements (Walker, 1988: 50–80; Giddens, 1994: 246–53). For radical pluralists, a new kind of cosmopolitan politics is located in non-governmental organizations such as human rights groups, women's movements and green movements, which have constructed their constituencies and invented new forms of resistant political practice to challenge global hegemonic powers (Walker, 1988: 62–3).

At the heart of radical democratic cosmopolitanism is the suggestion that international political institutions and practices which depend on the established principles of inter-state politics enshrined in existing international law and institutions are effectively (empirically and normatively) exhausted and a new form of politics is called for. Even though the effects of globalization are viewed as frequently operating to exclude and oppress, they are nevertheless seen as providing new opportunities for transnational grass roots political action and for the production of new global political cultures which have not existed before. The emphasis in the radical democratic approach is on civil society rather than state or international institutions as the key to genuinely democratic political cosmopolitanism. The normative values given priority are those of pluralism, difference and resistance as opposed to the universalist ethic of liberal internationalism and cosmopolitan democracy.

> I have suggested that one of the most persistent insights of critical social movements is that it is necessary to explore novel political spaces. These explorations occur in the context of far-reaching articulations of political space associated with global flows of capital, with new information and weapons technologies, with world-wide environmental problems, and so on. The disjunction between the global structures and processes that now have such a profound impact on people everywhere and these centres of political authority organized within separate territorial boundaries provides the setting for a major crisis in the way we understand political life. (Walker, 1988: 147–8)

Walker argues that the spatio-temporal parameters of inter-state politics are profoundly undermined by the impossibility of containing global structures and processes within them and that this in itself provides the opportunity for new forms of cosmopolitan politics. Critical assessment of radical pluralism therefore depends both on the claims it makes as to the effects of globalization in creating new articulations of political space and on the claims made for the new forms of politics which are linked to exploration of that space.

In general the radical democratic approach to political cosmopolitanism owes more to the sociological literature on economic and cultural globalization than does that of the liberal internationalists or even the cosmopolitan democrats. It is important therefore to look at the arguments of this body of work a little more carefully before assessing the conclusions drawn from it for this form of political cosmopolitanism. Fundamental to the globalization thesis in relation to the economy and culture is the argument that increasingly (this is in process, few would see it as complete) both operate at a global level, unconstrained and unmediated by state or national boundaries. It is important to distinguish this from claims to the increasing internationalization of economy and culture, which continue to presume the significance of nation-states as mediators of economic and cultural processes (Hirst and Thompson, 1996: 18–50). There are some profoundly pessimistic interpretations of globalization. Bauman, for example, identifies the process with the immiseration of the vast majority of the world's population, their increasing immobility and poverty (financial and informational) being the flip side of the increasing mobility and wealth (in material and information terms) of a small global elite (Bauman, 1998). Moreover, he identifies 'new tribalisms', the reactive politics of the excluded and oppressed, exemplified by bloody nationalist conflicts and the rise of religious fundamentalism as an inevitable consequence of the effects of globalization (Bauman, 1995: 163–222). Less wholly pessimistic is the argument of Giddens, who identifies globalization as offering new opportunities as well as risks in the contemporary world and who links those opportunities to the transition from an emancipatory politics of life chances in modern societies to a reflexive politics of lifestyle in late modernity.

> It becomes more and more apparent that lifestyle choices, within the settings of local–global interrelations, raise moral issues which cannot simply be pushed to one side. Such issues call for forms of political engagement which the new social movements both presage and serve to help initiate. 'Life politics' – concerned with human self-actualization, both on the level of the individual and collectively – emerges from the shadow which 'emancipatory politics' has cast. (Giddens, 1991: 9)

Giddens's distinction between emancipatory and life politics refers to the difference between a politics centred on the acquisition of rights in relation to life chances (this would include struggles for legal, political and material rights) and a politics centred on existential issues which flow from 'processes of self-actualization in post-traditional contexts' (Giddens, 1991: 214).

There is no doubt that arguments such as Bauman's and Giddens's resonate with the experience of certain political developments in certain parts of the world. The negative side of the globalization argument, which is now routinely used by liberal democratic governments to justify austere economic policies within state borders, accords with the experience of citizens of affluent Western states in the late twentieth century. It is also the case that the growth of 'life politics' and critical social movements, though by no means confined to such states, has been particularly marked within them, along with a disillusion with old style patriotic or class politics. Giddens includes environmental movements, peace movements, feminism and campaigns in relation to abortion and reproductive technology in his list of examples of life politics (Giddens, 1991: 227). However, the plausibility of the radical democrat's reading of the political implications of globalization depends on these kinds of developments representing new forms of democratic politics which are global in their implications and which break with both dependence on the state and dependence on fixed identities or universal moral law. Two things are particularly significant here: first, the distinction between the positively evaluated cosmopolitanism of new social movements and the much more suspiciously evaluated cosmopolitanism of the extension of international law and institutions; secondly, the distinction radical pluralists want to draw between critical social movements and new tribalisms.

In the first case, the departure of radical pluralism from both liberal internationalism and cosmopolitan democracy is marked. The problem with international law and institutions along with that of old-fashioned emancipatory politics is argued to be not simply that they are open to colonization by hegemonic interests, but that even when they operate benignly they do so on the assumption of the universal applicability of values and goals which are both culturally specific and inevitably exclusive of difference and otherness (McGrew, 1997: 246). However, as Giddens points out, it is actually very difficult to disentangle emancipatory from life politics, and to the extent that the latter depends on the former it is not clear that radical pluralism's rejection of the commitment of liberal internationalism and cosmopolitan democracy to global regimes for the institutionalization of different kinds of rights (juridical power) is sustainable (Giddens, 1991: 228). Walker locates the distinction in the second case as that between political movements which stick to traditional and fixed principles of political organization (such as nationalist, fundamentalist or class based movements) and those that in the process of political engagement re-interpret and re-invent principles of political organization which cut across established categories (Walker, 1988: 62–3). Underlying this argument is the claim that nationalist, fundamentalist and socialist movements mistake the kind of world in which they live, which is one in which identities are multiple and fluid rather than exclusive and fixed. This is a claim which readily transmutes into the associated claim that multiplicity and fluidity are in some sense normatively preferable to exclusivity and fixity, demonstrating again the tendency of postmodernist accounts of self-determination to translate the idea of the transgression of given limitation and respect for otherness into an abstract ideal for political action (Campbell, 1998a: 513; Walker, 1988: 166–70). Two questions emerge from the claims made for radical democratic pluralism: first, do radical pluralists tend to overestimate the degree of multiplicity and fluidity of identity in the contemporary world? Secondly, are radical pluralists able to account for the paradoxical consequences of the principle of 'respect for alterity' (which necessarily means that certain 'others' cannot be respected because their politics are reactive) without implicitly relying on universal principles which they claim to have rejected?

The reading of history

The models of political cosmopolitanism outlined above all depend on a certain reading of history mediated by a certain set of normative values which their particular version of democracy encapsulates. They clearly share certain arguments and differ over others, but they all rely on the identification of aspects of the current international order as having positive ethical potential, with particular criteria for what counts as such potential. The explication of these models and the ways in which they are locked into debate with each other and with anti-cosmopolitan perspectives repeats patterns with which we have become familiar in exploring the parameters of contemporary normative international theory in this book. Liberal cosmopolitans (internationalists) are locked into argument with realists and communitarians. Critical normative positions (within this debate notably critical theory and postmodernism in the models of cosmopolitan democracy and radical pluralism respectively) put themselves forward to transcend the familiar battle, but their own positions continue to echo aspects of the realist/idealist engagement which has structured the study of international politics in the twentieth century. In the previous chapter an attempt was made to assess the value of these different ways of structuring the reading of history in relation to the variety of debates surrounding the principle of self-determination in normative international theory. This assessment was based on the requirements of phenomenological adequacy and genealogical honesty which have been identified as the mark of the 'second best' normative theorizing for which I have been arguing in this book. In this section the same approach will be employed in relation to the models of political cosmopolitanism and their anti-cosmopolitan critics. The point of the exercise is not to identify the best model as such, but to reflect on both the conditions of possibility and the implications in principle of reading history in one way as opposed to another.

Liberal internationalism is the most prominent model of political cosmopolitanism and comes closest to the principles which already underlie international law and institutions. The conditions of possibility on which the liberal internationalist vision relies involve, as we have seen, the coming together of political and economic liberalism, democracy and the state, the analogy between individual and state (with both being understood as self-contained agents) and the politically liberalizing effects of a globalizing capitalist free market economy. The plausibility of all of these conditions is open to question in practice, but they are also questionable in principle when subject to phenomenological analysis. At the most basic level, liberal internationalism continues to operate with a conception of both individual and state as discrete entities within which the line between self- and other-determination is clearly distinguishable. A liberal state therefore, like a liberal individual, will act according to liberal democratic principles. However, as a description of the determination of either individual or state behaviour this is phenomenologically inadequate. This is not because, as realists would claim, individuals and states are always motivated by self-interest, but because neither individuals nor states are unitary, bounded, self-consciously self-determining actors. In any given context what the state is and what the state does will involve a host of relations of relative identity with a variety of other types of actor. These identities belie the firm inside/outside distinction upon which liberal internationalism is premised even if they sometimes work to sustain that distinction. A liberal constitution and culture will not be irrelevant to any given constellation of determinations, but it cannot be guaranteed to be decisive outside of an ideal 'first best' world in which states and individuals are conceived of as autonomous in a classically liberal or liberal Kantian sense. This does not necessarily invalidate liberal internationalist claims for the importance of liberal democracy but it does suggest that both realists and cosmopolitan democrats are right in stressing that the international context itself is as crucial for international politics as the internal structure of states.

Liberal internationalism oversimplifies accounts of states and the determination of state action and this problematizes its reliance on the influence of internally liberal democratic arrangements for external political practice. There are also, however, questions to be raised as to the phenomenological adequacy of the account of liberal democracy on which liberal internationalism also relies. It is communitarians and civic republicans who most commonly draw attention to the shortcomings of liberal democracy as a version of democracy. Since Rousseau it has been asserted repeatedly that liberal democracy is not genuine democracy because it relies on representative institutions and the rule of law rather than on the direct participation of the people in government. My concern here is not with the debate about what democracy really means but with the question to which such critiques of liberal democracy draw attention. This is, the question of how it is determined who the 'people' are. All accounts of democratic political cosmopolitanism rest on the view that the 'people' is a flexible category; for liberal internationalists it refers both to citizens of states and, more remotely and in relation to certain areas of global decision-making only, to humanity as such. But according to the civic republican tradition in democratic theory, the people cannot be understood in merely aggregative terms as bearers of rights or interests. Instead the people is defined in terms of strong solidarities which rely on shared culture and identity. Liberal internationalists gloss over the 'fudge' which has successfully linked individuals and states together and the question of what the implications of this fudge might be for attitudes of insiders to outsiders in the liberal internationalist state system (Canovan, 1996a, 1996b). This draws attention to Held's point that the establishment of liberal democracy relies on political will and political culture as well as constitutions and institutions. It raises the question as to whether liberal democratic culture is essentially self-sustaining or whether it relies, as Canovan suggests, on solidarities which are not themselves definable in liberal or democratic terms. Such arguments do not necessarily invalidate the liberal internationalist vision, but they do suggest that the institution of the state as such, even the liberal democratic state, may be too weak to carry it.

The link established by liberal internationalism between economic and political liberalization is equally vulnerable to phenomenological deconstruction. This is not because there are not demonstrable links between the two both in principle and practice, but because the relation between them has clearly always had the potential (in principle but also demonstrably in practice) for one to subvert the other. Massive increases in wealth and productivity are inevitably accompanied by massive increases in material inequality within competitive free market capitalism. This does not necessarily mean that the poor get poorer (though it may do so), but it does mean that material and therefore power inequalities exist side by side with legal, civil and political equality in liberal democratic, capitalist free market systems. This poses two problems for the liberal internationalist vision: first, there is a clash between the equal status of sovereign states within international law and institutions and the actual material inequalities of power between rich states and poor states; secondly, the differentiated effects of the global economy seem likely to block rather than enhance the development of internal liberal democratic institutions in poor states. Paradoxically, the implications of liberal internationalism push equally in realist and cosmopolitan democracy directions. Reliance on the state and global capital as such seems likely to return us to the realist world view; recognition of the problems with this reliance in the light of liberal internationalist ideals seems to lead us to a much more interventionist social democratic cosmopolitanism.

The thinking through of the liberal internationalist reading of history points to a range of difficulties with sustaining it in both principle and practice. The key principle through which liberal internationalists read the ethical potential of contemporary world politics is what Held refers to as the principle of autonomy – the familiar liberal ideal of self-determination which we discussed in the previous chapter. We have already seen that the ontological account of the 'self' of self-determination in liberal internationalism (as in contractarianism and Kantianism in the previous chapter) is phenomenologically unconvincing. If we shift from the phenomenology of the ontological categories in terms of which liberal internationalists understand the world to the phenomenology and genealogy of the theorist's ethical judgement then further issues arise. To begin with, it is clear that liberal internationalist theory reflects the identification of the theorist with the nexus of economic and political liberalism, democracy and the state. This in turn reflects not the necessary, but the contingent constellation of historical developments which have enabled the flourishing of all of these together in certain contexts. This means that the theorists must reflect carefully on their own understanding of the conditions of possibility of their judgement. The temptation is to translate contingency into necessity by reading these specific historical developments as either the expression of transcendentally universally valid principles or as the outcome of the inevitable development of history. If this move is made then the liberal internationalist vision is translated into some kind of ethical solution without remainder for the problems of international politics. This makes the theorist's judgement vulnerable on two counts: first because it opens them up to traditional realist charges of being out of touch with reality; secondly, because that kind of univeralist claim is neither redeemable in abstraction nor non-exclusive in its effects – although it has pretensions to be both. If, on the contrary, liberal internationalists are honest about the extent to which liberal internationalism is uneasily intertwined with its conditions of possibility and necessarily problematic in its effects and if, in addition, liberal internationalists are clear that their ethical commitment is not all-inclusive but shorthand for a way of doing politics which marginalizes certain alternatives, then at least it will be possible for readers to assess the adequacy of liberal internationalist analysis when applied to any particular aspect of international politics.

Realism, communitarianism, cosmopolitan democracy and radical pluralism all play on the phenomenological inadequacies of liberal internationalism to help sustain their own readings of history. Before moving on to look at the two alternative models of political cosmopolitanism, it is worth reflecting on what very little comfort the above discussion offers to realists and communitarians. Both realism and communitarianism as anti-cosmopolitanism positions share with liberal internationalism an inadequate ontology of collective or supra-individual agency. The account of the state as a self-contained self-interested actor or of the community as an exclusive culture are no more convincing than the liberal internationalist account of and analogy between the genuinely autonomous individual and state. This is not because it is not possible for states to act in a Hobbesian fashion or for communities to be experienced as radically other, it is because these phenomena are themselves only possible through a complex of relative identities which construct but simultaneously subvert them. Realism and communitarianism continue to express partial truths about contemporary international politics, but in treating these truths as abstractly given and necessary, rather than concretely constructed and contingent, they end up confounded by the lack of fit between the first best and second best worlds just as much as liberal internationalism. In terms of the phenomenology and genealogy of the theorist's judgement, realism and communitarianism both repeat the failure of many liberal internationalists to reflect carefully on the conditions of possibility of their claims. In the case of realism, a dimension of hypocrisy is added which is lacking in moral cosmopolitanism and critical normative approaches. This is because realists pretend to the abandonment of ethical judgement within the international context, whilst at the same time quite clearly sustaining a normative stance in which state is prioritized over inter-state, inside over outside. In the case of communitarianism, there is a persistent tendency to revert either to realism or to some form of liberalism, simply because communitarianism does not have the conceptual equipment to think about politics which transcends the boundaries of the culture, nation or state. To limit the scope of normative judgement of international politics, either because the international sphere is amoral or because morality exists only within community is not actually to limit it at all. If liberal internationalists can be criticized for idealism, so can realists and communitarians, because they equally operate in an ideal world in which self- and other-determination are clearly and necessarily distinguishable in a way which is radically at odds with the realities of both international politics and normative judgement.

It is unsurprising, in the light of the analysis in this and previous chapters, that I consider both cosmopolitan democracy and radical democratic pluralism as avoiding some of the phenomenological inadequacies to be found in liberal internationalism, realism and communitarianism. However, it should also be apparent from the discussion of the two models given above that there are questions to be raised in relation to the phenomenology of the ontological categories used and the phenomenology and genealogy of the theorist's judgement made in cosmopolitan democratic and radical pluralist theory. In the case of cosmopolitan democracy, it provides a much fuller account of the conditions of possibility for democracy and political agency in all their complexity and mutual tension than is to be found in liberal internationalism or the anti-cosmopolitan positions. However, it also relies on faith in the principle of autonomy underlying cosmopolitan democratic law to manage that complexity and those tensions. The principle of autonomy is essentially a liberal Kantian principle of self-determination. Cosmopolitan democracy as it is formulated by Held, but also in Habermas's work, therefore relies on both the plausibility and the universal reach of the Kantian account of genuine self-determination. As Held himself acknowledges, democracy cannot be established without a democratic political will and political culture – these are the product of a complex of historical circumstances, but they are also, it is claimed, the reflection of a universal truth about the nature and desirability of human freedom. In the model of cosmo-politan democracy the principle of autonomy is plucked out from its context and given the status of a transcendental ought and a necessary end of history. So that although cosmopolitan democracy introduces a more sophisticated understanding of how liberalism, democracy and the state are both mutually compatible and in tension than is offered by liberal internationalism, it nevertheless follows liberal internationalism in abstracting out its key normative principle from its own conditionality and politics. This renders models of cosmopolitan democracy prey to the same charges of idealism and imperialism which are standardly levelled at liberal internationalism (Jahn, 1998). From the point of view of Hegelian/Foucauldian normative theory, the problem with cosmopoli-tan democracy, and the insights of critical theory on which it draws, is not that it presents a model which implies fundamental change in international politics. The problem is rather that in abstracting out the principles of ethical judgement on which it relies, cosmopolitan democratic theory suggests that there are short cuts through interna-tional politics to a future ideal. Universal ethical principles of a liberal Kantian kind are inextricable from a complex history. The conditions of possibility for the realization of such principles also have the potential to subvert them, and their realization will always imply the exclusion of other ways of being.

Radical democratic pluralism shares with cosmopolitan democracy an account of political agency, at individual and supra-individual levels, which appreciates the complexity, contingency and contextual specificity of identity and self-determination. Moreover, it is premised on the explicit acknowledgement of the conditions of possibility and political implications of the theorist's judgement. However, there is still a sense in which radical pluralism, like cosmopolitan democracy, does not fully live up to the requirements of its own phenomenological and genealogical

sophistication. What emerges from consideration of the phenomenological adequacy of radical democracy is that it pays too little attention to
the conditions of possibility of the developments it is identifying as
carrying the cosmopolitan future. On examination, the distinctions
radical pluralism draws between emancipatory and life politics and
between resistant and reactive politics problematize the radical pluralist
critique of both liberal internationalist and cosmopolitan democratic
ethical universalism. In the former case this is because the two forms of
politics turn out to be mutually dependent; in the latter case because
there is a temptation to rest the distinction on the 'ought to be' of the
eternal transgression of limitation. The deconstructive element of judgement, in which the complexities and contingency of the conditions of
possibility of the theoretical object are made explicit, can become con-
fused with the actual deconstruction of that object. This is apparent in the
endorsement of difference over identity and resistance over law, not as a
matter of contextual judgement but as an absolute verdict on history,
which is to neglect the relative identity between individual and institution, state and civil society, international law and new social movement.

Conclusion

The discussion of the principle of self-determination in the previous
chapter and of democratic ideals of political cosmopolitanism in this has
not issued in any neat answers as to the meaning and value of either self-
determination or democratic political cosmopolitanism. In a positive
sense, my examination of the different perspectives has resulted in the
conclusion that none of them has nothing to add to normative debate in
contemporary international politics, but that none of them is fully
adequate to the challenges of that debate either. This matters only in so
far as the normative perspectives are applied as if they were fully
adequate to the matter in hand, a kind of theoretical hubris which I have
argued is particularly well developed in mainstream international theory
and the ethics of international politics, though it is not entirely absent in
more critical perspectives. The approach to normative international
theory for which I have been arguing establishes the inadequacy of
ethical thinking that is grounded and redeemable only in an ideal world,
defined in abstraction from the ontological complexity of the real and
thereby inevitably misrecognizing its own identification with that world.
At the same time, it is an approach which sees the heteronomy of action

and judgement not as a pretext for the abandonment of normative judgement but as the occasion of phenomenological care and genealogical honesty on the part of the theorist. In my view, for all the reservations which can be (and must be) noted in relation to them, critical theory, postmodernism and feminist theories come closest to the best kind of international normative theory because they supplement the priority they give to certain normative values with both attempts to grasp the conditions of possibility of political agency by individual and collective international political actors and with a recognition of the politics of their own theoretical practice.

Notes

1 This literature has expanded rapidly in recent years. Key contributors include: Habermas (1992, 1997, 1998); Held (1995, 1996); Falk (1995); Walker (1988, 1993); Linklater (1998); Giddens (1991, 1994). See also: Archibugi and Held (1995); Bohman and Lutz-Bachmann (1997); Archibugi, Held and Koehler (1998).

2 A broad range of analyses of the meaning and significance of contemporary democratization are offered in Parry and Moran (1994); Whitehead (1996); Dawisha and Parrott (1997); Potter et al. (1997). See also Global Society Vol. 12, No. 2, 1998. The most optimistic readings of these developments are associated with Fukuyama's end of history thesis (Fukuyama, 1992) and liberal democratic peace theory (Doyle, 1993; Russett, 1993; M.E. Brown et al. (1996) which are discussed below.

3 Debates over globalization are essentially twofold: they concern the extent to which economic and cultural globalization is a reality and the normative assessment of processes of globalization in so far as they are occurring. Thomson and Krasner (1996, first published in 1986) and Hirst and Thompson (1996) argue against strong economic globalization claims; for an opposing view see Lash and Urry (1987, 1994). Camilleri and Falk (1992), Giddens (1991, 1994), Shaw (1994), Scholte (1993), Appadurai (1996), Spybey (1996), Hoogvelt (1997) and Bauman (1998) present various aguments for the reality of globalization across a range of areas – economic, cultural and political – though they vary in their assessments as to whether this is a good or bad thing. There are basic disagreements as to whether the nature of international

politics is fundamentally affected by globalization or not (see Bayliss and Smith, 1997; Clark, 1997; 1998).

4   I have adjusted McGrew's terminology for purposes of clarity. He refers to the models as liberal internationalism, cosmopolitan democracy and radical communitarianism respectively (McGrew, 1997: 254). As we will see below, the models of democracy correspond to debates over the meaning of democracy within the state. Liberal internationalism is a version of liberal (libertarian or welfarist) democracy; cosmopolitan democracy corresponds to social/socialist models with elements of deliberative/discursive democracy; radical democratic pluralism is related to civic republican, participatory and direct democracy traditions (see Held, 1996). Treating these models as completely separate and distinctive inevitably leads to an element of caricature in my analysis. Many theorists debating democratic political cosmopolitanism draw on a range of models. This is particularly true of those I am labelling 'cosmopolitan democrats', who see their position as synthesizing the strengths of the other two.

5   The distinction between emancipatory and life politics is drawn by Giddens (Giddens, 1991: 209–31). It is a distinction between a politics focused on the acquisition of rights (legal, political and welfare) and a politics centred on what Giddens refers to as moral-existential questions of lifestyle, see discussion of radical democratic pluralism below.

6   There is a massive literature on the relation between capitalism and liberal democracy in practice and principle. The question of the relation between liberal democracy and capitalism is not simply a historical one since answers to it depend very much on the conceptions of liberalism, democracy and capitalism involved. In political theory, a Marxist tradition of thought argues for the necessary connection but ultimate contradiction between the values implicit in liberalism and free market capitalism (see Macpherson, 1962, 1973; Hunt, 1980; Bowles and Gintis, 1986; Nielsen, 1998). The collapse of Soviet socialism has fuelled increased debate on this issue (Fukuyama, 1992; Stephens, 1993; Held, 1993; Parry and Moran, 1994; Whitehead, 1996; Dawisha and Parrott, 1997; *Global Society*, Vol. 12, No. 2, 1998).

7   What is treated here as a perspective on cosmopolitan democracy is part of a broader trend in democratic theory which criticizes liberal democracy and aims to synthesize different elements of Marxist and republican conceptions of democracy with postmodernist and feminist insights into the construction and fluidity of identity. A significant proponent of radical democratic pluralism is Mouffe (1992, 1993). Mouffe argues that liberal political theories which are premised on universal moral values are mistaken about the nature of liberalism. The basis of liberal democracy, according to Mouffe, is not common recognition of universal rights or a principle of autonomy but the project of managing the play of identity and difference within a common polity. Mouffe understands the play of identity and difference in non-essentialist, discursive terms. Thus liberal democracy is not to do with the management of plural identities which are eternally given, but of contingent

and shifting identities which are always capable of reconstruction (Mouffe, 1993: 6; 146). Other recent examples of critical perspectives on liberal democracy which have been influential in debates over democratic political cosmopolitanism include: work on deliberative democracy (Dryzek, 1990; Bohman and Rehg, 1997) and work on democracy and difference in relation to feminism and multiculturalism (Young, 1990; Phillips, 1993; Benhabib, 1996; Willett, 1998). The revival of more classical republican models has also been significant (Barber, 1984; Miller, 1995, 1999; Pettit, 1997).

CONCLUSION

7

International Politics as Ethical Life

This book set out to realize two principal aims: first, to offer an overview of competing schools of thought in normative international theory; secondly, to present an argument for doing normative international theory as *international political theory* rather than as either *international relations theory* (realism) or *applied ethics* (idealism). The latter aim has been accomplished through tracing the implications of critical, post-modernist and feminist responses to mainstream normative international theory and fleshing out those implications with a reading of Hegel and Foucault. The conclusion drawn from this process has been that the fixed, idealized ontologies and abstractly authoritative epistemologies which have traditionally underpinned normative judgement need to be replaced by a concern with the phenomenological adequacy and genea-logical honesty of judgement. Whilst realist and idealist, cosmopolitan and communitarian ethical approaches repeat the same interminable and irresolvable arguments, I have argued for a conception of normative international theory which breaks out of this trap. This conception of international normative theory is, however, both more modest in its ambitions than the approaches of which it is critical and decisively shifts the emphasis as to what counts as the main task of such theory.

The most significant consequence of the re-thinking of how to do normative international theory recommended here is the move away from the articulation and defence of specific prescriptions as the primary aim of such theory. In the past the most important task facing normative international theory has been to argue for or against particular prescriptive positions on issues such as the justice of war, human rights, global distributive justice, rights to national self-determination and so on. This has led to a preoccupation within normative theory with the problem of accounting for the validity of such judgements, which in turn has resulted in the predominance of metatheoretical debate about the merits and demerits of rival moral ontologies and epistemologies. Critical theory, postmodernism and feminism share the insight that these ontologies and epistemologies are highly idealized and, for this reason, that they are unsatisfactory in their accounts both of international politics and the nature and power of normative judgement. In making this point, critical theory, postmodernism and feminism draw attention to the complexity of self- and other-determination in international politics and to the implication of normative judgement within it, thus challenging the idea of the normative theorist as 'moral doctor'. It is this challenge which is taken up in the work of Hegel and Foucault.

To argue that the articulation and defence of specific prescriptive positions is not the main purpose of normative theory is not to argue that argument over normative claims or the settlement of normative questions is not possible. It is, however, to argue that the normative theorist does not have privileged access to the ground of normative truth, which can somehow operate self-evidently as a short cut to universal normative agreement. The ground on which any person may argue for a particular normative prescription is the ground of their 'relative identity' with their ethical life and the principles, values, practices and institutions which it encompasses – in all their complexity and tension. It is therefore the exposition of international politics as ethical life which must be the primary purpose of the normative international theorist, most particularly if that theorist is concerned to defend and articulate particular prescriptive positions. This is because the validity of normative judgements of international politics relies ultimately on the identification of others with the conditions of possibility of the normative position in question. Where there is no such identification, the carrying through of that prescription in practice can only be a matter of coercion. This is why it is of primary importance that normative theorists should focus on the ethical potential of the world as it is rather than take refuge in the idea of truths of reason as the key to progress in history.

Both Hegel and Foucault have been accused of being conservative thinkers, and one can see the reasons for this in the resistance of both theorists to the idea of legislating for the future. However, such a judgement rests, in my view, on a profound misreading of the actual implications of doing normative theory in a Hegelian/Foucauldian mode as opposed to, for instance, a Kantian cosmopolitan approach. The prescriptions generated by the latter position indicate clearly what is wrong with the (second best) world and how it should be changed. However, because these prescriptions are apparently formulated in abstraction from the world to which they are being applied, they actually work to freeze the distinction between morality and politics and therefore leave the world untouched. Either normative theory is condemned as irrelevant to actuality or, given the actual implication of all specific prescriptions in broader political agendas, morality comes to be seen as *realpolitik* in disguise. In contrast to this, normative theory which makes explicit its grounding in the second best world locates itself within the dynamic processes of international politics. The fact that the ethical potential of the world is complex, contradictory and open to a variety of developments only underlines the importance of genealogical honesty on the part of the normative theorist. Such honesty offers no guarantees of the persuasiveness of the position which is being argued for, but it does open up possibilities of recognition and validation which are closed off by normative claims which block the acknowledgement of their own conditioning and politics. At the beginning of this book I stated that normative theory in itself changes nothing, but this is not entirely accurate. To the extent that normative theory presents an evaluation of international politics as ethical life which can be recognized by others, it can be said to be an integral part of the ways in which the world has changed or is changing.

Bibliography

Almond, B. and Hill, D. (eds) (1991) *Applied Philosophy: Morals and Metaphysics in Contemporary Debate*, London: Routledge.

Anscombe, E. (1970) 'War and Murder', in R. Wasserstrom (ed.), *War and Morality*, London: Belmont.

Appadurai, A. (1996) *Modernity at Large: Cultural Dimensions of Globalization*, Minneapolis: University of Minnesota Press.

Archibugi, D. (1995) 'Immanuel Kant, Cosmopolitan Law and Peace', *European Journal of International Relations*, 1: 429–56.

Archibugi, D. and Held, D. (eds) (1995) *Cosmopolitan Democracy*, Cambridge: Polity Press.

Archibugi, D., Held, D. and Koehler, M. (eds) (1998) *Re-imagining Political Community: Studies in Cosmopolitan Democracy*, Cambridge: Polity Press.

Ashley, R. (1988) 'Untying the Sovereign State: A Double Reading of the Anarchy Problematique', *Millennium*, 17 (2): 227–62.

Ashley, R. (1989) 'Living on the Border Lines: Man, Poststructuralism and War', in J. Der Derian and M. Shapiro (eds), *International/Intertextual Relations: Postmodern Readings of World Politics*, Lexington, MA: Lexington Books.

Ashley, R. (1996) 'The Achievements of Post-Structuralism', in S. Smith, K. Booth and M. Zalewski (eds), *International Theory: Positivism and Beyond*, Cambridge: Cambridge University Press.

Ashley, R.K. and Walker, R.J.B. (1990) 'Reading Dissidence/Writing the Discipline: Crisis and the Question of Sovereignty in International Studies', *International Studies Quarterly*, 34 (3): 367–416.

Attfield, R. and Wilkins, B. (eds) (1992) *International Justice and the Third World*, London: Routledge.

Bacchi, C. Lee (1990) *Same Difference: Feminism and Sexual Difference*, St Leonards, NSW: Allen & Unwin.

Balibar, E. (1988) 'Propositions on Citizenship', *Ethics*, 98: 723–30.

Bankowski, Z. and Scott, A. (1996) 'The European Union?', in R. Bellamy (ed.), *Constitutionalism, Democracy and Sovereignty*, Aldershot: Avebury Press.

Barber, B. (1984) *Strong Democracy*, Berkeley, CA: University of California Press.

Barry, B. (1989a) 'Humanity and Justice', in B. Barry (ed.), *Democracy, Power and Justice*, Oxford: Clarendon.

Barry, B. (1989b) 'Justice as Reciprocity', in B. Barry (ed.), *Democracy, Power and Justice*, Oxford: Clarendon.

Bartelson, J. (1995) *A Genealogy of Sovereignty*, Cambridge: Cambridge University Press.

Basu, A. (1995) 'Introduction' to A. Basu (ed.), *The Challenge of Local Feminisms: Women's Movements in Global Perspective*, Boulder, CO: Westview Press.

Bauman, Z. (1995) *Life in Fragments*, Oxford: Blackwell.

Bauman, Z. (1998) *Globalization*, Cambridge: Polity Press.

Bayliss, J. and Smith, S. (eds) (1997) *The Globalization of World Politics*, Oxford: Oxford University Press.

Beetham, D. (1993) 'Liberal Democracy and the Limits of Democratization', in D. Held (ed.), *Prospects for Democracy*, Cambridge: Polity Press.

Beetham, D. (ed.) (1995) *Political Studies Special Issue: Politics and Human Rights*, Vol. 43.

Beiner, R. and Booth, W. (eds) (1993) *Kant and Political Philosophy*, New Haven, CT and London: Yale University Press.

Beitz, C. (1979) *Political Theory and International Relations*, Princeton, NJ: Princeton University Press.

Beitz, C. (1983) 'Cosmopolitan Ideals and National Sentiment', *Journal of Philosophy*, LXXX: 591–600.

Beitz, C. (1994) 'Cosmopolitan Liberalism and the States System', in C. Brown (ed.), *Political Restructuring in Europe: Ethical Perspectives*, London: Routledge.

Bell, D. (1993) *Communitarianism and Its Critics*, Oxford: Clarendon.

Bellamy, R. and Warleigh, A. (1998) 'From an Ethics of Integration to an Ethics of Participation: Citizenship and the Future of the European Union', *Millennium*, 27 (3): 447–70.

Benhabib, S. (1992) *Situating the Self: Gender, Community and Postmodernism in Contemporary Ethics*, Cambridge: Polity Press.

Benhabib, S. (ed.) (1996) *Democracy and Difference: Contesting the Boundaries of the Political*, Princeton, NJ: Princeton University Press.

Benhabib, S. and Dallmyr, F. (eds) (1990) *The Communicative Ethics Controversy*, Cambridge, MA and London: MIT Press.

Bentham, J. (1843) *Principles of International Law*, in J. Bowring (ed.), *The Collected Works of Jeremy Bentham*, Vol. II, Edinburgh: William Tait.

Bentham, J. (1970) *Introduction to the Principles of Morals and Legislation* (J.H. Burns and H.L.A. Hart, eds), London: Methuen.

Bentham, J. (1992) 'Bentham – an International Code', in E. Luard (ed.), *Basic Texts in International Relations*, London, Macmillan. pp. 415–17.

Bobbio, N. (1995) 'Democracy and the International System', in D. Archibugi and D. Held (eds), *Cosmopolitan Democracy*, Cambridge: Polity.

Bock, G. and James, S. (eds) (1992) *Beyond Equality and Difference: Citizenship, Feminist Politics and Female Subjectivity*, London: Routledge.

Bohman, J. (1997) 'The Public Spheres of the World Citizen', in J. Bohman and M. Lutz-Bachmann (eds), *Perpetual Peace: Essays on Kant's Cosmopolitan Ideal*, Cambridge, MA: MIT Press.

Bohman, J. and M. Lutz-Bachmann (eds) (1997) *Perpetual Peace: Essays on Kant's Cosmopolitan Ideal*, Cambridge, MA: MIT Press.

Bohman, J. and Rehg, W. (eds) (1997) *Deliberative Democracy*, Cambridge, MA: MIT Press.

Bontekoe, R. and Stepaniants, M. (eds) (1997) *Justice and Democracy: Cross-Cultural Perspectives*, Honolulu: University of Hawai'i Press.

Boyle, J. (1992) 'Natural Law and International Ethics', in T. Nardin and D. Mapel (eds), *Traditions of International Ethics*, Cambridge: Cambridge University Press.

Bowles, S. and Gintis, H. (1986) *Democracy and Capitalism*, New York: Basic Books.

Brennan, T. (1997) 'At Home in the World: Cosmopolitanism Now', in E. Saïd (ed.), *Convergences: Inventories of the Present*, Cambridge, MA: Harvard University Press.

Brown, C. (1992a) *International Relations Theory: New Normative Approaches*, Hemel Hempstead: Harvester Wheatsheaf.

Brown, C. (1992b) 'Marxism and International Ethics', in T. Nardin and D. Mapel (eds), *Traditions of International Ethics*, Cambridge: Cambridge University Press.

Brown, C. (ed.) (1994a) *Political Restructuring in Europe: Ethical Perspectives*, London: Routledge.

Brown, C. (1994b) 'The Ethics of Political Restructuring in Europe – The Perspective of Constitutive Theory', in C. Brown (ed.), *Political Restructuring in Europe: Ethical Perspectives*, London: Routledge.

Brown, C. (1994c) 'Critical Theory and Postmodernism in International Relations', in A.J.R. Groom and M. Light (eds), *Contemporary International Relations: A Guide to Theory*, London: Pinter.

Brown, C. (1995) 'International Theory and International Society: the viability of the middle way', *Review of International Studies*, 21 (2): 183–96.

Brown, C. (1997a) *Understanding International Relations*, London: Macmillan.

Brown, C. (1997b) 'Theories of International Justice', *British Journal of Political Science*, 27: 273–97.

Brown, M.E., Lynn-Jones, S.M. and Miller, S.E. (eds) (1996) *Debating the Democratic Peace*, Cambridge, MA: MIT Press.

Bubner, R. (1991) 'Hegel and the End of History', *Bulletin of the Hegel Society of Great Britain*, Nos. 23–24: 15–23.

Bull, H. (1995) *The Anarchical Society: A Study of Order in World Politics*, 2nd edn, London: Macmillan.

Bull, H. and Watson, A. (eds) (1984) *The Expansion of International Society*, Oxford: Clarendon Press.

Bull, H., Kingsbury, B. and Roberts, A. (eds) (1990) *Hugo Grotius and International Relations*, Oxford: Clarendon.

Burchill, S. (1996a) 'Liberal Internationalism', in S. Burchill and A. Linklater (eds), *Theories of International Relations*, London: Macmillan.

Burchill, S. (1996b) 'Realism and Neo-Realism', in S. Burchill and A. Linklater (eds), *Theories of International Relations*, London: Macmillan.

Burchill, S. and Linklater, A. (eds) (1996) *Theories of International Relations*, London: Macmillan.

Burnham, P. (1998) 'The *Communist Manifesto* as International Relations Theory', in M. Cowling (ed.), *The Communist Manifesto: New Interpretations*, Edinburgh: Edinburgh University Press.

Buzan, B., Held, D. and MacGrew, A. (1998) 'Realism versus Cosmopolitanism: A Debate', *Review of International Studies*, 24 (3): 387–98.

Camilleri, J.A. and Falk, J. (1992) *The End of Sovereignty?*, Aldershot: Edward Elgar.

Campbell, D. (1998a) 'Why Fight: Humanitarianism, Principles and Post-structuralism', *Millennium*, 27 (3): 497–521.

Campbell, D. (1998b) *National Deconstruction: Violence, Identity and Justice in Bosnia*, Minneapolis and London: University of Minnesota Press.

Campbell, D. and Dillon, M. (eds) (1993) *The Political Subject of Violence*, Manchester: Manchester University Press.

Caney, S. (1996) 'Individuals, Nations and Obligations', in S. Caney, D. George and P. Jones (eds), *National Rights, International Obligations*, Boulder, CO: Westview Press.

Caney, S., George, D. and Jones, P. (eds) (1996) *National Rights, International Obligations*, Boulder, CO: Westview Press.

Canovan, M. (1996a) *Nationhood and Political Theory*, Cheltenham: Edward Elgar.

Canovan, M. (1996b) 'The Skeleton in the Cupboard: Nationhood, Patriotism and Limited Loyalties', in S. Caney, D. George and P. Jones (eds), *National Rights, International Obligations*, Boulder, CO: Westview Press.

Carr, E.H. (1946) *The Twenty Years' Crisis*, London: Macmillan.

Charles, N. and Hintjens, H. (1998) *Gender, Ethnicity and Political Ideologies*, London: Routledge.

Charvet, J. (1996) 'What Is Nationality, and Is there a Moral Right to National Self-Determination', in S. Caney, D. George and P. Jones (eds), *National Rights, International Obligations*, Boulder, CO: Westview Press.

Clancy, W. (ed.) (1961) *The Moral Dilemma of Nuclear Weapons*, New York.

Clark, I. (1990) *Waging War: A Philosophical Introduction*, Oxford: Clarendon Press.

Clark, I. (1997) *Globalization and Fragmentation: International Relations in the Twentieth Century*, Oxford: Oxford University Press.

Clark, I. (1998) 'Beyond the Great Divide: Globalization and the Theory of International Relations', *Review of International Studies*, 24 (4): 479–98.

Cohn, C. (1989) 'Sex and Death in the Rational World of Defense Intellectuals', in M. Malson, J.F. O'Barr, S. Westphal and M. Wyer (eds), *Feminist Theory in Practice and Process*, Chicago and London: Chicago University Press.

Copp, D., Hampton, J. and Roemer, J.E. (eds) (1993) *The Idea of Democracy*, Cambridge: Cambridge University Press.

Cowling, M. (ed.) (1998) *The Communist Manifesto: New Interpretations*, Edinburgh: Edinburgh University Press.

Cox, R. (1996a) 'On Thinking About Future World Order', in R. Cox and T. Sinclair, *Approaches to World Order*, Cambridge: Cambridge University Press.

Cox, R. (1996b) 'Social Forces, States and World Orders: Beyond International

Relations Theory', in R. Cox and T. Sinclair, *Approaches to World Order*, Cambridge: Cambridge University Press.

Cox, R. (1996c) 'Gramsci, Hegemony, and International Relations: an Essay in Method', in R. Cox and T. Sinclair, *Approaches to World Order*, Cambridge: Cambridge University Press.

Cox, R. and Sinclair, T. (1996) *Approaches to World Order*, Cambridge: Cambridge University Press.

Cranston, M. (1973) *What Are Human Rights?*, New York: Taplinger.

Cutler, C. (1991) 'The "Grotian" Tradition in International Relations', *Review of International Studies*, 17 (1): 41–65.

Dallmyr, F.R. (1993) *G.W.F. Hegel: Modernity and Politics*, London: Sage.

Dawisha, K. and Parrott, B. (eds) (1997) *Democratization and Authoritarianism in Postcommunist Societies, Vols 1–4*, Cambridge: Cambridge University Press.

Der Derian, J. (1987) *On Diplomacy*, Oxford: Blackwell.

Der Derian, J. and Shapiro, M. (eds) (1989) *International/Intertextual Relations: Postmodern Readings of World Politics*, Lexington, MA: Lexington Books.

Devetak, R. (1996a) 'Critical Theory', in S. Burchill and A. Linklater (eds), *Theories of International Relations*, London: Macmillan.

Devetak, R. (1996b) 'Postmodernism', in S. Burchill and A. Linklater (eds), *Theories of International Relations*, London: Macmillan.

Dietz, M. (1985) 'Citizenship with a Feminist Face: The Problem with Maternal Thinking', *Political Theory*, 13 (1): 19–37.

Diez, T. (1997) 'International Ethics and European Integration: Federal State or Network Horizon?', *Alternatives*, 22 (3): 287–312.

Dillon, M. (1998) 'Criminalising Social and Political Violence Internationally', *Millennium*, 27 (3): 543–67.

Donelan, M. (1990) *Elements of International Political Theory*, Oxford: Clarendon Press.

Donnelly, J. (1989) *Universal Human Rights in Theory and Practice*, Ithaca, NY: Cornell University Press.

Donnelly, J. (1992) 'Twentieth-Century Realism', in T. Nardin and D. Mapel (eds), *Traditions of International Ethics*, Cambridge: Cambridge University Press.

Donnelly, J. (1993) *International Human Rights*, Boulder, CO: Westview Press.

Dower, N. (1998) *World Ethics: The New Agenda*, Edinburgh: Edinburgh University Press.

Doyle, M. (1993) 'Liberalism and International Relations', in R. Beiner and W. Booth (eds), *Kant and Political Philosophy*, New Haven, CT and London: Yale University Press.

Dryzek, J.S. (1990) *Discursive Democracy*, Cambridge: Cambridge University Press.

Dryzek, J.S. (1995) 'Political and Ecological Communication', *Environmental Politics*, 4 (4): 13–30.

Dunne, T. (1997) 'Liberalism', in J. Bayliss and S. Smith (eds), *The Globalization of World Politics*, Oxford: Oxford University Press.

Dworkin, R. (1985) *A Matter of Principle*, Oxford: Oxford University Press.

Ellis, A. (1992) 'Utilitarianism and International Ethics', in T. Nardin and D. Mapel (eds), *Traditions of International Ethics*, Cambridge: Cambridge University Press.

Elshtain, J.B. (1981) *Public Man/Private Woman: Women in Social and Political Thought*, Princeton, NJ: Princeton University Press.

Elshtain, J.B. (ed.) (1982) *The Family in Political Thought*, London: Harvester Press.

Elshtain, J.B. (1985) 'Reflections on War and Political Discourse', *Political Theory*, 13 (1): 39–57.

Elshtain, J.B. (1987) *Women and War*, New York: Basic Books.

Elshtain, J.B. (ed.) (1992a) *Just War Theory*, Oxford: Blackwell.

Elshtain, J.B. (1992b) 'The Power and Powerlessness of Women', in G. Bock and S. James (eds), *Beyond Equality and Difference: Citizenship, Feminist Politics and Female Subjectivity*, London: Routledge.

Enloe, C. (1989) *Bananas, Beaches and Bases*, London: Pandora.

Falk, R. (1994) 'The Making of Global Citizenship', in Bart Van Steenbergen (ed.), *The Condition of Citizenship*, London: Sage.

Falk, R. (1995) *On Humane Governance*, Cambridge: Polity.

Forbes, I. and Hoffman, M. (eds) (1993) *Political Theory, International Relations and the Ethics of Intervention*, London: Macmillan.

Forde, S. (1992) 'Classical Realism', in T. Nardin and D. Mapel (eds), *Traditions of International Ethics*, Cambridge: Cambridge University Press.

Forster, M.N. (1998) *Hegel's Idea of a Phenomenology of Spirit*, Chicago: Chicago University Press.

Foucault, M. (1977) *Discipline and Punish*, Harmondsworth: Penguin.

Foucault, M. (1980) *Power/Knowledge* (C. Gordon, ed.), London: Harvester Wheatsheaf.

Foucault, M. (1981) 'The Order of Discourse', in R. Young (ed.), *Untying the Text: A Poststructuralist Reader*, London: Routledge & Kegan Paul.

Foucault, M. (1982) 'The Subject and Power', in H. Dreyfus and P. Rabinow (eds), *Michel Foucault: Beyond Structuralism and Hermeneutics*, London: Harvester Wheatsheaf.

Foucault, M. (1984) *The Foucault Reader* (P. Rabinow, ed.), Harmondsworth: Penguin.

Foucault, M. (1988) *Politics, Philosophy, Culture* (L.D. Kritzman, ed.), London: Routledge.

Foucault, M. (1990) *The History of Sexuality*, Vol. 1, Harmondsworth: Penguin.

Foucault, M. (1991) *Remarks On Marx*, New York: Semiotext(e).

Franke, M. (1995), 'Immanuel Kant and the (Im)Possibility of International Relations', *Alternatives*, 20 (3): 279–322.

Frankel, B. (ed.) (1996a) *Roots of Realism*, London: Frank Cass.

Frankel, B. (ed.) (1996b) *Realism: Restatements and Renewal*, London: Frank Cass.

Fraser, N. (1989) *Unruly Practices: Power, Discourse and Gender in Contemporary Social Theory*, Cambridge: Polity Press.

Frost, M. (1996) *Ethics in International Relations: a Constitutive Theory*, Cambridge: Cambridge University Press.

Fukuyama, F. (1992) *The End of History and the Last Man*, London: Penguin.

Gaddis, J.L. (1992–3) 'International Relations Theory and the End of the Cold War', *International Security*, 17 (3): 5–58.

George, D. (1996) 'National Identity and National Self-Determination', in S. Caney, D. George and P. Jones (eds), *National Rights, International Obligations*, Boulder, CO: Westview Press.

Giddens, A. (1991) *Modernity and Self-Identity*, Cambridge: Polity Press.

Giddens, A. (1994) *Beyond Left and Right*, Cambridge: Polity Press.

Gilbert, P. (1996) 'National Obligations: Political, Cultural or Societal?', in S. Caney, D. George and P. Jones (eds), *National Rights, International Obligations*, Boulder, CO: Westview Press.

Gilbert, P. (1998) *The Philosophy of Nationalism*, Boulder, CO: Westview Press.

Gilligan, C. (1982) *In A Different Voice: Psychological Theory and Women's Development*, Cambridge, MA and London: Harvard University Press.

Global Society (1998) *Special Issue: Democracy and Civil Society*, 12 (2): 155–271.

Grant, R. (1991) 'The Sources of Gender Bias in International Relations Theory', in R. Grant and K. Newland (eds), *Gender as International Relations*, Milton Keynes: Open University Press.

Grant, R. and Newland, K. (eds) (1991) *Gender and International Relations*, Milton Keynes: Open University Press.

Griffiths, M. (1992) *Realism, Idealism and International Politics*, London: Routledge.

Groom, A.J.R. and Light, M. (eds) (1994) *Contemporary International Relations: A Guide to Theory*, London: Pinter.

Gunew, Sneja (ed.) (1991) *A Reader in Feminist Knowledge*, London: Routledge.

Habermas, J. (1979) *Communication and the Evolution of Society*, Boston, MA: Beacon Press.

Habermas, J. (1984) *The Theory of Communicative Action*, Vol. 1, Boston, MA: Beacon Press.

Habermas, J. (1987) *The Theory of Communicative Action*, Vol. 2, Boston, MA: Beacon Press.

Habermas, J. (1990a) *Moral Consciousness and Communicative Action*, Cambridge: Polity Press.

Habermas, J. (1990b) *The Philosophical Discourse of Modernity*, Cambridge: Polity Press.

Habermas, J. (1992) 'Citizenship and National Identity: Some Reflections on the Future of Europe', *Praxis International*, 12 (1): 1–19.

Habermas, J. (1994) *The Past as Future*, Cambridge: Polity Press.

Habermas, J. (1996) *Between Facts and Norms: Contributions to a Discourse Theory of Law and Democracy*, Cambridge: Polity Press.

Habermas, J. (1997) 'Kant's Idea of Perpetual Peace, with the Benefit of Two Hundred Years' Hindsight', in J. Bohman and M. Lutz-Bachmann (eds), *Perpetual Peace: Essays on Kant's Cosmopolitan Ideal*, Cambridge, MA: MIT Press.

Habermas, J. (1998) 'Remarks on Legitimation through Human Rights', *Philosophy and Social Criticism*, 24 (2/3): 157–71.

Halliday, F. (1991) 'International Relations: Is there a New Agenda?', *Millennium*, 20 (1): 57–72.

Hardimon, M.O. (1994) *Hegel's Social Philosophy: The Project of Reconciliation*, Cambridge: Cambridge University Press.

Hardin, G. (1977) 'Lifeboat Ethics: The Case Against Helping the Poor', in W. Aiken and H. Lafollette (eds), *World Hunger and Moral Obligation*, Englewood Cliffs, NJ: Prentice Hall.

Hardin, R., Mearsheimer, J.J., Dworkin, G. and Goodin, R. (eds) (1985) *Nuclear Deterrence: Ethics and Strategy*, Chicago: Chicago University Press.

Harris, A. and King, Y. (1989) *Rocking the Ship of State: Towards a Feminist Peace Politics*, Boulder, CO: Westview Press.

Harris, E.E. (1980) 'Hegel's Theory of Sovereignty, International Relations and War', in D.P. Verene (ed.), *Hegel's Social and Political Thought*, Atlantic Highlands, NJ: Humanities Press.

Hartsock, N. (1987) 'The Feminist Standpoint: Developing the Ground for a Specifically Feminist Historical Materialism', in S. Harding (ed.), *Feminism and Methodology*, Milton Keynes: Open University Press.

Heater, D. (1996) *World Citizenship and Government: Cosmopolitan Ideas in the History of Political Thought*, Basingstoke: Macmillan.

Hegel, G.W.F. (1969) *Science of Logic*, Atlantic Highlands, NJ: Humanities Press.

Hegel, G.W.F. (1970) *Philosophy of Nature*, Oxford: Clarendon Press.

Hegel, G.W.F. (1971) *Philosophy of Mind*, Oxford: Clarendon Press.

Hegel, G.W.F. (1975) *Lectures on the Philosophy of World History: Introduction*, Cambridge: Cambridge University Press.

Hegel, G.W.F. (1977) *Phenomenology of Spirit*, Oxford: Oxford University Press.

Hegel, G.W.F. (1991a) *Elements of the Philosophy of Right*, Cambridge: Cambridge University Press.

Hegel, G.W.F. (1991b) *Encyclopaedia of Logic*, Indianapolis: Hackett.

Held, D. (ed.) (1993) *Prospects for Democracy*, Cambridge: Polity Press.

Held, D. (1995) *Democracy and the Global Order: From the Modern State to Cosmopolitan Governance*, Cambridge: Polity Press.

Held, D. (1996) *Models of Democracy*, Cambridge: Polity Press.

Hirsch, M. and Fox-Keller, E. (eds) (1990) *Conflicts in Feminism*, New York and London: Routledge.

Hirst, P. and Thompson, G. (1996) *Globalization in Question*, Cambridge: Polity Press.

Hobbes, T. (1991) *Leviathan*, Cambridge: Cambridge University Press.

Hockaday, A. (1987) 'Warfare Without War: Intervention in the International System: Observations on Ian Forbes's Paper', *Arms Control*, 8: 68–72.

Hoffman, M. (1987) 'Critical Theory and the Inter-Paradigm Debate', *Millennium*, 16 (2): 231–49.

Hoffman, M. (1988) 'Conversations on Critical International Relations Theory', *Millennium*, 17 (1): 91–5.

Hoffman, M. (1993) 'Agency, Identity and Intervention', in I. Forbes and M. Hoffman (eds), *Political Theory, International Relations and the Ethics of Intervention*, London: Macmillan.

Hoffmann, S. (1977) 'An American Social Science: International Relations', *Daedalus*, 106: 41–61.

Holmes, Robert (1989) *On War and Morality*, Princeton, NJ: Princeton University Press.

Honneth, A. (1995) *The Struggle for Recognition: The Moral Grammar of Social Conflicts*, Cambridge: Polity Press.

Hoogvelt, A. (ed.) (1997) *Globalisation and the Postcolonial World*, London: Macmillan.

Houlgate, S. (1991) *Freedom, Truth and History: An Introduction to Hegel's Philosophy*, London: Routledge.

Hunt, A. (ed.) (1980) *Marxism and Democracy*, London: Lawrence & Wishart.

Huntington, S.N. (1993) 'The Clash of Civilizations?', *Foreign Affairs*, 72 (3): 22–47.

Huntington, S.N. (1996), 'The West Unique, not Universal', *Foreign Affairs*, 75 (6): 28–46.

Hutchings, K. (1991) 'Perpetual War/Perpetual Peace: Kant, Hegel and the End of History', *Bulletin of the Hegel Society of Great Britain*, 23–24: 39–50.

Hutchings, K. (1992) 'The Possibility of Judgment: Moralizing and Theorizing in International Relations', *Review of International Studies*, 18: 51–62.

Hutchings, K. (1994a) 'Borderline Ethics: Feminist Morality and International Relations', *Paradigms: the Kent Journal of International Relations* (now *Global Society*), 8 (1): 23–35.

Hutchings, K. (1994b) 'The Personal is International: Feminist Epistemology and the Case of International Relations', in K. Lennon and M. Whitford (eds), *Knowing the Difference: Feminist Perspectives in Epistemology*, London: Routledge.

Hutchings, K. (1996a) 'The Idea of International Citizenship', in B. Holden (ed.), *The Ethical Dimensions of Global Change*, London: Macmillan.

Hutchings, K. (1996b) *Kant, Critique and Politics*, London: Routledge.

Hutchings, K. (1997) 'Foucault and International Relations Theory', in M. Lloyd and A. Thacker (eds), *The Impact of Michel Foucault on the Social Sciences and Humanities*, London: Macmillan.

Hutchings, K. (1999) 'Feminist Politics and Cosmopolitan Citizenship', in K. Hutchings and R. Dannreuther (eds), *Cosmopolitan Citizenship*, London: Macmillan.

Hutchings, K. and Dannreuther, R. (eds) (1999) *Cosmopolitan Citizenship*, London: Macmillan.

Jabri, V. (1998) 'Restyling the Subject of Responsibility in International Relations', *Millennium*, 27 (3): 591–611.

Jackson, R. (1996) 'Is There a Classical International Theory?', in S. Smith, K. Booth and M. Zalewski (eds), *International Theory: Positivism and Beyond*, Cambridge: Cambridge University Press.

Jad, I. (1995) 'Claiming Feminism, Claiming Nationalism: Women's Activism in the Occupied Territories', in A. Basu (ed.), *The Challenge of Local Feminisms: Women's Movements in Global Perspective*, Boulder, CO: Westview Press.

Jagentowicz Mills, P. (ed.) (1996) *Feminist Interpretations of G.W.F. Hegel*, Philadelphia, PA: Penn State Press.

Jahn, B. (1998) 'One Step Forward, Two Steps Back: Critical Theory as the Latest Edition of Liberal Idealism', *Millennium*, 27 (3): 613–41.

Kaldor, M. (1995) 'European Institutions, Nation-States and Nationalism', in D. Archibugi and D. Held (eds), *Cosmopolitan Democracy*, Cambridge: Polity Press.

Kant, I. (1969) *Foundations of the Metaphysics of Morals* (P. Wolff, ed.), Indianapolis: Bobbs–Merrill.

Kant, I. (1991a) *Political Writings* (H. Reiss, ed.), Cambridge: Cambridge University Press.

Kant, I. (1991b) *The Metaphysics of Morals*, Cambridge: Cambridge University Press.

Kenny, A. (1985) *The Logic of Deterrence*, London: Firethorne.

Keohane, R. (1988) 'International Institutions: Two Approaches', *International Studies Quarterly*, 32 (4): 379–96.

Kingsbury, B. and Roberts, A. (1990) 'Introduction: Grotian Thought in International Relations', in H. Bull, B. Kingsbury and A. Roberts (eds), *Hugo Grotius and International Relations*, Oxford: Clarendon Press.

Kojève, A. (1980) *Introduction to the Reading of Hegel*, Ithaca, NJ and London: Cornell University Press.

Kratochwil, F.V. (1989) *Rules, Norms and Decisions: On the Conditions of Practical and Legal Reasoning in International Relations and Domestic Affairs*, Cambridge: Cambridge University Press.

Krishna, S. (1993) 'The Importance of Being Ironic: A Postcolonial View on Critical International Relations Theory', *Alternatives*, 18 (3): 285–417.

Krombach, H. (1991) *Hegelian Reflections on the Idea of Nuclear War*, London: Macmillan.

Kymlicka, W. (1995) *Multicultural Citizenship*, Oxford: Clarendon Press.

Lash, S. and Urry, J. (1987) *The End of Organized Capitalism*, Cambridge: Polity Press.

Lash, S. and Urry, J. (1994) *Economies of Signs and Space*, London: Sage.

Lawson, S. (1998) 'Democracy and the Problem of Cultural Relativism: Normative Issue for International Politics', *Global Society*, 12 (2): 251–70.

Linklater, A. (1982) *Men and Citizens*, London: Macmillan.

Linklater, A. (1990) *Beyond Realism and Marxism*, London: Macmillan.

Linklater, A. (1992a) 'The Question of the Next Stage in International Relations Theory', *Millennium*, 21 (1): 77–100.

Linklater, A. (1992b) 'What is a Good International Citizen?', in P. Keal (ed.), *Ethics and Foreign Policy*, St Leonards, NSW: Allen & Unwin.

Linklater, A. (1996a) 'Rationalism', in S. Burchill and A. Linklater (eds), *Theories of International Relations*, London: Macmillan.

Linklater, A. (1996b) 'Marxism', in S. Burchill and A. Linklater (eds), *Theories of International Relations*, London: Macmillan.

Linklater, A. (1996c) 'The Achievements of Critical Theory', in S. Smith, K. Booth and M. Zalewski (eds), *International Theory: Positivism and Beyond*, Cambridge: Cambridge University Press.

Linklater, A. (1998) *The Transformation of Political Community*, Cambridge: Polity Press.

Linklater, A. (1999) 'Cosmopolitan Citizenship', in K. Hutchings and R. Dannreuther (eds), *Cosmopolitan Citizenship*, London: Macmillan.

Lipschutz, R.D. and Conca, K. (eds) (1994) *The State and Social Power in Global Environmental Politics*, New York: Columbia University Press.

Little, R. and Smith, M. (eds) (1991) *Perspectives On World Politics*, London: Routledge.

Locke, J. (1988) *Two Treatises of Government*, Cambridge: Cambridge University Press.

MacCarthy, L. (1993) 'International Anarchy, Realism and Non-Intervention', in I. Forbes and M. Hoffman (eds), *Political Theory, International Relations and the Ethics of Intervention*, London: Macmillan.

MacCormick, N. (1996) 'What Place for Nationalism in the Modern World?', in S. Caney, D. George and P. Jones (eds), *National Rights, International Obligations*, Boulder, CO: Westview Press.

McGrew, A. (1997) *The Transformation of Democracy? Globalization and Territorial Democracy*, Milton Keynes: Polity & Open University Press.

MacIntyre, A. (1981) *After Virtue*, London: Duckworth.

MacKinnon, C. (1993) 'Crimes of War, Crimes of Peace', in S. Shute and S. Hurley (eds), *On Human Rights: The Oxford Amnesty Lectures 1993*, New York: Basic Books.

Macmillan, J. (1998) '"The Power of the Pen": Liberalism's Ethical Dynamic and World Politics', *Millennium*, 27 (3): 643–67.

McNay, L. (1992) *Foucault and Feminism*, Cambridge: Polity Press.

Macpherson, C.B. (1962) *The Political Theory of Possessive Individualism*, Oxford: Oxford University Press.

Macpherson, C.B. (1973) *Democratic Theory: Essays in Retrieval*, Oxford: Clarendon Press.

Mapel, D. (1992) 'The Contractarian Tradition and International Ethics', in T. Nardin and D. Mapel (eds), *Traditions of International Ethics*, Cambridge: Cambridge University Press.

Marchand, M.H. and Papart, J.L. (eds) (1995) *Feminism, Postmodernism, Development*, London: Routledge.

Marx, K. (1975) *Early Writings*, Harmondsworth: Penguin.

Marx, K. (1976) *Capital*, Vol. I, Harmondsworth: Penguin.

Marx. K. and Engels, F. (1970) *The German Ideology*, London: Lawrence & Wishart.

Marx, K. and Engels, F. (1998) 'Manifesto of the Communist Party', in M. Cowling (ed.), *The Communist Manifesto: New Interpretations*, Edinburgh: Edinburgh University Press.

Meehan, E. (1993) *Citizenship and the European Community*, London: Sage.

Mill, J.S. (1962) *Utilitarianism* (M. Warnock, ed.), London: Fontana.

Mill, J.S. (1992) 'The Right to Intervene Against An Oppressive Alien Government', in E. Luard (ed.), *Basic Texts in International Relations*, London: Macmillan.

Miller, D. (1995) *On Nationality*, Oxford: Clarendon Press.

Miller, D. (1999) 'Bounded Citizenship', in K. Hutchings and D. Dannreuther (eds), *Cosmopolitan Citizenship*, London: Macmillan.

Mittelman, J.H. (1998) 'Coxian Historicism as an Alternative Perspective in International Studies', *Alternatives*, 23: 63–92.

Mohanty, C., Russo, A. and Torres, L. (eds) (1991) *Third World Women and the Politics of Feminism*, Bloomington and Indianapolis: Indiana University Press.

Morgenthau, H. (1958) *Dilemmas of Politics*, Chicago: University of Chicago Press.

Morgenthau, H. (1985) *Politics Among Nations: The Struggle for Power and Peace*, 6th edn, New York: Arnold Knopf.

Mouffe, C. (ed.) (1992) *Dimensions of Radical Democracy*, London: Verso.

Mouffe, C. (1993) *The Return of the Political*, London: Verso.

Mulhall, S. and Swift, A. (1996) *Liberals and Communitarians*, 2nd edn, Oxford: Blackwell.

Murray, A.J.H. (1997) *Reconstructing Realism: Between Power Politics and Cosmopolitan Ethics*, Edinburgh: Keele University Press.

Nardin, T. (1983) *Law, Morality and the Relations of States*, Princeton, NJ: Princeton University Press.

Nardin, T. and Mapel, D. (eds) (1992a) *Traditions of International Ethics*, Cambridge: Cambridge University Press.

Nardin, T. and Mapel, D. (1992b) 'Convergence and Divergence in International Ethics', in T. Nardin and D. Mapel (eds), *Traditions of International Ethics*, Cambridge: Cambridge University Press.

Neumann, I.B. and Waever, O. (eds) (1997) *The Future of International Relations*, London: Routledge.

Neumann, I.B. and Welsh, J.M. (1991) 'The Other in European Self-Definition: an addendum to the literature on international society', *Review of International Studies*, 17 (4): 327–48.

Nicholson, L. (ed.) (1990) *Feminism/Postmodernism*, London: Routledge.

Nickel, J.W. (1987) *Making Sense of Human Rights*, Berkeley, CA: University of California Press.

Niebuhr, R. (1946) *Moral Man and Immoral Society*, London and New York: Charles Scribner's Sons.

Niebuhr, R. (1959) *Nations and Empires: Recurring Patterns in the Political Order*, London: Faber & Faber.

Nielsen, K. (1998) 'Is Global Justice Impossible', *Res Publica*, IV (2): 131–66.

Norman, R. (1995) *Ethics, Killing and War*, Cambridge: Cambridge University Press.

Nussbaum, M.C. (1996), 'Patriotism and Cosmopolitanism', in M.C. Nussbaum (ed.), *For Love of Country: Debating the Limits of Patriotism*, Boston, MA: Beacon Press.

Nussbaum, M.C. and Sen, A. (1993a) *The Quality of Life*, Oxford: Clarendon Press.

Nussbaum, M.C. and Sen, A. (1993b) 'Introduction', in M.C. Nussbaum and A. Sen (eds), *The Quality of Life*, Oxford: Clarendon Press.

Nussbaum, M.C. with respondents and J.C. Cohen (ed.) (1996) *For Love of Country: Debating the Limits of Patriotism*, Boston, MA: Beacon Press.

O'Neill, O. (1989a) *Constructions of Reason*, Cambridge: Cambridge University Press.

O'Neill, O. (1989b) *Faces of Hunger – An Essay on Poverty, Justice and Development*, London: Allen & Unwin.

O'Neill, O. (1991) 'Transnational Justice', in D. Held (ed.), *Political Theory Today*, Cambridge: Polity Press.

O'Neill, O. (1992) 'Commentary: Magic Associations and Imperfect People', in B. Barry and R. Goodin (eds), *Free Movement: Ethical Issues in the Transnational Migration of People and Money*, London: Harvester Wheatsheaf.

Onuf, N.G. (1989) *World of our Making: Rules and Rule in Social Theory and International Relations*, Columbia, SC: University of South Carolina Press.

Parekh, B. (1992) 'The Cultural Particularity of Liberal Democracy', *Political Studies*, 40: 160–75.

Parry, G. and Moran, M. (eds) (1994) *Democracy and Democratization*, London: Routledge.

Pateman, C. (1988) *The Sexual Contract*, Cambridge, Polity Press.

Pateman, C. (1992) 'Equality, Difference, Subordination: the politics of motherhood and women's citizenship', in G. Bock and S. James (eds), *Beyond Equality and Difference: Citizenship, Feminist Politics and Female Subjectivity*, London: Routledge.

Paul, E.F., Miller, F.D., Paul, J. and Ahrens, J. (eds) (1986) *Nuclear Rights/Nuclear Wrongs*, Oxford: Blackwell.

Paul, E.F., Miller, F.D. and Paul, J. (eds) (1996) *The Communitarian Challenge to Liberalism*, Cambridge: Cambridge University Press.

Pelczynski, Z.A. (ed.) (1984) *The State and Civil Society: Studies in Hegel's Political Philosophy*, Cambridge: Cambridge University Press.

Pettit, P. (1997) *Republicanism: A Theory of Freedom and Government*, Oxford: Clarendon Press.

Pettman, J.J. (1996) *Worlding Women: A Feminist International Politics*, London: Routledge.

Phillips, A. (1993) *Democracy and Difference*, Cambridge: Polity Press.

Pinkard, T. (1994) *Hegel's Phenomenology: The Sociality of Reason*, Cambridge: Cambridge University Press.

Pogge, T.W. (1994) 'Cosmopolitanism and Sovereignty', in C. Brown (ed.), *Political Restructuring in Europe: Ethical Perspectives*, London: Routledge.

Pompa, L. (1991) 'Philosophical History and the End of History', *Bulletin of the Hegel Society of Great Britain*, Nos. 23–24: 24–38.

Popper, K. (1944–5) *The Open Society and Its Enemies*, Vol. 2, London: Routledge & Kegan Paul.

Potter, D., Goldblatt, D., Kiloh, M. and Lewis, P. (1997) *Democratization*, Milton Keynes: Polity and Open University Press.

Ramsey, P. (1961) *War and the Christian Conscience*, Durham, NC: Duke University Press.

Ramsey, P. (1968) *The Just War*, New York: Charles Scribner's Sons.

Rawls, J. (1972) *A Theory of Justice*, Oxford: Oxford University Press.

Rawls, J. (1993) 'The Law of Peoples', in S. Shute and S. Hurley (eds), *On Human Rights: The Oxford Amnesty Lectures 1993*, New York: Basic Books.

Raz, J. (1986) *The Morality of Freedom*, Oxford: Oxford University Press.

Rengger, N. (1988) 'Going Critical? A Response to Hoffman', *Millennium*, 17 (1): 81–9.

Rengger, N. (1993) 'Contextuality, Interdependence and the Ethics of Intervention', in I. Forbes and M. Hoffman (eds), *Political Theory, International Relations and the Ethics of Intervention*, London: Macmillan.

Renteln, A. (1990) *International Human Rights: Universalism versus Relativism*, London: Sage.

Review of International Studies (1999) Forum on A. Linklater's *Transformation of Political Community*, 25: 139–75.

Roberson, B. (ed.) (1998) *International Society and the Development of International Relations Theory*, London and Washington, DC: Pinter.

Rorty, R. (1993) 'Human Rights, Rationality and Sentimentality', in S. Shute and S. Hurley (eds), *On Human Rights: The Oxford Amnesty Lectures 1993*, New York: Basic Books.

Rose, G. (1981) *Hegel Contra Sociology*, London: Athlone.

Rothstein, R.L. (1991) 'On the Costs of Realism', in R. Little and M. Smith (eds), *Perspectives on World Politics*, London: Routledge.

Rousseau, J-J. (1973) *The Social Contract and Discourses*, New York: Dent Dutton.

Ruddick, S. (1990) *Maternal Thinking: Towards a Politics of Peace*, London: Women's Press.

Russett, B. (1993) *Grasping the Democratic Peace*, Princeton, NJ: Princeton University Press.

Sandel, M.J. (1982) *Liberalism and the Limits of Justice*, Cambridge: Cambridge University Press.

Scholte, J.A. (1993) *International Relations of Social Change*, Buckingham: Open University Press.

Shanley, M.L. and Pateman, C. (1991) *Feminist Interpretations of Political Theory*, Cambridge: Polity Press.

Shaw, M. (1994) *Global Society and International Relations*, Cambridge: Polity Press.

Shue, H. (1996) *Basic Rights: Subsistence, Affluence and US Foreign Policy*, 2nd edn, Princeton, NJ: Princeton University Press.

Shute, S. and Hurley, S. (eds) (1993) *On Human Rights: The Oxford Amnesty Lectures 1993*, New York: Basic Books.

Singer, P. (1972) 'Famine, Affluence and Morality', *Philosophy and Public Affairs*, 1: 229–43.

Smith, H. (1994) 'Marxism and International Relations Theory', in A.J.R. Groom and M. Light (eds), *Contemporary International Relations: A Guide to Theory*, London: Pinter.

Smith, M.J. (1992) 'Liberalism and International Reform', in T. Nardin and D. Mapel (eds), *Traditions of International Ethics*, Cambridge: Cambridge University Press.

Smith, S.B. (1989) *Hegel's Critique of Liberalism*, Chicago: University of Chicago Press.

Smith, S., Booth, K. and Zalewski, M. (eds) (1996) *International Theory: Positivism and Beyond*, Cambridge: Cambridge University Press.

Spegele, R.D. (1996) *Political Realism in International Theory*, Cambridge: Cambridge University Press.

Spike Peterson, V. and Sisson-Runyan, A. (1993) *Global Gender Issues*, Boulder, CO: Westview Press.

Spike Peterson (1990) 'Whose Rights? A Critique of the "Givens" in Human Rights Discourse', *Alternatives*, XV: 303–44.

Spike Peterson, V. (ed.) (1992) *Gendered States: Feminist (Re)Visions of International Relations Theory*, Boulder, CO: Lynne Reiner.

Spirtas, M. (1996) 'A House Divided: Tragedy and Evil in Realist Theory', in B. Frankel (ed.), *Realism: Restatements and Renewal*, London: Frank Cass.

Spybey, T. (1996) *Globalization and World Society*, Cambridge: Polity Press.

Steiner, H. (1992) 'Libertarianism and the Transnational Migration of People', in B. Barry and R. Goodin (eds), *Free Movement: Ethical Issues in the Transnational Migration of People and Money*, London: Harvester Wheatsheaf.

Steiner, H. (1996) 'Territorial Justice', in S. Caney, D. George and P. Jones (eds), *National Rights, International Obligations*, Boulder, CO: Westview Press.

Steans, J. (1998) *Gender and International Relations*, Cambridge: Polity Press.

Stephens, J.D. (1993) 'Capitalist Development and Democracy', in D. Copp, J. Hampton and J.E. Roemer (eds), *The Idea of Democracy*, Cambridge: Cambridge University Press.

Stewart, J. (ed.) (1996) *The Hegel Myths and Legends*, Evanston, IL: Northwestern University Press.

Stewart, J. (ed.) (1998) *The Phenomenology of Spirit Reader*, Albany, NY: State University of New York Press.

Sylvester, C. (1994) *Feminist Theory and International Relations in a Postmodern Era*, Cambridge: Cambridge University Press.

Sylvester, C. (1996) 'The Contributions of Feminist Theory to International Relations', in S. Smith, K. Booth and M. Zalewski (eds), *International Theory: Positivism and Beyond*, Cambridge: Cambridge University Press.

Tamir, Y. (1993) *Liberal Nationalism*, Princeton, NJ: Princeton University Press.

Tamir, Y. (1996) 'Reconstructing the Landscape of Imagination', in S. Caney, D. George and P. Jones (eds), *National Rights, International Obligations*, Boulder, CO: Westview Press.

Taylor, C. (1984) 'Foucault on Freedom and Truth', *Political Theory*, 12 (2): 152–83.

Taylor, C. (1990) *Sources of the Self*, Cambridge: Cambridge University Press.

Taylor, C. (1994) 'The Politics of Recognition', in A. Gutmann (ed.), *Multiculturalism*, Princeton, NJ: Princeton University Press.

Thomson, J.E. and Krasner, S.D. (1996) 'Global Transactions and the

Consolidation of Sovereignty', R.J. Art and R. Jervis (eds), *International Politics: Enduring Concepts and Contemporary Issues*, New York: HarperCollins.

Tickner, J.A. (1991) 'Hans Morgenthau's Principles of Political Realism: a Feminist Reformulation', in R. Grant and K. Newland (eds), *Gender and International Relations*, Milton Keynes: Open University Press.

Tickner, A. (1992) *Gender in International Relations: Feminist Perspectives On Achieving Global Security*, New York: Columbia University Press.

Toulmin, S. (1992) *Cosmopolis: the Hidden Agenda of Modernity*, Chicago: Chicago University Press.

Verene, D.P. (1971) 'Hegel's Account of War', in Z. Pelczynski (ed.), *Hegel's Political Philosophy: Problems and Perspectives*, Cambridge: Cambridge University Press.

Vincent, R.J. (1974) *Nonintervention and International Order*, Princeton, NJ: Princeton University Press.

Vincent, R.J. (1986) *Human Rights and International Relations*, Cambridge: Cambridge University Press.

Vincent, R.J. (1992) 'The Idea of Rights in International Ethics', in T. Nardin and D. Mapel (eds), *Traditions of International Ethics*, Cambridge: Cambridge University Press.

Waever, O. (1997) 'Figures of International Thought: Introducing Persons Instead of Paradigms', in I.B. Neumann and O. Waever (eds), *The Future of International Relations*, London: Routledge.

Walby, S. (1996) 'Woman and Nation', in G. Balakrishnan (ed.), *Mapping the Nation*, London: Verso.

Walker, R.B.J. (1988) *One World, Many Worlds: Struggles for Just World Peace*, Boulder, CO: Lynne Reiner.

Walker, R.B.J. (1993) *Inside/Outside: International Relations as a Political Theory*, Cambridge: Cambridge University Press.

Walker, R.B.J. (1999) 'Citizenship After the Modern Subject', in K. Hutchings and R. Dannreuther (eds), *Cosmopolitan Citizenship*. London: Macmillan.

Walt, S. (1989) 'Hegel On War: Another Look', *History of Political Thought*, 10 (1): 113–24.

Waltz, K.N. (1959) *Man, the State and War*, New York: Columbia University Press.

Waltz, K.N. (1979) *The Theory of International Politics*, Reading, MA: Addison-Wesley.

Walzer, M. (1981) 'The Distribution of Membership', in P.G. Brown and H. Shue (eds), *Boundaries: National Autonomy and Its Limits*, Totowa, NJ: Rowman & Littlefield.

Walzer, M. (1983) *Spheres of Justice: a Defence of Pluralism and Equality*, Oxford: Blackwell.

Walzer, M. (1992) *Just and Unjust Wars*, 2nd edn, New York: Basic Books.

Walzer, M. (1994a) *Thick and Thin: Moral Argument at Home and Abroad*, Southbend, IN: University of Notre Dame Press.

Walzer, M. (1994b) 'Notes on the New Tribalism', in C. Brown (ed.), *Political Restructuring in Europe: Ethical Perspectives*, London: Routledge.

Walzer, M. (1994c) 'Spheres of Affection', *Boston Review*, 19 (5): 29.

Warren, K. and Cady, D. (eds) (1994) *Hypatia Special Issue: Feminism and Peace*, 9 (2).

Wasserstrom, R. (ed.) (1970) *War and Morality*, London: Belmont.

Watson, A. (1992) *The Evolution of International Society*, London: Routledge.

Watson, A. (1998) 'The Practice Outruns the Theory', in B. Roberson (ed.), *International Society and the Development of International Relations Theory*, London and Washington, DC: Pinter.

Wendt, A. (1992) 'Anarchy Is What States Make of It: the Social Construction of Power Politics', *International Organization*, 46 (2): 391–425.

Wendt, A. (1995) 'Constructing International Politics', *International Security*, 19: 71–81.

Westphal, M. (1979) *History and Truth in Hegel's Phenomenology*, Atlantic Highlands, NJ: Humanities Press International.

Whitehead, L. (ed.) (1996) *The International Dimensions of Democratization: Europe and the Americas*, Oxford: Oxford University Press.

Wight, M. (1991) *International Theory: The Three Traditions*, G. Wight and B. Porter (eds), London: Leicester University Press.

Willett, C. (ed.) (1998) *Theorizing Multiculturalism*, Oxford: Blackwell.

Williams, H. (1983) *Kant's Political Philosophy*, Oxford: Blackwell.

Williams, H. (1992a) *International Relations in Political Theory*, Milton Keynes: Open University Press.

Williams, H. (ed.) (1992b) *Essays on Kant's Political Philosophy*, Cardiff: Wales University Press.

Williams, H., Sullivan, D. and Matthews, G. (1997) *Francis Fukuyama and the End of History*, Cardiff: University of Wales Press.

Wood, A. (1990) *Hegel's Ethical Thought*, Cambridge: Cambridge University Press.

Young, I.M. (1990) *Justice and the Politics of Difference*, Princeton, NJ: Princeton University Press.

Yuval-Davis, N. (1997) *Gender and Nation*, London: Sage.

Yuval-Davis, N. (1998) 'Beyond Differences: Women, Empowerment and Coalition Politics', in N. Charles and H. Hintjens (eds), *Gender, Ethnicity and Political Ideologies*, London: Routledge.

Zolo, D. (1997) *Cosmopolis: Prospects for World Government*, Cambridge: Polity Press.

INDEX

abortion 145, 170
absolute knowledge, (Hegel) 99, 100–2
accountability 34, 156, 161, 167
achievement, discourse of 139–41, 168
Adorno, Th. 72–3
agency: achievement of 139–41; conditions of possibility of political 143–4, 146–7, 148–50; inadequate ontology of 175–8; and normative judgements 147–51
aid policy 39, 86
alienation 65
Almond, B. 28
American Revolution 120
anarchy 20, 57–9, 63, 79
Anscombe, E. 34
applied ethics xii, 28–9, 53, 182
Aquinas, Saint Thomas 52
Arab-Israeli conflict 43
arbitration 158
archaeology 77, 110
Archibugi, D. 154
Aristotelianism 51, *see also* neo-Aristotelianism
Ashley, R. 67, 80, 81, 82, 90, 139
'Reading Dissidence' 77–8
asylum, rights to 133
Augustine, Saint 15, 17, 52
autonomy: cultural 156; democratic principle of 159–62, 175, 177; feminism and individual 141–3; freedom as 133–4; individual 53, 137; meaning of 139–40; as reason 10, 12, 16, 23; respect for individual (Kant) 129, 130–1, 136; *see also* self-determination, individual

balance of power 14, 19, 21, 22
Bankowski, Z. 155
Barry, B. 38, 39–40, 52
Bartelson, J. 89
Basu, A. 167
Bauman, Z. 154, 169–70
Bayliss, J. xii, 14
Beetham, D. 125, 163
Beitz, C. 38
Bellamy, R. xi, 47, 155
Benhabib, S. 86
Bentham, Jeremy 10–11
Bobbio, N. 159
Bock, G. 142
Bohman, J. 162
Bontekoe, R. 163
borders: closed 127–8; opening of state 137–8, 140–1
boundaries, fluid permeable 139–41, 143

bourgeois state 66
Brown, C. xi, xii, 2, 12, 30, 47, 48, 54, 56, 66, 67, 70, 154, 165
'The Ethics of Political Restructuring in Europe' 96–7
Brown, M.E. 158, 165
Bull, H. 73
The Anarchical Society 57–9
Burchill, S. 11, 14, 165
Buzan, B. 163

Cady, D. 86
Camilleri, J.A. 154, 156
Campbell, D. 80, 81, 139, 140, 141, 168, 171
Canada, nationalism in 125
Caney, S. 126, 131
Canovan, M. 128, 136, 151, 174
capital punishment 124
capitalism 65, 66, 84
globalization of 158; and liberal democracy 158, 180; and liberalism 165
care, ethic of 83–6
Carr, E.H. 15, 16, 17, 20, 22, 66
categorical imperative 26–7, 37, 39, 124, 139, 147
categories: dominant 77; gendered 85; subversion of 78–82
Charles, N. 167
Charvet, J. 126, 127, 131
children's rights 112
Christianity 14, 16, 17, 32–3, 60
citizenship: cosmopolitan 2, 51, 118; extension of notion of 73; transnational 154; world 154
citizenship rights, sex-differentiated 142
civic republican communitarianism 53–4, 132–3, 150, 173–4
civil conflict 160
civil society: democratization of 161–2; global 154, 166, 167, 168–9
Clark, I. 166
class relations 64–6, 67
coercion 183
Cohn, C. 86
Cold War 14, 24, 25, 69–70, 158, 165
end of the 24, 64, 125, 154, 155
collective right 43–4, 46, 147
and minority groups 130–1; as state right 127–9; to self-determination, and national identity 132, 134
common interests 58

commonality of condition 143
communication, domination-free 72, 146
communitarianism xii, 29, 31, 42, 44, 47, 147
and collective right to national self-determination 132; and realism 44, 45–6; and specificity of political culture 165–6; static account of the normative 62; vs. cosmopolitanism 44–5, 175–6; *see also* civic republican communitarianism; moral communitarianism; organic communitarianism
community 62, 160
moral and moral cosmopolis 36, 47–50, 51; as ongoing achievement 168
competition 26
Conca, K. 167
conditions of possibility xiii, xv, 68–9, 117, 146, 147, 177, 183–4
of knowledge 139–40; of political agency 148–50, 179
confederation of republics (Kant) 158
consciousness 119–20
history of 100–1, 110, 119
consequentialism 28–9, 36, 40, 54
constitutional law 160
constitutional state, and ethical life (Hegel) 105–9
constitutive theory, individual and state 47–8, 96–7
contract theory 45
contractarianism 32, 33–4
and individual natural right 123–4, 125
control 156, 158, 162
cooperation, international 7, 26, 159, 164–5, 167
cosmopolis 35, 51
moral, and moral community 47–50
cosmopolitan democracy 13, 27, 29, 34, 36, 154, 156, 159–62, 180
criticism of 167–8; modelling 157–66; phenomenological adequacy of 176–8
cosmopolitan democratic law 9, 154, 161, 177
cosmopolitan institutions: interventionist 157; regulatory 157